Chicken Soup
for the Soul®

What I Learned from the Cat

Chicken Soup for the Soul: What I Learned from the Cat
101 Stories about Life, Love, and Lessons
Jack Canfield, Mark Victor Hansen, Amy Newmark

Published by Chicken Soup for the Soul Publishing, LLC   www.chickensoup.com

The publisher gratefully acknowledges the many publishers and individuals who granted Chicken Soup for the Soul permission to reprint the cited material.

Front cover photo courtesy of Getty Images / David Tipling. Back cover photo courtesy of iStockphoto.com/mariusFM77. Interior photograph courtesy of iStockphoto.com/flibustier

Cover and Interior Design & Layout by Pneuma Books, LLC
For more info on Pneuma Books, visit www.pneumabooks.com

Distributed to the booktrade by Simon & Schuster. SAN: 200-2442

Publisher's Cataloging-in-Publication Data
(Prepared by The Donohue Group)

Chicken soup for the soul : what I learned from the cat : 101 stories about
 life, love, and lessons / [compiled by] Jack Canfield, Mark Victor Hansen,
 [and] Amy Newmark.

   p. ; cm.

 ISBN: 978-1-935096-37-5

1. Cats--Literary collections. 2. Cats--Anecdotes. 3. Cat owners--Literary collections.
4. Cat owners--Anecdotes. 5. Human-animal relationships--Anecdotes. I. Canfield,
Jack, 1944- II. Hansen, Mark Victor. III. Newmark, Amy. IV. Title: What I learned
from the cat

PN6071.C3 C455 2009
810.8/02/03629752   2009933199

PRINTED IN THE UNITED STATES OF AMERICA
on acid∞free paper
18 17 16 15 14 13 12 11 10 09   01 02 03 04 05 06 07 08 09 10

Chicken Soup for the Soul®
What I Learned from the Cat

101 Stories about Life, Love, and Lessons

Jack Canfield
Mark Victor Hansen
Amy Newmark

CSS

Chicken Soup for the Soul Publishing, LLC
Cos Cob, CT

Contents

❻

~Learning to Play~

❼

~Learning What's Important~

❽
~Learning to Believe~

❾
~Learning about Love~

❿
~Learning to Let Go~

Foreword

What have I learned from my cat?

Everything!

Poet May Sarton said, "Time spent with cats is never wasted," and it's no wonder cats have been some of the greatest muses in history. Wordsworth, Hemingway, Poe, Twain, Dickens, the Brontes, Elliot and a number of other writers have all personified their love for cats onto the page. Now, this collection of stories aims to do the same.

I love my cat, and I love yours too. I have spent my whole career trying to keep our cats safe and happy. I am so excited that Chicken Soup for the Soul has put together another one of their heartwarming collections for cat lovers, and this one is on such a special topic, with 101 true tales offering insights about life, love, and the fundamental wisdom we can learn from our cats. This book makes me smile, laugh out loud, cry, and pick up the phone to share my favorite stories. Meanwhile, the book makes my cat Pasha jump, leap, paw, scratch, and caterwaul—all positive signs of truly loving the text.

What do we learn from our cats? Perhaps the most important thing is to make time to enjoy life. The Victorian novelist Samuel Butler said "All of the animals except man know that the principal business of life is to enjoy it." In this book, you will read about Kimberly Garrow, who always noticed her "cats stretched out across the floor, absorbing every ounce of the glorious sunlight streaming through the window. I placed myself right there next to the cats on the floor, mingling with the sun spot. My 'to do' list faded away, replaced by the contentment of just being." Kimberly and her husband eventually used the magic of the sun spot to persuade their reluctant three-year-old to take a nap and now the whole family enjoys the sun with the cats. If only I could nap as much as our cats do, I know I would enjoy life a little bit more.

Cats help us put things in perspective too. Do cats ever have a "bad day"? Good day or bad, life goes on and there is always reason to be optimistic. Terri Elders and her family were experiencing a variety of health and other problems when she decided to adopt a new attitude after watching her cat, Chico, fruitlessly bird-hunting in the middle of February. Terri writes that "Chico is the only cat I've ever known who dedicates herself to the principles of the Law of Attraction. This means that if you believe good things are going to happen to you, then they simply will. And for Chico, they often do. Her message gets through to me. Maybe good things don't have to happen [I]every[I] day."

We cat lovers have a special mission in life — educating "dog people" who don't appreciate cats… because they don't know them! This book will arm you with a whole chapter of stories called "Learning to Love the Cat." You'll read about Rebecca Hill's father, who loved dogs and hated cats, but took in Commander, who needed a new home, for a "trial period." You know what happened next. Rebecca's parents ended up designing a new house with lots of nooks and crannies for the cat and her father "even took the time to measure Commander with a ruler so that the window ledges would be made wide enough for him to easily lie on them with comfort." It still boggles my mind to think about people not liking cats, but just not having yet discovered them.

That brings me to the subject of homeless cats and adoption. You all know how passionate I am about animal rescue. I rescued my Russian Blue, Pasha, and my Maltese, Lucky, from pounds. I proudly support many animal rescue organizations and am happy to report that the tragedy of abandoned cats and dogs is steadily being addressed. Chicken Soup for the Soul shares in this passion, and this book is filled with stories of rescued cats… and rescued people!

When Peg Kehret's husband died unexpectedly, she decided to turn his workshop into a foster home for abandoned cats. She writes in her story that "the cats helped me as much as I helped them. I still miss Carl but his workshop is no longer a sad, empty space. It's now known as the cat room, complete with a 'Strays Welcome' sign. Even when I'm between cats, there is a sense of anticipation and the knowledge that the emptiness is only temporary and that soon the room will once again come alive with love and purpose."

I hope you will enjoy this book as much as I have. The Chicken Soup for the Soul team is dedicated to our cats and their wellbeing, and it is a pleasure and a privilege to introduce this book to you. These stories are a great way to relax and learn to re-appreciate your feline pals. So if you have a ragdoll cat, now's the time to get him or her on your lap, raise your reading glasses and just dive into this feline non-fiction.

My boy Pasha needs to be fed and loved every day, no matter what else I have going on. And he loves me right back. There is a rhythm to life with a cat that calms us and puts things in perspective. We have so much to learn about life from our cats. Their simple faith in the fact that the sun will come up every morning, their feed dish will be filled, and that life is meant to be enjoyed, helps give us a positive outlook. As the French historian Hippolyte Taine said, "I have studied many philosophers and many cats. The wisdom of cats is infinitely superior."

So stretch a little, purr a lot, love your cat, love yourself, and learn from each other.

~Wendy Diamond

What I Learned from the Cat

Chapter 1

Learning Who's in Charge

As every cat owner knows, nobody owns a cat.

~Ellen Perry Berkeley

Dibbs!

I had been told that the training procedure with cats was difficult.
It's not. Mine had me trained in two days.
~Bill Dana

Having two cats is like having two children, where you must never, ever, bring something home for one without buying the exact same thing for the other.

For example, we brought home a new throw rug for the kitchen floor. Nothing fancy, just a basic woven throw with tassels on the ends.

We laid it on the floor.

"What do you think?" I asked my husband.

"Looks good," he said. "I..."

A rumbling, rushing sound filled the air as two cats careened around the corner. Eyes bulging, ears laid flat, they were neck and neck racing for the rug. In a surprise move, the kitten took a Herculean leap and was the first to land victoriously on the bounty.

"Mrrowr!" she screeched, spread-eagled across the fabric.

"Rowr-rrrr!" the cat yelped, looking to us as if for a judge's call. She screeched to a halt at the edge of the rug as if an invisible barrier protected it.

The kitten smirked as she pranced around the new rug.

"Well, it was nice for the thirty seconds we could call it ours," said my husband. "I'm going to watch TV."

I glared at his retreating back. Yet again, I was left to single-parent the situation. Fortunately, I had the deft touch.

"You share," I told the kitten. "Be a good kitty. Share."

The kitten's idea of sharing was to settle into the middle of the rug and begin cleaning her private parts. I decided parenting was overrated and joined my husband in front of the TV.

The kitten didn't move for the next four hours. Our entering the kitchen didn't deter her in the least, and she went so far as to let us step over and around her as we fumbled through trying to cook and set the table.

My husband made the mistake of standing on the carpet as he stirred something at the stove.

A rumble emanated from deep in the kitten's throat.

"I'd move if I were you," I told him.

"Why?" he asked.

The kitten walked over and glared at the portion of his shoe on the mat.

"You're on somebody's turf," I said.

He looked down at the scowling kitten. "I pay the mortgage," he said. "If I want to stand on my new carpet, in my kitchen, no cat is going to stop me."

I shrugged and went back to rinsing off lettuce.

The kitten nudged his ankle with her head. When subtlety didn't work, she went for an all out head-butt.

"Hey, cut that out," said my husband.

The kitten whipped out her claws and targeted his sock, which unfortunately had his foot in it at the time.

"Ow. Hey. OW!" He hopped off the rug.

"Us, zero. Cats, 391," I said. My husband glared at me.

The cat moped in the doorway, watching the kitten. But older and wiser, she bided her time.

At dinnertime, the cat sashayed over and planted herself in front of the kitten's dish. The kitten sat up, alarmed. The cat smiled, and then sank her head deep into the kitten's food.

"Rowr, rowr, psst!" yelled the kitten. My husband and I came into the kitchen. The kitten stared accusingly at the cat. "Mrow, mow, mow!"

"Well, go get your food then," I said.

The cat hummed as she patrolled the perimeter of the rug.

The kitten bit her lip and lay back down.

The cat wasn't through. She started splashing in the water dish. Hear the water? When is the last time you went the bathroom? Ho, hum. Splash, splash. I love playing in the runny water.

The kitten crossed her legs. She looked worried.

Splish-splash. Splish-splash. Oh, how I love the runny, full, wet, drippy water.

The kitten turned a deep shade of purple as she held her breath. Unable to bear it any longer, she tore off the carpet toward the litter box. Doing her business in record time, she raced back to the mat, coming to a dismayed stop at the edge.

The cat squatted at the corner of the rug, flipping a tassel back and forth. "Do you mind?" she asked the kitten. "I own this rug now."

Me, I'm fed up. It's impossible to be in the kitchen with territorial cats nipping at my heels, and both cats toying alternatively with starvation and kidney explosion so as not to lose their claim on the rug.

"We have to take action," I tell my husband.

He sighs. "You're right. We've spoiled them. But with hard work and commitment on our part, I'm sure we can do better."

I stare at him. "What?"

He stares back. "Weren't you going to lecture me that we need to find new ways of reward and discipline, so as to create a more fair, harmonious environment where we all learn a lesson about love and sharing?"

"Uh, no. I was going to suggest we go buy two small, crappy rugs for the hall and let them duke it out there."

He thought for a moment. "Okay, that's good too."

Too bad we don't have kids. We'd make great parents.

~Dena Harris

Top 15 Lessons Learned

In ancient times cats were worshipped as gods;
they have not forgotten this.
~Terry Pratchett

I have learned that...

... it doesn't matter what I'm doing, they are more important.

... if I'm on the computer, they need to be, literally, on the computer.

... my bed is actually their bed, and I should be grateful I get half of it to share.

... you are nobody until you've been ignored by the cat.

... pens are fun to chew on.

... although they may look cute, they are always up to something.

... head bonking is showing some form of love.

... they know they are cute. It saves them from more than enough trouble.

... food can solve any problem.

... cats have selective hearing.

... what I say doesn't matter—what the cat has to say matters more.

... everything is on their agenda, not mine.

... if they want something, they will get it themselves if you don't.

... the whole purpose of purring is to keep you awake until they fall asleep.

... I don't know what I'd do without them. A home is not a home without a cat.

~Katie Matthews

Feline Wiles

*Always the cat remains a little beyond the limits we try to set for him
in our blind folly.*
~Andre Norton

I t wasn't exactly catastrophic, but our Middy kitty was giving us community relations problems. We had moved temporarily into our son's rental in town while our country home was being refurbished. Middy, accustomed to being confined indoors due to roving dogs and coyotes, was delighted with the freedom to roam here in the "civilization" of town. However, our first mistake was to allow her to discover the three elegant backyard birdfeeders in our neighbor's yard. She promptly began polishing her bird harvesting skills.

We had two cats: Midnight — Middy, for short — an all-black, young female, and Snowshoe, an all-white elderly male. Black cats blend with shadows and have a special talent for sneaking up on birds. Our Middy was no exception. Seemingly spring-loaded, she rarely missed in her early morning bird hunts. Snowshoe never left dismembered bodies and feathers on the front step. He had learned that capturing wild things required more stealth than his white coat would permit and more speed than his mature bones could muster.

Long ago, we ceased hanging birdfeeders in our trees as our concession to the rules of Audubon. But Middy, undeterred, crossed the street to the home of our neighbors. She sneaked onto the neighbors' property at dawn when the finches and song sparrows first stretched their wings and scarfed up seeds. At the right moment, Middy pounced.

Our resourceful neighbors tried everything from shouts and chasing with a broom to spray bottles and garden hose—to no avail. Sneaky Middy outwitted them as well as the birds.

These neighbors came to discuss the matter, averting their eyes as they stepped over the latest scattering of feathers that Middy delivered to our door. I invited them in. "Would you consider putting a bell on Middy, if we purchase it?" Albert asked. We readily agreed.

The bell arrived—a tiny brass noisemaker. Fastened to its handsome red collar it looked great against kitty's black coat. The collar's beauty did not impress Midnight, however. She went wild the moment it circled her neck. She raced from couch to stairwell to lampshade to kitchen sink board trying to escape the jingle that must have sounded like the clang of a freight train to her bird-sensitive ears. Exhausted and frustrated, Middy finally stopped, dead still. She wouldn't move and she wouldn't eat or drink. Her little head was frozen on her body. Only her eyes moved whenever we approached trying to coax her with kibble. For two days, she crouched near the food bowl but did not approach it. I was concerned that Midnight would wither away from starvation or dehydration. Snowshoe gave her a wide berth, nibbling food from his side of the bowl as though turning his back on her might somehow transfer that loathsome bell to him. Not only was Middy ostracized from the human kingdom and deterred from avian haunts, she was shunned by her feline ilk.

I was about to plead with our country-based friends to adopt Middy, when hunger overcame her fear of the bell. Cautiously she crept to the water and food bowl. Within a few days she accepted the bell as part of her life. As important, this determined little birder did not give up on her favorite sport.

Within a few days we learned that our neighbors were wakened each morning by Midnight's bell as she sneaked along their bedroom windowsill—instead of creeping on the ground. The height of the sill apparently gave her about two seconds advantage as she leaped onto the birdfeeder before the bell alerted the birds. In short, she had outwitted us all and was back to garnering at least one bird on her morning forays.

But all was not lost. Albert did not give up in his quest to preserve his birds. He rigged up a motion detection device. The entire yard's sprinkler system went on the moment Midnight sneaked under their gate.

Hooray! Technology to the rescue. But our Middy was not without her own ingenious resources. One morning, shortly after the motion-sensitive sprinkler was installed, I looked out to see—silhouetted against the dawn sky—a small form, unmistakably feline, creeping along the roofline of the neighbors' house. My bet is that she learned to quiet the bell on her collar with one paw as she made a flying leap to the birdfeeder.

Fortunately for Middy and our friendship with our neighbors, our country home was remodeled in a timely fashion, and Middy was back to being an indoors cat, sheltered from wandering dogs and free-range coyotes. She now has to content herself with tapping the glass with her paw as she watches pigeons strut on the windowsill of our second-story bedroom.

~Willma Willis Gore

The Guardian Cat

The problem with cats is that they get the exact same look on their face whether they see a moth or an axe-murderer.
~Paula Poundstone

A Grizzly lived down the street from me. Not an actual grizzly bear, but a gigantic German Shepherd named Grizzly. And he did not like me or anyone else, as far as I could tell.

When I went jogging past his house, Grizzly nipped at my heels. When I rode my bike, he would chase me for blocks. Sometimes when I went to the mailbox for the morning newspaper, Grizzly would run down the sidewalk at me, barking and growling.

I had even called his owner, Mr. Albertson, to complain, but that wasn't much help.

"It's your own fault," Mr. Albertson nonchalantly explained. "You've shown fear. Grizzly can sense that and now he knows you don't like him."

Well, that was true. I didn't like Grizzly. In general, I didn't much care for dogs or cats at all. Actually, I was the only resident on the whole street without a pet — until the cat came into my life.

He arrived the way many cats seem to come into people's lives. He chose me. I was leaving for work early one January morning and I found him on the front porch. He stared me in the eye and meowed loudly.

I had no idea where the scruffy orange tiger cat had come from. And he certainly wasn't pretty. His fur desperately needed brushing, most of his left ear was missing and he walked with a limp. This cat needed a home—but not mine.

Pointing down the road, since that is where I assumed he'd come from, I firmly commanded: "Go home! Go home!" The cat didn't move, so I went off to work.

This ritual was repeated again that evening when I returned and numerous times throughout the next two days. "Go home! Go home," I would tell the cat. To my knowledge it never left the porch.

Why me? I complained to myself. I can't just leave it out there staring at me! Why did it have to pick me? I don't need a pet! What am I going to do with a cat?

Finally, one especially cold evening, I gave in and opened the front door. Within a day the cat had completely and comfortably made himself at home.

Now this cat had some serious aggression issues. That was obvious from the look of him. He seemed to get along with humans, but every time I let him outside he got into an altercation with some neighborhood creature. The tabby cat from across the street, the Collie that lived next door, even the woodchuck who resided behind my garage. He was definitely a fighter, so I named him Agamemnon after the great warrior king who fought alongside Ulysses in the Trojan War. I just hoped Agamemnon never met Grizzly.

For his own safety, and the safety of all the other animals in the area, I kept Agamemnon inside during the day while I was at work. He seemed quite content to fill his daytime hours with running up and down the stairs, wrestling with my houseplants and capturing dust bunnies under the bed. In the evenings he would go outside to wander around the yard, no doubt looking for a fight, and then stretch out on the railing of the porch.

For weeks I tried to find someone else who would adopt Agamemnon, but whenever anyone asked about his disposition, I couldn't lie. No one seemed to be interested in a scruffy one-eared cat with social difficulties.

A few months went by, Agamemnon continued to get in fights,

and I continued to ask: Why me? For what reason did this cat come to my porch?

Spring arrived late that year, so by the time the ground was dry enough to start gardening I was anxious to get to work. Agamemnon sometimes joined me as I worked around the yard, but usually he spent his time perched on his porch railing, relaxing in the sunshine and taking long naps.

One Saturday afternoon I was working along the front of the house, putting in rows of marigolds and petunias while Agamemnon napped on his railing throne. I was intent on my work, pulling weeds, planting flowers and spreading mulch.

Then a strange feeling came over me, like I was being watched. Still on my knees, I put down my spade and slowly looked around.

There was Grizzly! The dog had managed to sneak up on me and he was about five feet behind me. He pulled back his lips and snarled at me, stepping closer. There was nothing I could do on my hands and knees with the dog blocking my path to the front door. I was too scared to make a sound, but the dog kept growling. This time I felt sure I was going to get bitten, or worse.

Suddenly a hissing orange streak flew from the porch railing and Agamemnon landed on the dog's back. Grizzly began yelping furiously. The huge dog immediately ignored me and ran around the yard, then down the street, with the cat attached to his back. The sounds of the terrified dog echoed throughout the neighborhood as he scrambled towards his house.

A few minutes later, Agamemnon strolled home, jumped up on his porch railing and went back to sleep.

And although Grizzly had not been seriously injured, just a couple of minor scratches from what I heard, the dog never left his yard again.

Agamemnon became a bit of a hero around the neighborhood. The lady across the street often brought over fresh catnip for him. The family next door made a wooden sign to hang on my porch that stated "BEWARE OF THE ATTACK CAT!" Kids rode past on their bikes and called to Agamemnon when he was out on the porch.

I no longer questioned why the cat had come to me. Obviously, my guardian angel sent him!

~David Hull

Patches Goes to Camp

Children make you want to start life over.
~Muhammad Ali

Each summer, children from several surrounding inner cities flock to Camp Scully in a rural area of upstate New York. Living just up the road from the camp, our cat, Patches, probably caught the sounds of merriment which drifted her way from a multitude of voices mingled in glee. Maybe she wondered what opportunities awaited her there, or it could be she decided a communal atmosphere was more to her liking. For whatever reason, without asking our permission, Patches packed her bags and set off for camp.

One evening in late May, my husband and I returned home from celebrating our first wedding anniversary to find a cryptic note from my stepdaughter. "Camp Scully returned Patches a few hours ago. She's in my room now," the note read.

Patches had been missing for several days. My husband assured me there was no need to fret. She usually took these sabbaticals as soon as the weather turned warmer. Since we had only been married for a short period, this was the first time I experienced these jaunts of Patches, and I must say they made me extremely uneasy. My cats had never even been outdoors. Furthermore, while I was glad to have Patches under our roof once again, I puzzled over the meaning of my stepdaughter's message. I went upstairs and knocked on her door.

"What's this about Camp Scully?" I asked.

"Someone from Camp Scully called and said they had Patches. They brought her back about eight o'clock," she answered in typical non-explanatory fourteen-year-old fashion.

"How did she get to Camp Scully?" I questioned, thinking I hadn't even filled out an application, let alone put down a deposit.

"I don't know. Someone just told me she was there," she said, already moving on to other more important teenage concerns.

A few nights later, my questions were answered. Patches had again disappeared and around 8:30 the doorbell rang. The young woman who ran the camp stood silhouetted under the porch light, a decidedly unhappy calico cat cradled in her arms. As I ushered her in, she explained how Patches first wandered up to her during the lull before the opening day of camp. Susan knew from her collar and name tag that a meal ticket waited to be cashed in elsewhere. Yet, no matter how she tried to ignore her overtures of friendship, Patches showed up daily, finally opting to move in completely.

"Patches hasn't been very happy since I moved in with my three cats," I told her, while Susan warily watched our strapping black and white male, dubbed the resident bully. "Especially him," I concluded.

Perhaps the thought of eight-pound Patches living with this towering menace unnerved Susan somewhat, because eventually she gave in to Patches' wishes. After a few more transfers between her rightful home and her dream escape, we all agreed that Patches would be better off at camp.

Patches settled into the routine of camp almost immediately. Rather than the campers intimidating her, as I had worried, she welcomed the chance to be cuddled and petted at every turn. Plus, she liked the many different diversions that camp offered, from supervising an arts and crafts session to lounging on the beach while reluctant ten-year-olds attempted the back stroke. Hanging around the mess hall had its rewards, too. Usually someone surreptitiously pulled a tidbit from a slightly bulging pocket or just happened to drop a leftover morsel of dinner. Patches adored the children, and they her. Soon she reigned as the camp mascot, at times surpassing Susan's leadership role.

The effect she had upon the children illustrated this well. Many of them had never been away from their families or out in the country for any length of time. The utter quiet and open spaces overwhelmed them when they first arrived. Patches provided just that necessary familiar touch, like the smell of grandma's home-baked cookies or the feel of a well-worn blanket on a nippy autumn night. In her, the children could confide their fears in ways they could not do with each other, and somehow Patches made them feel all right.

More importantly, the campers learned about responsibility from Patches, which in turn gave them a truer sense of belonging. Many of the children appointed themselves as Patches' official caretakers. Invariably, each morning and evening several willing servers showed up at Susan's cabin and helped prepare Patches' meals. Susan showed them how much food to put in the dish and made sure they changed her water. Soon, Patches took to parking herself on the porch to prepare for the arrival of her young wait staff.

I like to think that because of Patches, a few children left camp with a bit more than they brought with them. Perhaps it was an added air of confidence, perhaps a new understanding of compassion, or perhaps the sense of wonder which nature brings. In countless ways, Patches touched those around her and taught them to see as they hadn't seen before.

Several months prior to what would have been her fourth camp session, Patches succumbed to kidney failure at the age of fourteen. A marker commemorates the spot where Susan buried her, near a towering pine tree on the camp's front lawn. I suspect, though, that her spirit refuses to be likewise confined. Often on a summer's night, as I hear the sound of taps carried on the breeze, I picture Patches with one paw placed against her heart, giving thanks for another day at camp.

~Carolyn M. Trombe

Midwife Cat

Cats conspire to keep us at arm's length.
~Frank Perkins

Somehow Hazel knew we'd been told our baby would die. I carried my three-year-old son in from the garage, and as I opened the door to our house, I tripped over the cat. She stood before the door, chin tilted up, eyes round and decidedly worried.

I made my way to the couch, still processing the doctor's words. I was five months pregnant, and my baby had a fatal birth defect. She would live and grow perfectly until I gave birth in four months. After she was born, she could survive an hour or two, and then she would die.

Hazel joined me on the couch. She put her head under my hands, then crawled onto my lap. There she remained, purring.

Two hours later, I realized Hazel hadn't left me, not even once. When I moved to the computer to research my baby's condition, she followed. When we ordered a pizza so our son could have dinner, she remained. While I cried on the phone to my best friend, Hazel sat beside my leg, always purring.

How had she known to be waiting at the door? Usually little more than a tortoise-shell throw pillow with feet, Hazel spent her days lolling on the sofa or sunning in the kitchen. The door between the garage and the house is a tight seal, so she couldn't have scented my distress before I got into the house. I'm convinced she knew because she loves me.

I'd seen cats offer comfort before. My stepmother's cat—also an aloof tortie—could sense her migraines, climbing onto her lap and purring, eyes distressed. Even more striking had been my mother's cat, who had comforted my husband when he underwent radiation therapy. During his treatment, he stayed in my childhood bedroom at my mother's house. Two weeks earlier she had adopted a bedraggled stray, inches away from dying, and that cat—yet a third tortie—stayed in my childhood bedroom as well. This cat loathed people, especially men, and hissed or snapped at anyone who tried to touch her. We suspected abuse. As the cat recovered from her ordeal, my husband recovered from his cancer treatments. The cat began to sleep at the foot of his bed, then on his lap, and afterward would rub her face (forbidden territory to the rest of us) against his hands so he could pet her. They recovered together, and she loved him for it.

My stepmother's migraines always ended. My husband had been cancer-free for ten years. Now my daughter was going to die, and Hazel knew this made me sad.

For the rest of the pregnancy, Hazel followed me. For four months, whenever I lay down for a nap, Hazel settled herself on the bed at my side. Our other cat didn't change her behavior, remaining a friendly but otherwise immobile couch fixture. Hazel would sit on the growing lump of baby, purring for her, sometimes giving me offended looks when the baby kicked both our tummies. I did a lot of crying, and Hazel did a lot of sitting beside me. She didn't let me stay alone until after the baby was born—and died.

Five months later, my husband and I thought I was pregnant, but test results wouldn't be reliable for another four days. As it turned out, I didn't need to take a test. Whenever I sat at my computer or in the rocking chair or on the couch, Hazel would trot from any part of the house—her sunny spots or her soft kitty beds—in order to sit on my lap. While there, she didn't relax. She didn't purr. She acted like a guard.

Even my husband noticed. "Why do you think she's doing that?"

I looked down at Hazel in my lap. "Maybe she thinks I'm pregnant."

"She never did that before," he said. "Why would she do it now?"

Seeing her sitting like the Sphinx on sentry duty, all I could say was, "She's protecting the baby."

Three days later, I confirmed the pregnancy Hazel had diagnosed. She remained on my lap, ever vigilant. For weeks, when I lay down at night, she sat on my stomach, looking into my eyes. We've always understood Hazel has highly confident notions, and I imagine she thought, "You clearly can't protect this baby properly, so I'll do it for you." I told everyone that cats were immune to the Evil Eye, and that she was drawing the Evil Eye away from the baby and into herself. She certainly behaved as if she were.

It was our other cat who "induced" my labor. She weighs twenty pounds, and while I slept, she settled herself on the pedestal of my belly and ruptured my membranes; we had our baby an hour later.

Given the way Hazel guarded my pregnancy, we wondered what she would do once the new baby arrived. Our first baby had frightened her. We expected that having nurtured this baby for nine months, she would be watchful of her afterward as well.

Instead, our aristocratic tortie ignored the baby the way she ignored everyone else in the house. She returned to ignoring me too! She wanted no thanks for "helping" me grow a healthy baby. When I'd pet her, she would give a disdainful look, turn her shoulder, and venture off in search of a new sunny spot. The message was clear: "You have your moist, noisy, milk-smelling little human. My work here is complete."

~Jane Lebak

Tank

*Most of us rather like our cats to have a streak of wickedness.
I should not feel quite easy in the company of any cat that walked about
the house with a saintly expression.*
~Beverly Nichols

It wasn't until after a couple of weeks that I noticed something was wrong. Unlike the other kittens, who'd already begun crawling on their tummies, he was rolling like a ball down a hill.

I brought him to one of the local vets who coldly offered to put him down. He said the little guy had neurological damage and would never be able to walk. As a specialist in developmental and physical disabilities, I never put anyone or anything in a defined box.

Tank was all black and was originally named Tink, after Tinkerbelle in *Peter Pan* because of his fluttering and unstable movements. When he was weaned, I had to hold him steady so he could eat, and as he ate, he just wobbled like a foal just born. I never held him securely. I would place my hands just on either side of him and let him wobble into them as he ate. By the time he was a year old, he still wobbled but ate without any help at all.

His walk was a clumsy trot and at first he would bump into walls and table legs. In time, he gained enough muscle control to move more slowly and learned to lean on the walls for balance. The base of his tail was always bald from his using it for balance as he walked by chairs and table legs.

As for getting on the sofa, he just clawed his way up to curl up and go to sleep. If you have ever seen anyone with a palsied condition, you have an idea of how he walked, sat and perched himself. Tank had a way of always getting what he wanted and, to compensate for his disability, grew into a formidable bully! We had a household of multiple cats and three big dogs, one Golden Retriever and two yellow Lab mixes, but when Tank sauntered by they all cleared the way for him. If they didn't, he would give a blood curling yowl that would send them all into hiding.

I remember one night sitting up in bed reading. Our dogs were all curled up nicely on the old sofa we kept for them in our bedroom when Tank came in. He looked about and then settled his eyes on the sofa. I knew this was his destination. He wobbled over and sat, staring each dog in the eye one at a time. Each one picked up his head and looked at him and then at each other. He swung one paw onto the sofa, claw grabbing cloth and in one instant all three dogs gave up their spot on the sofa. Tank climbed up and sprawled outstretched right in the middle of the sofa. I had heard of people clearing out a room and this little guy could clear out a sofa when he wanted it. In fact, he ruled the house.

In all my years of working in the disabilities field I have learned that compensating for one's disability is greatly underestimated by most people. The power of adaptation is amazing to witness as I have many times in my work. Tank truly demonstrated the real meaning of adapting to one's circumstances and fully utilizing the environment to the fullest to live a normal life.

Tank could not jump to where I kept the dry cat food. It wasn't necessary anyway. Like everyone else, he had me trained. When he was hungry, he would walk over to me and stare. I would ask him, "Do you want to eat?" and he would turn tail and scamper to the porch to be fed.

He was born neurologically damaged and most would have taken the advice of that vet who wanted to put him down. In so doing, they would have been denied the blessing of seeing the true meaning of a valiant, brave and indomitable spirit taking the hand given and playing it to the fullest.

Tank passed away at the age of seventeen. Not bad. Not bad at all.

~Cate Cavanagh

Perfect Love

Some people say man is the most dangerous animal on the planet.
Obviously those people have never met an angry cat.
~Lillian Johnson

I was sitting in my veterinarian's office when a young family rushed in. The father held a bundle of blood-soaked towels in his arms. He was followed by a young boy carrying the largest, fattest, yellow-striped tomcat I'd ever seen draped across his shoulder and crying as if his little heart was completely broken. The mother held the door and followed up the rear, comforting the sobbing boy. The cat simply viewed everyone with disinterest and remained as calm as a rag doll, lying across the boy's shoulder.

A medical team hustled the man and his precious bundle into the examining rooms. As the mother, boy and cat settled in on the seats in the waiting room, I couldn't help but ask what this was all about. I assumed that the pet in the bloody towels, a dog or another cat, must have been hit by a car. What unfolded was one of the most bizarre and yet heartwarming stories I had ever heard.

The cat, named Tom, was the first family pet, now an old codger of twelve years. They had rescued him as an abandoned kitten. He was a typical tomcat, aloof, self-centered, and quite independent, but very gentle. He had grudgingly acknowledged the birth of their son and finally accepted the little boy's pokings and proddings as the child grew. Although he accepted everyone in the family—on his own terms, of course—Tom was not overly affectionate, and definitely not a "lap cat." He wanted a good meal and a pat now and then, but preferred to be left alone to bask in the sun on his favorite windowsill.

Then, a year before this incident, a pup came into the picture. A gift from the maternal grandparents, Scotty was a West Highland White Terrier of noble bloodlines. The family was at first fearful about how Tom would accept the newcomer, but a strange thing happened. The old cat took to the pup as if he were a long lost little brother. He absolutely adored the little guy. He allowed the pup to chew his tail. He played for hours with him as if the dog were his own personal pet. When the boy was playing with Scotty, and Tom felt he was getting too rough, he would slip his huge yellow body between them and gently swat at the boy as if to say, "Okay. Enough is enough."

The family told everyone, took videos of the pair together, and marveled at the way the old cat and young dog bonded.

The family lived in a new housing tract in an upscale area near the hills in the west San Fernando Valley. We had experienced a fairly wet winter in Southern California that year, which meant that both the fauna and flora was overabundant that summer. We get used to the opossums and raccoons turning trash cans, and make sure to bring in all pet food and clean up fruit dropped from trees to slow down the critters a bit. The biggest problem is coyotes who stalk the populated areas at night, searching for cats and other small pets that make easy meals.

Tom and Scotty were kept in at night and even though their yard had a six-foot brick wall around it, the family often heard the predators scrabbling at the trash cans on the outside of the fence. Nobody ever thought there would be a problem in the daylight, however.

That Sunday afternoon, the family had returned from church and let Scotty out into the yard to romp. Suddenly, the air was filled with barking, then snarls and finally screams of pain. The family rushed to the sliding glass doors in time to see a coyote with Scotty in his jaws. The small white dog was fighting bravely but the coyote had the definite advantage.

The father grabbed a nearby chair and rushed out the door just in time to see a blazing flash of yellow fly past his head. Tom, seeing "his" pet in the jaws of the coyote, had leaped from the upper bedroom balcony and onto the coyote's head. Screaming and spitting, with claws flying like a buzz saw, the old tom lit into the beast, shocking him enough so that he dropped the little dog.

The father followed suit, swinging the chair at the coyote, who immediately decided that the meal wasn't worth losing an eye to an insane cat or getting thrashed by a wild man, and leapt back over the six-foot wall as if it weren't even there.

Scotty lay in a bloody heap, with Tom meowing and licking him gently. The little dog was still breathing. The mother ran out and wrapped him in a towel and they rushed to the vet's office.

Now we waited for news. The cat watched all of us as if he knew there was nothing to worry about, and he was right. Soon the father came out and told us that Scotty was going to be fine. He had been chewed up, but had no broken bones or internal damage. After some stitches, antibiotics, and one night in the hospital just for observation, he would be fine and could go home.

When the family started to leave, the cat squirmed from the boy's arms and ran back to the door that led to the inner examination room area. He meowed loudly and rubbed back and forth against the door. The family and an orderly tried several times to get the cat into a box to carry him out, but he hissed and spat at them.

Finally, one of the doctors came out and said that Tom could stay with Scotty in a divided cage overnight. They could not let him in the same cage as the dog for sanitation reasons, but they could put them in side by side recovery cages where they could see each other. When the door was opened the cat literally dashed into the back kennels.

I went out to my car, my heart feeling lighter than it had in a long time. I never saw the family, Scotty, or Tom again, but I will never forget their story and the most dramatic example I had ever heard of "perfect love casting out fear."

~Joyce Laird

The Great Hunters

Prowling his own quiet backyard or asleep by the fire,
he is still only a whisker away from the wilds.
~Jean Burden

Even though our cats grew up in an urban setting, they never lost their instinct to hunt. For ten years we had two cats, Blackie and Sam, and no matter how well fed with store-bought cat food, the primitive urge to find their own food in the wild (a.k.a. our backyard) was still strong.

Blackie in particular was a formidable hunter. One house we lived in had a deck off the back door, skirted by lattice woodwork. Blackie, ever on the prowl, discovered a nest of mice under the deck and eliminated them one by one. Every morning I'd find a dead mouse just outside the back door, a gesture I chose to think of as an expression of my cat's love.

We moved to a smaller city surrounded by farmland. One year a lot of grain was left unharvested in the fields because the early winter had prevented the farmers from getting to it. As a result, the vole population skyrocketed the next spring because they'd had so much to eat over the winter. I'd never even heard of a vole before. It turns out they're about the size of a field mouse with a snout similar to a mole's. Because we lived only a couple of streets from an open field, we were inundated with the tiny creatures.

One afternoon my oldest daughter went out into the yard to jump on the trampoline. A short time later she dragged me into the yard to show me what she'd found. Under the trampoline, several dead voles had been deposited, a sort of miniature graveyard. The cats never actually ate any of the voles; they just played them to death. I later observed Sam repeatedly catching and releasing her quarry. She'd let the little rodent escape and briefly taste freedom before pouncing on it a moment later, obviously enjoying the game immensely. On the other hand, the vole wasn't having nearly as much fun.

Not all the cats' prey was of the rodent kind. They had a particular fondness for birds. Our backyard had beautiful trees that attracted an assortment of birds. The cats would lie in wait, hiding under the branches of the weeping birch, ready to pounce on an unsuspecting bird. To give the birds a fighting chance, we belled the cats, using the biggest, loudest bells we could find. I could hear them wherever they were in the house, and when they were outside, I heard them coming from half a block away.

Unfortunately the birds didn't seem to have hearing as sensitive as mine. The cats still managed to catch some of the less wary. One evening Blackie tried to bring a terrified live sparrow into the house. Fortunately, I managed to pry the poor bird out of her jaws and set it free. Even after I had Sam declawed, I watched in amazement as she made a two-foot vertical leap to capture a bird between her soft paws.

Instinct in cats is a powerful force. No matter how much we think we've domesticated, trained, or humanized them, they still retain the qualities they developed eons ago that allowed their species to survive. Although I tried, I couldn't get them to stop hunting. But maybe that was for the best. Who am I to mess with what comes naturally?

~Judy Reynolds

Boundary Lessons

The cat seldom interferes with other people's rights. His intelligence keeps
him from doing many of the fool things that complicate life.
~Carl Van Vechten

Raised as a people pleaser, I have spent most of my adult life learning how to establish clear boundaries between myself and others, making sure that I don't lose track of my own needs by always doing what other people want. Cats don't have this problem. Cats are clear about what belongs to them (everything), and nothing is more important than their own delight.

My black cat, Muggins, has been my teacher in this regard — showing me how to get what I want by loosening up the very boundaries I have tried so hard to maintain. Through a variety of boundary issues with neighbors over the years, Muggins has taught me how even the most highly guarded boundaries can be dissolved when two beings (feline or human) agree to let love in.

The first lesson involved a dispute over Muggins himself. Soon after finding him at an animal shelter, I took him to the vet for neutering and to have his front paws de-clawed. The first action was politically correct, something the Humane Society encouraged. Not so with de-clawing, I soon discovered, when a neighbor returned Muggins one day, setting him inside the house and taping a note to the door saying: "Your cat accidentally got out. I know that you would want him inside since he is de-clawed."

Several days later, she knocked on the kitchen door, holding

Muggins in her arms and returning him once again. This time I was there. "This cat should not be outside. You are risking his life," she said, reluctantly handing him over as if I were a criminal.

"How am I risking his life?" I innocently replied.

"He cannot defend himself!" she said, throwing her hands up in the air. "If I see him outside again, I will have to call the animal control center." And she stomped off, indignantly.

"He seems to have done all right so far," I muttered under my breath, holding the warm, purring body of my cat in my arms. And yet in that moment, I couldn't help feeling a bit guilty. Was I endangering his life? I would never intentionally do anything that would hurt Muggins. I decided to call the vet.

"In all of my twenty-five years in practice," he said, "I've never seen a cat injured because of a lack of front claws. It's the back claws that are most important in their defense."

Not satisfied, I called the animal control center. Apparently, my neighbor had already called them.

"Oh, so you're the one she was talking about," the guy said on the other end of the phone. "She was really distressed."

"So what did you tell her?" I asked meekly, wishing that I hadn't identified myself.

"We would never recommend de-clawing a cat that goes outside," the man said. "But I guess it really isn't a problem in a residential neighborhood." He also told my neighbor she had no legal recourse.

Well that's a relief, I thought. So why didn't I feel it? And was that going to be enough to keep my neighbor from showing up at my kitchen door again, like a recurring nightmare?

Summoning my courage, I walked through several yards, across the back alley and knocked on her door. As I stood there, hyperventilating, I noticed a beautiful white, blue-eyed cat propped up on the windowsill looking out at me. My neighbor answered the door.

"So this is the reason Muggins comes over here," I said pointing to her cat. "He has good taste."

"Yes," the woman said. "They love staring at each other through the window. He makes her purr."

"Ah," I said. "Must be love."

"Perhaps," she said. "She's an inside cat."

There we were again, back to our favorite issue.

"Yeah, well. That's why I'm here," I said. Tears were forming in my eyes. I couldn't believe that I was about to cry in front of this woman. "I want to thank you for caring about my cat," I said. That was not what I had planned to say, and my words startled both of us. "We have that in common. We both care about my cat." There were other things on my list — reasons, justifications, owner's rights. None of them seemed to matter.

"I understand," she said. "I know you do." We stood there for a few seconds staring at each other.

"Well, I guess that's all I wanted to say," I said.

"Okay," she said. "Thanks for coming by."

To this day, I think that my neighbor and I were inspired by our cats. If Muggins and his girlfriend could let love have its way with them, blocked as they were by a window, why couldn't we? Finding common ground was key.

Six years later, I married the man of my dreams, and Muggins and I found ourselves in a new home on the other side of the country. Within a week of moving in, our new next-door neighbor, Sylvia, came over to tell me that she was a bird lover, not a cat lover, and that if she shooed our cat, Muggins, away from her birdfeeders, not to take it personally.

"Muggins is just being a cat," she said with a strange mix of compassion and disdain. "Cats don't understand boundaries, so I don't expect him to stay out of my yard. But if he bothers my birds, I will send him home."

"Fair enough," I said.

I liked this spunky, white-haired woman. As a retired psychotherapist living alone, Sylvia knew how to articulate her boundaries and I appreciated that. I was sorry, however, that she didn't seem to think much of my precious cat.

It didn't take long, however, for Muggins to work his magic once again. It was a sunny spring day when Sylvia charged over to me as I sat at the picnic table on our deck eating lunch. Oh no, I wondered. What has Muggins done now?

"Mary, I've got to tell you what Muggins did the other day," she said, with an incredulous look on her face. "He was sitting under my birdfeeder, watching the birds, when I saw him from my living room window. So I walked out to the feeder, looked down at him, and in the same voice I am using with you now, I said, 'Muggins, it is time to go home.' And do you know what he did?" She leaned closer to me as she neared the punch line.

"He just looked up at me, got up and walked back to your house. Just like that. That is one amazing cat."

I nodded and smiled. "I know." Leave it to Muggins, I thought, to respect a boundary, and by doing so, find his way into someone's heart.

~Mary Knight

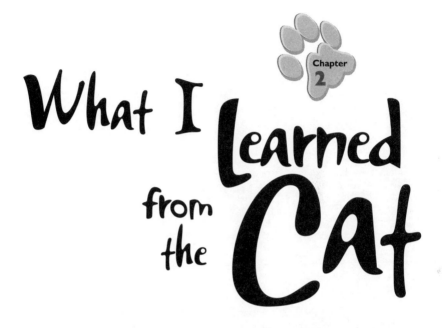

Chapter 2

What I Learned from the Cat

Learning to Love the Cat

Some people say that cats are sneaky, evil, and cruel. True, and they have many other fine qualities as well.

~Missy Dizick

When a Cat Decides He's Moving In

Any conditioned cat-hater can be won over by any cat
who chooses to make the effort.
~Paul Corey

A big, beautiful, black Persian cat named Commander taught me that not even the most adamant-dog-loving-cat-hating human being in the world can resist the charms of a cat once the cat decides he's moving in.

Commander was my parents' cat but I knew him first. Originally, Commander was my college roommate's cat. My roommate was supposed to be selling Commander because he was "a show cat." When potential buyers saw the magnificence of Commander's appearance and his impressive bloodline, they thought he would be a blue ribbon champion. But, unlike his brothers and sisters, Commander would not tolerate the show cat lifestyle. He would not sit serenely in his crate nor would he tolerate his eyes, teeth, ears and body being examined by a judge.

Because of his prideful and uncooperative behavior, no one would buy Commander. My roommate grew frustrated with Commander and began to neglect him. Commander was often kept in the bathroom (which my roommate pointed out was much bigger than the crates his brothers and sisters lived in) but the bathroom was not big enough for Commander's spirit. Commander ripped up and ate some of the bathroom tile and out of boredom played with a razor blade leaving little bloody paw prints all over the bathroom.

My roommate was unhappy, Commander was unhappy, and I was unhappy. In desperation I called my parents to see if they would like to adopt Commander. My mom had always loved cats but my dad disliked cats intensely. (Apparently, when he was young he had known some feral cats who bit and scratched him and that had made a bad impression on him.) As predicted my dad said, "No way. No cats." So, being the ever-obedient daughter that I am, I brought Commander home for Christmas break. Fortunately for me, my dad was out of town at a math conference. By the time he returned, both my mom and Commander had decided that Commander was going to stay.

My mom broke it to my dad by saying that Commander was going to live at their house for a "trial period" while we looked for a buyer. My dad looked at Commander with great apprehension and was very leery when I sat Commander on his lap. As the weeks, then months, went by there was absolutely no effort to sell Commander and it became clear to my dad that Commander was there to stay. Commander started sitting by my dad as he read the newspaper and slowly my dad began to pet Commander—just a little bit.

By the time I came home that summer I was surprised to see my dad carrying Commander around the house and holding him up to each of the windows so "kitty" could be on "bug patrol." Over the years, my parents' love for Commander grew to the point that they could not imagine life without him.

Once my brother and I finished college and there was no more tuition to pay, my parents built their dream house and they named the floor plan The Commander! They worked with the architect to design every nook and cranny of the house so that it was perfectly suited for both of them and for Commander. For my mom, they designed a beautiful living room and parlor. For my dad, they created a fantastic office and beautiful places for my dad to display his African art collection. For Commander, they designed windows that went to the floor so he could "see all of the bugs and birds" and my dad even took the time to measure Commander with a ruler so that the window ledges would be made wide enough for him to easily lie on them with comfort.

Commander died at the age of eighteen. That was four years ago. My mom still talks about Commander often and misses him tremendously... and so does my dad, which proves that not even the most adamant-dog-loving-cat-hating human being in the world can resist the charms of a cat once the cat decides he's moving in... to your heart.

~Rebecca Hill

Reprinted by permission of Off the Mark
and Mark Parisi ©2008

Lucky 8

*By and large, people who enjoy teaching animals to roll over
will find themselves happier with a dog.*
~Barbara Holland

The rain had turned from a light mist to a steady, gray drizzle. I knew the path would be slick so I slowed the cart down as we neared a sharp bend.

"Whoa!" I yelled, jerking the steering wheel to the left.

"What?" asked Kathy, my wife.

The golf cart tumbled into the light brush beside the path.

"There was a cat back there, just sitting in the middle of the path."

Kathy and I jumped out of the cart and began walking back up the path. I wasn't exactly happy. We had decided to spend a week in Puerto Vallarta, Mexico. We had been married for less than a year, and wanted to get away for some fun and sun. Instead, all we had seen was a lot of rain.

As we approached the crest of the hill, the cat was sitting off to the right of the path. It had managed to dart away just in time, narrowly avoiding certain death. The cat was actually a kitten, and a pathetic one at that. She was a shorthair calico and her entire coat was soaked through with rain. You could see every bone in her body. She weighed no more than two or three pounds. Ticks covered her body, several jutting out from her head. Her eyes and ears were huge, seemingly much too big for her body. The kitten didn't move an inch.

Kathy bent down to scoop her up. I thought for sure this kitty was going to bolt for the nearest bush. She didn't. Instead, the kitten settled into my wife's arms.

"Jim, she's adorable," my wife cooed.

I knew right then my round of golf was over. I had grown up with dogs my entire life. Kathy and I had a Siberian Husky back home. I loved that dog. I didn't like cats. Here is all of the knowledge on cats I had accumulated in thirty years of living:

1) You couldn't play with them or teach them cool tricks like "play dead."

2) You basically got to pet them for about two seconds every thirty-five days or so.

3) They were essentially miniature ninjas that would use those wicked claws to carve you up like a Thanksgiving turkey.

We took the kitten to a vet to have her checked out. The doctor removed all of the ticks, gave her a complete exam and fed her. He pronounced her healthy, disease-free and said she was about eight weeks old.

"So, señor, what would you like to do?" the good doctor asked me.

I paused. What I wanted to do was to leave the cat with the vet. However, almost a year of marriage had taught me well. "I need to speak with my wife," I responded instead.

A quick smile split the doctor's face and he hurried off. We decided to take the cat back to the hotel with us, hang on to it for the remainder of the trip, and then drop it off at a shelter near the airport on our way out of town. This way, at least the kitten would know a few days of comfort, and we could return to a cat-free, dog-only house.

At the hotel, the kitten settled in, exploring every nook and cranny. She ate cat food until her belly bulged. She used the litter box immediately. That first night she slept by Kathy's side. I could see where all of this was headed.

The next few days passed quickly. When we would return from exploring Puerto Vallarta, the kitten was always there, happy to see us. She began to really turn on the charm and I found myself thinking more and more about the kitten, as she slowly won me over.

Our last evening in Mexico arrived quickly. The next day Miss Kitty was headed for the shelter. By this time, I was completely torn. In a matter of days this little kitten had captured my heart. As the evening closed, the cat jumped up on the bed, climbed onto my knee, and crawled her way up to my chest, her sharp claws jabbing me the entire way. I didn't move. She sat in the center of my chest, curled up into a tight ball, and went to sleep.

"You know, we can't leave her," I found myself saying.

"I know," was all Kathy said, smiling.

We hadn't named the cat, for fear of becoming too attached. Obviously, we had disproved that theory. Since we had found her on the 8th hole of a golf course and *ocho* means eight in Spanish, we named her Ocha, adding the feminine "a" at the end. The name was perfect. She was too.

In Chicago, Ocha thrived. She ate three square meals a day, quickly gaining weight. You couldn't see her ribs anymore. She explored the house, slept under bed covers, and always found the sunniest spots on the most comfortable of furniture. She even earned the respect of Chloe, the Siberian Husky, with a few quick ninja swipes to the nose.

However, Ocha was a very timid cat. Who knows what type of trauma she experienced before Kathy and I found her? She always hid when company visited.

The years rolled by and Ocha became my cat. I fed her and changed her litter and made a point of petting and playing with her every single day. Eventually, she progressed to exploring the backyard while under my close supervision. On cold winter nights, Ocha would crawl underneath the covers of our bed and plaster herself to my right hip, purring intently. She became a warmth freak, lying on the heating vents during winter months.

As the bond between Ocha and me grew, unfortunately, the bond between Kathy and me became strained. There was a miscarriage and arguing. Eventually, that bond dissolved completely. We divorced after six years of marriage and my life, my dreams, were blown apart.

Ocha came with me while Chloe went with Kathy. The divorce was the most difficult thing I've had to go through in my life. It caused me to doubt myself and to question everything I knew. I felt lost, afraid, and alone.

Many nights, after all of the lawyers were done arguing and all of the paperwork had been signed, I would look to Ocha for strength and inspiration. Here is a cat, now fully grown, who had a horrible start in life. She had no reason to live, and indeed, would probably have died had she not been found. Yet, she started over, with complete trust in me, leaving everything behind, for a totally new life. She made it. She survived and has become a beloved pet and friend that I lean on to this day. If she can survive difficult circumstances, and flourish, so can I. I draw strength from the story of her life and know, even in my darkest moments, hope lives, and a better life is just around the bend.

~Jimmy Tang

It's Not about the Cat!

It's really the cat's house — we just pay the mortgage.
~Author Unknown

"**H**oney, Tigger doesn't seem well," I told my husband Eric one evening. My dear domestic cat was usually perfectly content to lay on my pillow, even when my head wasn't on it. But tonight, he repeatedly climbed right in my lap, stared me in the face, and meowed loudly. I knew he was trying to tell me something.

"He seems to be in pain," I said. Eric agreed to run him to the vet right then. And when he called me from their office an hour later, the news wasn't good.

"He has a blockage in his urinary tract. It's a common problem with male cats," he explained.

"Okay, so let's get him taken care of," I said with a shrug. If it was a common problem, it shouldn't be a big deal for the vet to fix. I was convinced that Tigger would be on my pillow by bedtime.

My husband sighed and said, "It's not as easy as that. The treatment is going to take several days and it could cost as much as a grand."

"A thousand dollars?" I gasped, thinking of our two young children, our hefty mortgage payment, and my part-time teacher's paycheck. I swallowed hard. "What other options do we have?"

"We pay to treat him or we pay to put him to sleep."

"Oh, my gosh! We can't let him die!" I said through my tears.

"He's a cat," Eric said flatly. "We got him for free, and now you want to spend a thousand dollars to fix him."

"He's part of our family," I insisted. "We have no choice."

"Look, they said that they wouldn't do anything for him until tomorrow morning anyway. Why don't I come home and we can make the decision overnight?"

I agreed, although in my mind, the decision was already made.

That night, we went around and around about "the cat."

He mentioned the cat allergy he had discovered he had since Tigger had come into the family. I shrugged and handed him his Zyrtec. I brought up how much the children loved Tigger and how sad they would be if he were no longer with us.

He brought up some outstanding financial obligations, as well as the fact that I had decided to work part-time since the birth of our second child. He even mentioned that our upcoming vacation plans might have to be cancelled if we decided to treat Tigger's condition.

Finally I threw up my hands and said, "I can't even believe we're discussing this. Tigger is worth whatever it costs."

"Maybe to you, but not to me," he said stubbornly. "I don't want to spend our vacation money on your cat."

I sighed and gently put my hand on my husband's cheek. "You do realize that this is not about the cat, right?"

He stared at me blankly. "Of course it is. You want to spend a thousand dollars on a cat we got for free."

"But it's not about the cat." Another blank stare. "Look, do you love me?"

It was his turn to sigh. "You know I do."

"Then you need to change the way you're thinking. Don't think of it as spending a thousand dollars on a cat."

"A cat that I'm allergic to," he interrupted.

"Don't think of it that way. Think of it as spending a thousand dollars to keep your wife from being heartbroken. To prevent your kids from losing their pet. That's where this money is going. To save your family's feelings, not the cat's life."

"But it's so much money, and our vacation plans..."

"I know, honey, I know. You were going to take your family on a lovely vacation to show them how much you love them, but your family decided that they would rather have you spend that money on something else. So..."

"So I'm going to spend a thousand dollars on a cat to show my family how much I love them," he finished. "A cat we got for free."

I nodded and smiled gently.

"It doesn't make sense," he insisted.

"But it's not about the cat, remember?"

A few days later, Tigger was recovering and my husband was writing an extremely hefty check to the vet's office.

And under his breath, I could swear I heard him mutter, "It's not about the cat."

~Diane Stark

That Canal-Cat Nuisance!

To err is human, to purr is feline.

~Robert Byrne

I knew that canal cat was going to prove a problem the day I came home from work to find my wife, Jeanne, and our sixth-grader, Dixon, hovering over a cardboard box in his room.

A bedraggled bit of matted, black and white fur lay on a soft towel with a warm water bottle tucked under it. Jeanne, a nurse, was hand-feeding it some special food. The poor little kitten was so weak it could scarcely lick the food off Jeanne's finger. ("Careful!" I warned myself. "Don't think of it that way in this house of pet collectors. Think, instead, of another mouth to feed.") Dixon hugged me as I put down my briefcase. "Somebody tried to drown her, Dad," he said. "Her fur was all wet. The vet gave her a shot of antibiotics to ward off an infection and told us to feed her this until she can tolerate regular cat food."

"I see," I said, eyeing the eighty-five-dollar vet bill on the dresser. "Just remember you can't keep this cat because you already have one."

"But we're supposed to help the helpless, Dad," Dixon rebutted. "Just last Sunday our lesson was 'Cast your bread on the water for you will find it after many days.'" (Ecclesiastes 11:01)

"I agree to help the helpless," I said. "But when she's well, the canal cat has to be given away. This house isn't big enough."

"Meanwhile, she can stay in my room with Kiff and me," Dixon said. "Kiff doesn't mind her and, with my bed hoisted up to the ceiling, there is plenty of room on the floor below it." I wished he hadn't mentioned that bed. Jeanne had been worried about that bed ever since Dixon and I raised it high off the floor to imitate a ship hammock, suiting Dixon's new seafaring room motif. Jeanne was afraid he might fall out of bed onto the tile and concrete floor. She only agreed to the bed being raised when I said it was scarcely higher than an upper bunk bed and we could get a soft rug for his floor.

That was weeks ago and he'd vetoed every rug sample Jeanne brought home. Nor had he given the cat away, though she was now fat, her coat shiny and her green eyes mischievous. I hadn't exactly been rewarded, either, for casting my bread on the water to help that rascal. "Sparky," as Dixon named her, had behavior problems. In spite of our efforts to train her, Sparky chewed electric cords. I figured some day she would live up to her name. Though we'd partly solved that problem by attaching the cords tightly to the walls, she also ate house plants. My study's big brass bowl of Creeping Charley was the first victim, down to the last leaf. Then she ravaged the front room ivy while Jeanne was at the grocery store. But she committed her worst sin the day she dirtied on my lecture notes for my bridge design course. "Dad, Sparky still has delicate bowels," Dixon said. "She couldn't help it."

"Dixon, you've excused that furry culprit's every crime! But her dirtying on my lecture notes is the last straw! Tomorrow, I'll help you write an ad to give her away."

That evening was quiet. Even Kiff was away, scaring a field mouse from a neighbor's store room. We watched TV and played chess before we went to bed early.

But the quiet was short lived. About 1:30 A.M., Jeanne and I woke up to loud, eerie screams! We both bolted upright in bed. "What is that noise?" I yelled, as I leaped out of bed and hit the light switch. "What's wrong?"

"The cat, I think!" Jeanne grabbed her robe and flew down the hall to Dixon's room.

I sprinted ahead of her, jerked open the door and snapped on the light. Sparky was running around and around the room. But the cat stopped short when we entered. I looked up at Dixon's bed. He wasn't in it! Suddenly we heard a moan from across the room and saw Dixon there, in a heap on the floor. He must have had a bad dream and literally pitched out of that bed.

As we ran toward him, I saw a gigantic lump on Dixon's head. Just then he started gagging. Though his eyes were shut and he was unconscious, he was starting to vomit. "Hurry!" Jeanne ordered. "Help me turn him on his side, so he doesn't get vomit in his lungs and drown!" I obeyed. "Sparky called us just in the nick of time," Jeanne said, as I dialed an ambulance.

At the hospital, X-rays showed that his skull was not fractured under that gigantic bump. But he was still not conscious. "He's got a nasty concussion," the doctor said. "We'll keep him hospitalized until we're sure there is no blood clot requiring surgery."

By sun up Dixon was conscious and talking coherently so I went home to shower and go to work. When I got home, I lowered that bed the first thing. Then I opened a can of cat food and Sparky came purring. As I knelt down and petted her, I remembered the Bible verse Dixon had quoted the day he'd rescued Sparky.

When the doctor decided there was no blood clot, we brought Dixon home. As Dixon climbed into his bed, I set Sparky beside him. Petting her black and white fur, he said, "Dad, are you still going to make me give her away?"

"No," I said, raising my hand in a swearing-in position, "I hereby declare that Sparky has a permanent home with us for the rest of her life!" Ever since, I've sworn off complaining about nuisances. You never know when one will turn out to be God's blessing in disguise.

~Louis A. Hill, Jr.

A Tale of Two Kitties

One cat just leads to another.
~Ernest Hemingway

In September 2003, Hurricane Isabel hit Maryland hard, felling trees and knocking out power. Much to the delight of the kids, no power meant no school. At the time, we lived in a townhouse development, and more construction was in progress. No school meant more time for my boys and all the neighborhood kids to get muddy and explore the construction site. So while I was busy trying to figure out how I'd ever get a cup of coffee or prepare meals without electricity, my sons and their friends were trying to figure out which neighborhood mom would be most likely to take in the litter of kittens they'd just discovered huddled in a drain pipe. They voted for me.

The power eventually came back on and the kids returned to school, but those five little kittens lived in our downstairs bathroom for weeks. Every day after school the boys and their friends would race in to see the kittens—to feed them, play with them, and cuddle them. I, of course, set about the task of finding homes for them. Eventually four went to new homes, and one stayed with us.

The light-colored calico of the litter had stolen our hearts, and we, perhaps predictably, named her Isabel. It was a fitting name considering her powerful personality. When she wasn't much bigger than a pork chop herself, she jumped on the table while my husband was eating dinner, stuck her claws in his pork chop, and dragged it off his plate. She seemed to approach all of life that way. Isabel was unstoppable and would simply not conform to life as an indoor cat. She regularly slipped out of the house for adventures in the neighborhood. Yet whenever she returned, she was eager to jump in your lap to knead, snuggle, and purr. It didn't take long before it felt like Isabel had always been a part of our family. As time passed, we stopped calling her Isabel and started calling her Kitty.

Two years after the boys had brought her home, Kitty got sick. My husband took her to the vet and returned home with terrible news: Kitty had only twenty percent of her lung capacity left and likely had FIP, a fatal disease. We would have to put her to sleep. The boys had found this cat and loved her, but I was devastated too. She slept with me that final night, snuggled up beside me in bed.

The next morning my husband, my oldest son, and I took her to the vet. As we drove, we discussed the new kitten that everyone wanted—everyone but me, that is. My husband had spotted the kitten in the vet's office the day before. Her brothers were all variations on gray and white, but this kitten was a dark calico with a checkerboard for a face. I was adamantly opposed. As our friend so aptly put it, I feared the new kitten would always be "death kitty." I wanted some space first. Time to grieve. I was overruled.

On the way home I held Kitty's body wrapped in a blanket and cried. In the back seat, my son held the new kitten that my husband had named Checkers. We buried Kitty in the backyard. In the house, Checkers hid under the couch. She would only come out to dash under the nearby loveseat. Everyone already adored Checkers, but I insisted that she was a terrible cat and would never come out of hiding.

Somehow, though, kittens find a way to win you over. They hop sideways, stretch out for tummy scratches, and jump into bathroom sinks to nap. The cute factor dismantles your defenses. Oddly enough, though my husband had chosen Checkers, for two years he could not get anywhere near her. If he did get a chance to pet her, she would run away and proceed to bathe herself thoroughly. We joked that she thought he was repulsive. He'd tell Checkers that she owed her life to him, but it was my lap she'd jump into.

Checkers is both feisty and sweet, and it's been a long time since she has needed to hide under the couch. My husband is now allowed to pet her and she'll occasionally jump into his lap too. The boys still adore her, and I always tell her that she's my favorite pretty girl. Checkers is a wonderful reminder that good can come from bad, that blessings can come out of sad situations, and that—sometimes anyway—I can be wrong and my husband can be right.

~Nina Taylor

The Man Who Hated Cats

She clawed her way into my heart and wouldn't let go.
~Missy Altijd

My father did not like cats. He'd say so himself in his gruff, no-nonsense voice every time the subject came up. Raised during the Great Depression, he took pride in the fact that he'd been doing a man's work and receiving a man's pay for it ever since the age of eight when he landed his first job in a local dairy. Implied in that notion was that real men didn't like cats. They might tolerate dogs, preferably large hunting dogs, but certainly not small, fluffy cats.

None of the other tool-and-dye makers my father worked with cared for cats. If one showed up at the back door of the factory, certainly no one ever put down a saucer of milk or a can of tuna. Instead, the poor creature would be quickly shooed away. After all, real men didn't like cats.

Around the time my father retired, however, a scraggly tiger cat showed up in the neighborhood. The skinny fellow would peer in the window at night and meow sadly. Clearly he had once been someone's pet but whether he'd been lost or abandoned, we were never to know.

"I don't like cats," my father told my mother one night. "But I don't think it would hurt if you put out some food for that tiger cat. He looks starved half to death."

Since my mother was already entertaining thoughts in that direction, she started putting out a dish of cat food by the back door. Quickly realizing he was on to a good thing, the tiger cat soon started hanging out full time in our backyard. As he plumped out, he lost his sense of fear and gained a name. He went from "that tiger cat" to "Tiger Cat" and finally, "Tiger." Now when he arrived for breakfast, he began to be less interested in food than in attention. He'd arch his back and rub up against our legs, purring happily.

My father continued to profess his dislike of cats, but every now and then we'd catch him leaning down to give Tiger a pat on the head. However, with winter approaching my mother began to fret about where he would find shelter from the snow and the wind. All the forecasters were predicting one of the harshest winters in years. A small animal would need to find a snug home or perish in the cold.

"Well, I don't care much for cats," Dad said. "But I don't suppose it would hurt if we took care of him through the winter. Let me see what I can do for a box."

He rooted through the junk in his tool shed and came up with an old wooden whiskey crate. It would provide Tiger protection on four sides but the wind would still be able to whistle in through the opening on the fifth side. So my father nailed a covering across it. He cut a hole in it just big enough for Tiger to wriggle in and out.

It didn't end there, though. The man who hated cats seemed determined to provide this particular cat with the finest of winter resorts. He lined the box with insulation to keep out the cold. To make it more comfortable, he covered the insulation with carpet samples. Then, worried that Tiger would still be able to feel the cold, he tucked his old woolen army blanket inside.

When my mother raised an eyebrow and asked why he was doing this if he disliked cats so much, he defensively replied, "Just because I don't like cats doesn't mean I want to see him suffer."

That winter, Tiger was very grateful that my father disliked cats so much. The winter that blew in early that November was even crueler than the weather forecasters had predicted. By February the temperature had remained below zero for weeks. One particularly bitter morning, Tiger stumbled out of his whiskey crate half frozen to death. Even the layers of wood, insulation, carpet, and wool couldn't keep him warm. When my mother suggested moving Tiger into the heated garage, my father didn't object.

"I don't like cats," began his familiar refrain, "but I don't think it would hurt anything to keep him in the garage for the rest of the winter."

So Tiger exchanged his box outdoors for an equally luxurious box next to my father's workbench. However, now that he had crossed the threshold from outdoors to indoors, Tiger didn't see why he should be kept out of the rest of the house. Whenever he heard my parents inside, he scratched at the door, meowing plaintively.

This time, my mother didn't even have to suggest it to my father. One night as Tiger was making his usual racket outside the kitchen door, my father pointed out, "I'm not much of a one for cats, but it would at least be quieter if we brought him all the way inside."

That night, Tiger made his final transition from unwanted stray to pampered pet. He wandered through the carpeted rooms as though unable to believe his good fortune. He finally settled down on a cushion next to the fireplace. His contented purr rumbled through the room.

After that, there was no question that Tiger would ever again be anything but an indoor cat. My father, however, still tried to maintain his dislike of cats.

"I don't like cats," he'd still say. "But this guy is something special."

My mother and I never disputed that statement. Instead, we just exchanged smiles.

Several years later, as Tiger grew into old age, another tiger cat appeared in the raspberry bushes at the edge of the yard. She had six kittens in tow.

"You know, I don't much like cats," my father said, peering out the kitchen window. "But maybe we should bring them inside...."

~Amy Merrill-Wyatt

A Little Cat Can Change a Campo

Cats are intended to teach us that not everything in nature has a purpose.
~Garrison Keillor

It was my first week in my new Peace Corps assignment in a small campo in the Dominican Republic. I had just moved in with my new host family, and was feeling fairly alienated by my less than mediocre Spanish. Communication was difficult and frustrating. I had never been a cat person before, but the family had a kitten that was a few weeks old running around the house; it was a small boney thing of fluff that had just shown up one day. It was white, with a black patch over one eye; very sweet. It didn't speak Spanish either... we bonded instantly.

That week, on my trip into the local town, I purchased a bag of cat food to bring back to the undernourished kitten. I thought nothing of this action, as I assumed the cat was small because my host family was too poor to buy food for her, and that they would be pleased by the contribution. I had no idea the repercussions of this action would reverberate throughout the entire community.

It was explained to me that in campo life in the Dominican Republic, a cat has one sole purpose: to kill and eat rats. If a cat is underfed, it is because it hasn't done its job. If it dies from this condition, that's the consequence of not serving its purpose. The fact that I had purchased cat food, when there was an abundance of rats and undernourished children in the population, was regarded as more than just a strange phenomenon, but somewhat of an affront to the community. I tried to explain that in the U.S., our pets are considered part of the family, often supplying much love and comfort. My explanations, in faulty Spanish, only served to further confuse the natives.

During the next week, twice a day I would call out, "Mishu" (the word for "cat" in our campo) and put out the cat food. By the end of the week, every time I called out to her, she came, often from great distances, meowing replies to the call, which mystified people in the campo greatly. They had never seen a cat respond to a human in such a way, but of course, they had never seen a human treat a cat in such a way either.

The following week, I became ill, and was confined to my bed. When I finally arose, I noticed the kitten was no longer in the house. I asked my host family what had happened to her, and was told one of the neighbors had taken her, and had tied her up at their house. I was shocked. I asked why no one had gone to get her, but wasn't too surprised to hear the response of "It's just a cat."

I went to the neighbor to ask why he had taken the kitten. The man looked at me, and said roughly, "It's my cat." He was lying, but to avoid confrontation, I offered to buy the cat from him. "No, this cat needs to eat rats." I felt desperate as I looked at Mishu tied there, straining against the twine cord crudely tied around her neck, meowing in discomfort and frustration as she tried to come to me.

I went back to my host family's house and began to cry. It felt like such a helpless situation, struggling against the language and cultural barrier, but then something happened. People started coming to console me. They had never seen a person so distraught over an animal, and though they didn't understand, they were sympathetic. The community began to talk, and the original owner of the kitten was soon tracked down and brought to me. I was incredibly moved by the community effort.

The owner went and collected the kitten, and offered to gift her to me, but I insisted on paying for the trouble. I had no idea how much a cat cost, and offered 500 pesos (the equivalent of fifteen U.S.

dollars). The community couldn't believe I would place such a high value on a kitten. After that, there was never any doubt that Mishu was mine.

Well... there was a little doubt that Mishu was mine, as she was convinced that I was hers. When I finally moved out of my host family's house, into a house of my own, she was decidedly discontent. She didn't want to move, and apparently hadn't given me permission to either. She would come to the new home, sit in front of me and meow non-stop until I returned to visit my host family. When it was time to go back to our new home, she would follow me all the way, meowing intensely. People joked that I hadn't consulted her about the move. This was a first for the community—acknowledging an animal could have an opinion.

During my time with Mishu, she provided many "firsts" for the campo. She was the first cat to ever have a bath, the weekly provision of which provided many humorous stories for the people of the campo. She was the first cat to sleep in a bed, despite all the warnings that if you sleep with a cat, it will wake up in the night and claw out your throat. She was the first cat to be loving and cuddly—anyone could approach her and be greeted with love. She was the first cat to go for walks in the campo, often accompanying me on short visits. She was the first cat to change the way people saw animals, exceeding every preconceived expectation they had... and she was the first cat in the campo to kill rats for the sport of it, and not from overwhelming hunger.

When Mishu disappeared the following year, people went out and searched for her, without being asked. She was considered a member of the community by then. When they found her body, people cried and consoled me. No one said, "It's just a cat." She had served as more than just an odd conversation piece in the campo, and had indeed taught these people, through interaction, love and an occasional humorous mishap, what a wonderful addition a cat can be to the life of a family.

~Mei Emerald Gaffey-Hernandez

A Little Cat Can Change a Campo : Learning to Love the Cat

Fish Out of Water

Some circumstantial evidence is very strong,
as when you find a trout in the milk.
~Henry David Thoreau

One hot summer day my best friend Danielle appeared at my doorstep. She was holding a small lime green tank and inside was her beloved Chinese fighting fish named Lil' Blue. Alongside was her mother with the keys to her house and a long list of instructions. Their family was going away on a three-week vacation and they trusted me to look after their two cats and the fish. This was my first "real" job and I was determined to do an excellent job. I'd walk to their house twice a day to care for the cats, and the fish would remain under my watchful eye on my bedside table. "Don't worry," I called as they drove down the driveway, "I'll take care of them. Your pets are safe with me."

And I kept true to my word. The fish got fresh water and a tank cleaning on a regular basis, the cats' meals never came a minute late, and the litter box was cleaned daily. Time flew by and before I knew it my job was coming to an end. In just two short days, Danielle and her family would be returning home and greeting their wonderful pets. There would be a twenty-dollar bill with my name on it.

My entire family was gathered on the living room floor playing a game of *Cat-opoly*, with one of our cats watching intently. Just as I landed on the Cat-astrophe square (what traditional *Monopoly* players would know as Chance), my other cat dashed onto our game board, knocking over the game pieces. This was not unusual behavior for Abby, as she'd always been rather hyper and carefree. She gently released something onto the game board and then looked up at us with proud eyes. It looked almost like a wet feather sticking to our game. "What is that?" my mother questioned. We all bent forward to get a closer look and not a moment later I heard my mother begin to scream. My sisters joined in and soon after, I too was screaming at the top of my lungs. It was Lil' Blue! He was lying there; limp, with what looked to be not a speck of life left in him. "Abby! How could you! Bad cat!" we were all yelling ferociously. Her head sunk as she ran off as fast as she could. That stupid cat had killed my friend's fish. I couldn't help but cry knowing how disappointed Danielle and her family would be. They trusted me and I had broken my promise in keeping the pets safe.

My mom was the only one who had the composure to swipe that fish up and get it back into water. Lil' Blue just floated on top, his once bright blue colour shifted to gray. I went to my bedroom to check the crime scene. It appeared that the fish tank had been knocked off my table and all of its water had drained out. "Megan," my mom hollered, "Get back here!" I quickly ran to the bathroom and noticed Lil' Blue finally starting to quiver and move. Slowly but surely, his colour returned. By the end of the night he was swimming around healthily as if nothing had happened. This was surely a miracle, I thought to myself.

But it wasn't a miracle that happened that day. It was the kind, thoughtful heart of Abby that saved the fish. Clearly the tank had been knocked over. How? We would never know. Abby was probably playing around or something. Regardless, the fish was rescued. Abby brought him directly to us. She left no bite marks, not even the tiniest dent, in his gills. It would have been so easy for her to just savor him as a light snack or leave him on the floor for me to find later on. But Abby wasn't the evil cat we made her out to be; she was a hero that day and I will always feel sorry for yelling at and blaming her.

In the end, I got Lil' Blue back home to Danielle safe and sound. He lived on for more than two years after that. I cannot thank Abby enough for her choice to save the fish that day. This cat taught me two very important lessons: One being that things aren't always how they appear and you should never blame someone for something without knowing all of the facts. And two, be careful where you leave the fish tank.

~Megan Carty

Reprinted by permission of Off the Mark
and Mark Parisi ©1999

You Don't Know Jack

Does the father figure in your cat's life ever clean the litter box?
My husband claims that men lack the scooping gene.
~Barbara L. Diamond

We love cats. Well, I love cats, and my husband is a sort of transient in the world of animal lovers, finding himself standing on the outside and looking in with a tepid interest in how the other half lives.

An overzealous pet owner he is not, but he can mildly tolerate dogs that live outdoors. He claims allergies. When he met me, however, he had to resign himself to living among the enemy.

To date, we have had five adult cats and approximately thirty-three kittens scattered throughout eighteen years of marriage.

The system that works around our house is that I feed the cats, I clean up after the cats, I shop for the cats, and I care for the cats. My spouse still complains.

"Cats are a lot of work. Why do we need all these cats?" he asked me years ago.

"We only have two."

"They don't do anything but eat, sleep, and use the litter box. What good are cats?"

"The kids love them."

"But the kids will leave someday, and we'll be stuck with all these cats. What then?"

"I'll take care of them. Don't worry, dear."

I knew the addition of one more cat would be reckless, but one chilly evening fate had other plans.

The kids and I stopped to get some burgers for dinner at Jack in the Box. Intending to run in and out, we almost missed a woman kneeling on the ground with French fries in her hand.

"Will you take this kitten home?" she asked. "My husband will just kill me if I bring home one more stray!"

"Ohhhhhhh," I sympathized with an apologetic chuckle, the same version of her story (different husband) quick on my lips. "I don't think..." But then I looked down at the helpless creature, and I could feel my heart begin to soften. He was the picture of innocence.

However, because stray cats usually have unfavorable personalities, a certain people-less, independent air about them, I could feel myself gain the confidence to walk through the restaurant's glass doors and not look back.

Teetering on the precipice of refusal, I accidentally caught a glimpse of my toddler cradling the kitten inside her pudgy embrace. He lay there like a limp doll and allowed my daughter to fondle him with the unstable, brutish pawing of four-year-old hands. He didn't move. He purred.

This wasn't a typical alley cat.

This couldn't be! Why me? Why now? I could NOT take another cat!

"Of course I'll take him," I heard some foreign voice say from inside my body. It sounded like my voice, but surely I wouldn't have conceded so quickly, not with such a potentially volatile, six-foot-four-inch consequence looming at home.

Yet there we were—plus one—driving away with our burgers and fries.

I worried through dinner what I would say to my husband. We left the vagrant kitten sleeping in the car until I could introduce him in a way that would soften the inevitable firestorm that would shoot from my husband's mouth like sparks from an exploding brick of firecrackers. Would this be the final straw? Would the man finally just leave me to my feline friends in exchange for a life free from allergies and the pungent odor of litter box deposits?

I would know soon enough. At the first opportunity, I bathed the cat, named him, and counted the minutes for the hammer to fall.

"No!"

It was a singular word, but it carried the meaning of so many conversations before it. My husband took one look at the kitten, his freshly washed fur shining beneath the glaring fluorescent kitchen lights, and his eyes narrowed.

"No," he repeated. "We aren't keeping another cat. You shouldn't have brought him home. Look at him! Where'd you get him? We are not keeping him. We don't need another stray!"

"But you don't know Jack," I cooed, my hand extending to touch Jack's clean fur. "He seems thankful to us for rescuing him."

"Jack?" His brows arched in an I-can't-believe-you-named-him way.

"Yes!" I smiled. "We found him at Jack in the Box, and he was so hungry and dirty, you should have seen him! I couldn't just leave him there." That's it, pull on his heartstrings. "He had nowhere to go."

My husband's eyes darted from the kitten to me, over to the kids' expectant faces, and back to Jack. I could tell he wanted to assert his authority as Head of the Household, King of the Castle, and simply demand that we turn Jack loose, but to his credit, he couldn't.

I saw hesitation flicker across his face as he contemplated what he would say next. The kids and I waited for the verdict.

It never came.

With a defeated shrug, our hero quietly resigned himself to the idea of another cat and padded down the hall to bed. His tacit surrender was all Jack needed to become an integral part of the family.

Unfortunately, we did not get to keep Jack forever. After nine years, one day he just disappeared. He slipped from our lives as unexpectedly as he'd entered. We never saw him again, but he left his mark on our hearts.

After sharing a real home with us, Jack seemed undamaged by the life of a typical alley cat; he forgot what it was like to forage for food or dodge traffic. He slept on the bed at night. He took uninter-rupted naps. He made fast friends with the other cats in the house.

Jack proved his amiability, even as a stray. We loved him.

We didn't get Jack from a pet store or from an ad for free kittens. Jack spent the first few weeks of his life on a highway avoiding cars and sponging fries off good Samaritans. All he needed was a chance to show his worth.

The lesson here is that things may not always be as they first appear. Jack was a stray... but in name only. If you are still skeptical about stray cats, if you think they won't make good pets, or if you buy into the opinion that strays are unable to become lovable ani-mals—then, quite frankly—you don't know Jack.

~Dana Martin

On Probation

Success in marriage does not come merely through finding the right mate,
but through being the right mate.
~Barnett R. Brickner

When a chomping noise in our master bathroom woke me for the fifth night in a row, I nudged my husband. "Honey, are you awake? I'm hearing it again."

"So am I," Hal said. "It has to be rats in the drainpipes."

I shivered. "Rats? In this neighborhood?"

"They probably come up from the creek in back."

The thought of rats turned my stomach, as well as raising the hair on the back of my neck. Then I had a brilliant idea. "Time for a cat," I said.

"You know I'm allergic to cats. I'll put out traps in the morning." Hal turned over, preventing any further discussion.

I lay in bed getting more irritated by the minute. I had wanted a cat for a long time, having grown up with one, and now we really needed a ratter. But Hal wouldn't even consider one. I thought he overestimated his hay fever.

Hal put out well-baited traps the next morning, but the rats avoided them and continued dining on our house. "Time for a cat," I said as Hal and I worked in the garden.

"You want a cat?" A neighbor, overhearing me, called across the fence. "A friend of mine is moving and his cat needs a home. A one-year-old male. Big cat."

"Is he a hunter?" I asked.

"I hear he's a great hunter."

"Thanks, but no thanks," Hal told our neighbor. "I'm allergic to cats."

"Come on, honey," I begged. "Please give him a chance. We can always give him back."

Our neighbor looked from Hal to me, not wanting to get into a family argument. "My eyes itch just thinking about it, but I guess we have to try something," Hal relented.

I hugged him and went inside to tell our three kids.

As soon as I saw Snooper, I fell in love. A big, gray cat with a perfect white star on his chest, Snooper retracted his claws the minute I swooped him up, put his paws around my neck, and kissed my cheek with his sandpaper tongue.

Then Tami, Ben, and Joel each got a turn holding him, stroking his cheeks, and listening to him purr his appreciation.

"You have to catch a lot of rats if you want to stay," I whispered into his furry neck when it was my turn, again, to cuddle him.

I swear Snooper understood. He caught nine rats the first week, and five the second, laying them out carefully on the front steps.

"Fourteen rats in two weeks. Can we keep him?" I asked Hal.

"He's a samurai warrior, all right. But if I so much as touch him, my whole face runs. Sorry, hon."

I looked at Hal more closely. "Wow. Your eyes are all puffy," I said, putting my hand on his arm. Suppose he wasn't exaggerating his allergies? "I'll keep him off the furniture and have him sleep outside. See if that helps."

Snooper seemed to know he was still on probation. The third week he caught another five rats, and added two moles for good measure. When he wasn't hunting, he played family therapist, jumping into the lap of whichever kid seemed in most need of attention, and turning on his purr motor.

As if that weren't enough to please us, he appointed himself my personal bodyguard. I'd recently taken up jogging while Hal got ready for work. One morning when I was running alone I saw movement in the shrubs along the road. Was someone following me? I gathered my courage and looked again. I'd heard the safest course is to confront a pursuer. The shrubs rustled and Snooper shot out, loping across the yard next to me.

"Hey, Snooper," I called to him, delighted.

From then on, whenever I ran he kept a careful, yellow eye on me. I wasn't sure exactly what he'd do if I fell and twisted an ankle. Would he run home and yowl until someone followed him? But somehow I felt safer.

Hal appreciated him out there with me too. "A watch cat?" he said when I told him about Snooper. "Maybe he would come for us if something happened to you."

"So is Snooper off probation?" I asked.

"I hate to say it, but the allergy thing is a real hassle. What about a dog that hunts? Some kind of retriever. I'd like a big guy dog."

I chewed my lip in frustration. I'd like a dog too, but not if it meant losing Snooper. Still, I had to respect Hal's allergies. He'd made a real effort.

I combed the ads for the perfect dog. One morning an ad for Rex, a large Golden Retriever, appeared. I'd enjoy him, I knew, but I teared up just thinking about giving up Snooper.

The kids went with me to get Rex while Hal finished up a house project. I hadn't told them we probably couldn't keep Snooper. Once they had Rex, hopefully they wouldn't feel as bad. As soon as we turned in the driveway, Hal and Snooper wandered up to the car to meet our new dog.

Rex emerged, regal head first, then long, feathered legs, his burnished copper coat gleaming in the sun. "That's the most beautiful dog I've seen." Hal's eyes were wide with admiration. "Good job, honey."

Snooper took a step toward Rex. "Atta cat," I said, hoping, against hope, that through some miracle I could keep them both.

Rex promptly emitted a big "woof" and chased Snooper into a thicket of tall grasses and vine maple.

"No," I shouted at Rex, terrified for Snooper.

I could have saved my breath. Within seconds Rex tore out the other side of the brush, his tail between his legs, Snooper nipping at his heels.

Hal laughed so hard tears sparkled in his eyes. "I'm starting to really like this cat," he said. "Samurai Warrior? Bodyguard? That's all good. But a fifteen-pound cat that will take on a ninety-pound dog? That's great."

"Which means?"

"The dog is gorgeous. We can't send him back. Snooper? He's unique among cats, isn't he? I guess we can't send him back either."

Hal reached down and patted Rex. I swooped Snooper into my arms. "You did it," I whispered, ruffling his fur. "You're off probation."

Then I looked at Hal. He smiled, his eyes soft.

"Thank you," I said, finally getting it. True, Snooper was a very remarkable cat. But Hal also cared enough about the kids and my attachment to Snooper to grant him tenure.

~Samantha Ducloux Waltz

What I Learned from the Cat

Learning to Be My Best

Many times a day I realize how much my own life is built upon the labors of my fellowmen, and how earnestly I must exert myself in order to give in return as much as I have received.

~Albert Einstein

The Cat and Toad Exercise Plan

Even overweight, cats instinctively know the cardinal rule:
when fat, arrange yourself in slim poses.
~John Weitz

Katrina, my plus-sized Manx cat, and I are on a weight reduction program. I exercise at the gym three nights a week. Well, not exactly three times a week, but I seriously consider it that often. I take my workout clothes to the office and usually think twice before I accept a dinner invitation that conflicts with my exercise schedule. This is an improvement over prior attempts to squeeze into my skinny jeans. One of my more noteworthy failures was when I stopped exercising to Denise Austin's "Hit the Spot Abs" video. After an initial thirty-day burst of energy, I began to watch it while lying on the couch with Katrina on my lap.

Katrina, on the other hand, blissfully unaware of her obesity, yowls until I fill her dish with cat food. In warm weather, she supplements her diet with a huntress lifestyle. On cold days, I let her stay inside and laze around the house. Her belly pooches out as she waddles from the sunny spot in the kitchen to the sunny spot in front of the living room patio door. Her only exercise is watching squirrels scamper along the deck railing.

I double check the date on the appointment card from the vet. "Well, Katrina, we might as well go get our butts chewed out."

Katrina's vet is great with animals, but impatient with owners who allow their pets to gain too much weight. He is sure to give me a stern lecture now that Katrina has become a barrel-bellied beast. She swishes her short stubby tail and closes her green eyes as I brush her fur to a glossy sheen.

I cram her rear-first into a one-size-fits-most pet carrier for the trip to the vet's office.

"This cat needs to lose weight," Dr. Gough says as he runs his hands down her sides in a futile effort to feel her ribs.

"Somehow I knew you would say that."

"She has worms too," he continues. "I'm surprised she can catch anything as fat as she is."

I try to stuff an uncooperative Katrina back into the carrier. "She's really quick when she's chasing something," I say. Just last week, a snake tried to slither into a hole with Katrina hot on his tail. He finally got tired of her claws raking his slick backside and turned on her—hissing and chomping the air—while she continued to aggravate him. Not sure what kind of snake the little spitfire was, I threw walnuts at him and grabbed the scratching, clawing cat. I retreated into my house, slamming and bolting the door as if the snake would follow me inside.

"Apparently, she isn't getting enough exercise to offset what she eats," Dr. Gough said. "She needs diet food, and worm medication."

I gather up Katrina's new supplies and leave Dr. Gough's office. I briefly consider going to the gym while I'm in town. I have Katrina with me and, well, I just couldn't possibly leave her in the car, yowling in the pet carrier.

When we get home, I measure out a miniscule portion of Katrina's new diet food. She gazes at me with a bewildered expression, and her eyes shift from feed sack to her bowl, where the fish skeleton design is barely covered.

"Don't give me that look," I say. "You heard what Dr. Gough said as well as I did. This is it—all you get."

I grab a bag of chips, plop down on the couch and turn on the news. The brand of cat food I just fed Katrina has been recalled due to a few isolated deaths. Oh, crap! Here we are, two girls on a health kick and now one of us has eaten possibly tainted food. I fire up my computer and am somewhat comforted by the knowledge that Katrina's specific formula is not included in the recall.

After six weeks, we return for a moment-of-truth weigh-in. Katrina lost three pounds, and now weighs a svelte fourteen pounds. Her skin flops loosely around her belly when she trots and waves from side to side like a furry flag flapping in the breeze.

I tell Dr. Gough, "She acts like she's starving all the time."

Unconvinced, he says, "She still needs to lose a little more weight." I sympathize with her because I heard the exact same news at my doctor's appointment last week.

When we get home from the vet's office, I take the carrier out of the car and notice it feels heavier than the barbells at the gym. The weather has cooled slightly, and I decide it is no longer too hot for a girl wearing a fur coat. I open the carrier door and leave Katrina outside to play until evening.

The next morning, I let Katrina outside and notice the carrier on the porch. I'm ready for work and carrying my satchel and purse. I set them down and grunt as I bend to pick up the carrier. "Bending's hard on fat girls," I tell Katrina, as if she doesn't already know that.

When I plunk the carrier just inside the door, a toad leaps off it and lands on the kitchen carpet. I don't want a toad loose in the house so I contemplate how to catch the little critter.

I grab a paper towel and cup it inside my hand like a catcher's mitt. I reach for the toad and he takes a flying leap down the hallway where he sits defiantly on the floor. I creep a few steps closer and reach for him. Hop! Reach. Hop! Reach. Hop! Gotcha!

Just as success seems imminent, he jumps out of my paper-toweled hand and back onto the floor. The chase is on. Finally I grab him not so gently. I open the door and toss the toad onto the front porch. Luckily for him, Katrina is in the yard chasing something else.

I wash my hands thoroughly with anti-bacterial soap although my skin has not come into contact with the toad. I don't want my hands to break out in warts. Or, is that just one of those old superstitions?

I lock the door and notice the toad motionless in the exact spot where I tossed him. He is as gray as the weathered boards beneath him, tilted slightly on his side, one tiny webbed foot wedged in the crack between the boards.

"Oh, no! I killed him." Katrina, unaware of the lifeless toad, pounces in the opposite direction in pursuit of a squirrel.

Feeling remorse for my rough handling of the toad, I reach to touch the leathery skin I had carefully avoided earlier. As my finger nears the tiny still body, he leaps to the edge of the porch to make his escape.

The movement attracts Katrina's interest, and she streaks across the yard with youthful enthusiasm. I watch her and contemplate how winded I am after the additional activity this morning. Not to be outdone by an injured toad and an overweight cat, I slip my key into the lock and return for my exercise clothes.

~L. S. Fisher

Lucky

You will always be lucky if you know how to make friends with strange cats.
~Proverb

"I had a weird dream last night."

This line has become a private joke between my wife and me during our twenty-one years of marriage. Denise is one of those people who seem to think that only she has "weird" dreams. And Denise is always absolutely certain that I desperately want to hear every detail. And so, my rote, sarcastic-as-heck response:

"Can you share?"

"Well, I had this dream that we adopted another kitty," she continued.

This was not a new dream. Throughout our marriage we had always had at least one—and sometimes as many as four—felines that we both adored. We were down to just two cats. As a result, every few weeks Denise conveniently had a dream about adopting another cat.

"What's so weird about that?" I asked.

"This kitten was sooo unusual. He was gray, but with white, well, white... spirals. And he really needed us," she said.

I thought nothing more of it as we lay in bed that Saturday morning.

***

I'd been going through a rough patch in my career. I was counting the days until I would be checking out of a high-stress job with a think tank in downtown Washington, DC. I spent most of my workday debating with myself whether the three-hour commute sucked more than the nine hours spent working in a job that left me numb. At least the debate kept my mind active.

The Friday following Denise's weird dream, I woke with a jolt. Unlike Denise, who can amazingly remember all of her dreams in vivid detail, I have always had a bit of a memory disorder in that regard.

This morning was different. I had a distinct but fleeting image of a little gray kitten, with spiraling white circles.

I immediately put it out of my mind, and again began debating the suck-worthiness of the commute versus the job as I got ready for work.

***

My commute into Washington essentially consisted of one continuous construction site interrupted only by occasional stalled and sometimes abandoned cars. On this particular Friday, traffic was particularly heavy, particularly for a Friday, particularly in the summer.

The stream of barely moving cars in which I sat inched along an endless row of concrete "Jersey barriers" walling off the construction area along the roadside. At the same time other cars zipped by on the shoulder, bypassing the slow moving traffic as they merged onto the adjoining freeway. It made me a little nauseous, the flash of cars moving so quickly by in my peripheral vision.

I fingered the yellow Post-it note on the dashboard that I used to mark off the days I had remaining in the job that I so hated. Five days after today.

I thought about the sun deck I was building off our kitchen, and how much time I'd be able to devote to it after next week.

And then I saw him. At first I thought it was just a dust ball, blowing along the narrow strip of road filth alongside the Jersey barriers. But then I realized that the gray blur was headed against traffic, just inches from the cars whirring by on the shoulder. No inanimate object could blow into the turbulence of the oncoming cars.

A moment later I saw the face—the panicked, precious, perfect face—of the gray dust ball. It was the face in my dream.

Like most people, I've rarely been placed in a position where I have ever had a chance to do anything truly heroic.

Once, a few years ago, I saw an elderly man collapse at a local Oktoberfest celebration. Having just completed a first aid course, I was convinced that the man was having a heart attack, and I was rather oddly excited by that prospect. As is often the case with heart attack victims, I noticed upon closer examination that he had vomited on himself. Despite my initial enthusiasm for saving the man's life by performing mouth-to-mouth resuscitation and CPR, I admit that I hesitated at least momentarily when I noticed the fresh, bratwurst-based vomit.

In that moment when I knelt over the white-haired man in indecision, his wife, a substantial woman, rushed up.

Pulling him to his feet by the collar of his coat, she bellowed "God damn it Harry, I told you you'd puke if you kept drinking all that damn Lowenbrau!" and off they went.

I reassured myself later that, if needed, I would have done what was necessary, but I was left wondering by that interrupted brush with heroism.

So, in light of my limited and questionable prior experience as a hero, I still don't fully understand my actions that Friday morning. Without even a split second of conscious thought, I swerved onto the shoulder, swung open the door, and jumped into the freeway traffic. I ran down the narrow berm alongside the Jersey barriers, retracing the route traveled by the gray kitten.

Cars swerved, horns blared, and brakes squealed. More than once a car came so close to hitting me that I was forced to flatten myself against the Jersey barriers and hope for the best. Amidst the chaos, a woman rolled down her window.

"God bless you sir! Save that kitten! Please save that kitten!" she yelled, giving me the thumbs-up, a somewhat similar yet entirely different hand gesture than the one being offered by other passing motorists.

Bolstered by my new supporter's admiration, but mostly by the lingering image of panic on the poor kitten's face, I continued sprinting down the shoulder.

Just as I was losing hope, I saw the gray puff ball cowering under the shredded remains of a radial tire. I scooped him up in my right hand, not certain if he was dead or alive, but fairly certain that I would be dead shortly if I didn't make haste. Before I reached my truck, he began struggling against my grip and I knew I had arrived in time.

***

There was no debate whatsoever about a name. "Lucky" (full name: "Lucky 2B Alive") was named the day we found him, after our vet confirmed that he would live, despite a broken pelvis and other signs of a short but hard life in the urban wilds. And, to our great relief, our other two cats welcomed their new brother with uncommon hospitality and generosity.

***

The following Friday I finally crossed the last day off the countdown calendar taped to my dashboard. I had ended a chapter in my life that seemed as if it would never end. I was free to begin a new chapter, once I figured out just what that would be.

In the following months, I granted myself the luxury of pursuing all kinds of things I'd always wanted to do. I spent long overdue time with family and friends. I undertook home improvement projects on a scale rivaling the building of the Great Pyramids. I started a small antique business, and even tried to turn my longtime passion for raising bonsai plants into a cottage industry.

I also began writing. Not the kind of business writing I'd spent so much time doing since my nose met the grindstone, but the kind of story telling that was once a passion of mine. In the beginning it was just another hobby I indulged, but gradually I began to think it would be my next career, as far-fetched as that seemed at the time.

Lucky became part of my new daily ritual from the beginning, napping most of the day on my cluttered desk, fittingly next to the mouse pad, while I pecked away at the keyboard. Despite very limited interest from the outside world in my writing, I remained undeterred and uncharacteristically optimistic that this was the course I should pursue. In fact, it was with more a sense of fate than surprise that I reacted when my big break came nearly a year later.

Lucky stirred slightly from his nap when I opened the mysterious e-mail and a let out an audible "Huh?"

As a result of a contest in *The Washington Post* that I had entered—and lost—*The Today Show* had indirectly learned about me and seen some of my humor writing related to personal finances. Within a week I was appearing live on *Today*, chatting it up with Matt Lauer, and suddenly literary agents were anxious to work with me on a book project and national magazines were approaching me about buying exclusive rights to my previously unpublished work (fortunately, the vast majority of my portfolio).

***

Often times, as I watch Lucky sleep on my desk, my mind wanders back to that morning in June when I rescued him from the freeway. I always recall the horrific sight of him running into the oncoming traffic—toward me—and wonder why that was.

Why didn't he run to safety, away from the frightening rush of the traffic? Where was he coming from, and was it possible that he was in fact coming to me? And his name, the name we agreed on so easily and that at the time seemed a natural fit for him, now seems more fortuitous for me and the new direction our lives have taken since he came to live with us.

Of course, I also think a lot about the dreams. And as he lies sleeping on my desk, I often wonder, "Do cats dream?"

~Jeff Yeager

Editors' Note: A version of this story was first published in *Amazing Cat Tales*, Linden Hill Publishing, 2006.

A Winning Attitude

Attitude is a little thing that makes a big difference.
~Winston Churchill

I was born with a rare bone disease called osteogenesis imperfecta. My parents were told that I would never live to be a day old... then a week old... then a month old. But I was a fighter from day one and even though I have broken hundreds of bones in my lifetime, I never let that break my spirit.

When I was eight, I was going through a really hard time. I was about to go into a very dangerous neck surgery and my whole family was nervous. One day, my mom and I were on our way back from a particularly painful appointment at the hospital and she said, "Brianne, what would make you most happy in the world, anything, just name it." In her mind, I think she was hoping that I was going to ask for an ice cream cone from McDonald's or a pair of new shoes. Instead, at that moment, we passed a sign on the side of the road advertising "free kittens." Noticing my mischievous smile, she knew what my answer was and pulled into the driveway of an old farm house where the kittens were.

Mom held my hand as we entered the dark garage where about six of the cutest kittens you can imagine were scampering around and chasing each other on the dusty cement floor. However, when I knelt down on the floor to play with them, I noticed another little kitten sitting by herself in the corner. I walked over to get a closer look and saw that there was something odd about this little gray cat—she didn't have a tail and her back legs were all twisted like a rabbit.

Noticing my interest in this kitten, the owner matter-of-factly told us, "Yeah, that one right there has some leg problems. But don't worry, because we're going to send her up North so that the other animals can take care of her." Knowing that was basically a death sentence, my mom didn't say another word. She just took off her jacket, used it to scoop up the little cat, and walked us both back to the car.

My dad and little sister were surprised to see us return from the hospital with a kitten, and happily helped us give her a bath. To our amazement, this little gray cat (whom I named Chica) was actually a gorgeous calico but because of the neglect of her former owners, she had just really, really needed a bath. At the vet's office, we learned that her condition was a problem for a number of calico Manx cats and resulted from a genetic mutation.

Because of her small size and problems walking, at first we were nervous about how she would be able to interact with our other pets, which included another cat and two big dogs. However, we quickly learned that no one ever had to worry about Chica. She would enter a room and immediately control the situation. The dogs wouldn't dare bark at her or attempt to chase her around. Because of her small size and inability to run really fast, she would intimidate the other animals and they quickly learned not to mess with her.

I too learned a lot from my cat. When she became the "alpha animal" in our house, she taught me that with the right attitude, anything is possible. When she would win fights with our neighbor's Golden Retriever who was about ten times her size, she taught me that anyone can be brave and fearless. And when it took her weeks of practice to learn how to climb into the front window despite the fact that she could only jump about an inch off the ground, she taught me that with perseverance, any obstacle can be overcome.

Chica passed away fourteen years later. I had moved out to Washington, DC, to start my first job after college and Chica waited until the day I came home for Thanksgiving before she decided it was time to say goodbye. I carried her into the vet's office knowing that I would never find another friend who knew so precisely what it was like to be me. But every time in the future when I am confronted with a problem or an obstacle that seems too big to overcome, I will remember the lessons I learned from my cat and know that anything is possible.

~Brianne Schwantes

Simple Joy

Follow your passion, and success will follow you.
~Arthur Buddhold

I was in the middle of a busy day working at the restaurant where I was a line cook when I received a call from my younger sister, who was also my roommate.

"Don't be mad!" she said to me.

I wondered what new drama was headed our way.

"There's a cat in the apartment," she said. "I just had to take him!" Her co-worker had asked if anyone would take this kitten. It had been abandoned near his parents' home along with its siblings and mother. This one kitten was the sole survivor. The co-worker's mother had bottle-fed the little creature, but had to keep it in the porch attached to the house, because her husband was not fond of cats. The kitten needed a home!

I arrived home to find a chubby bundle of orange-and-white kitten staring up at me as if to say, "Here I am, figure out how to take care of me!" I made a makeshift litter box from a cardboard box and went to the store to buy a bag of litter and a box of cat food. From then on, I was responsible for the needs of that little ball of fluff.

I had no idea what to call the beast. "Let's call her Princess!" my sister insisted.

"Princess?" I exclaimed. "That's not a real name!"

"Yes, Princess Abigail!" She said. So, Princess Abigail it was and I called her Abby for short. As "Princess Abigail" grew, we soon discovered that she was a he. Try as we might, we could not get another more gender-appropriate name to stick even after he ripped off his pink collar in protest. Abby remains his moniker to this day.

The years ahead were filled with working full time and going to university part-time. They, of course, were also filled with change and, yes, more cats. My sister moved to her own apartment and my boyfriend, Adam, moved in with his own cat, Gizmo, pure white with lots of attitude. Abby and the "new girl" worked out their differences fairly quickly. They could often be found lazily grooming each other in the middle of the bed, enjoying a patch of sunshine. They settled into a comfortable life together, feasting on only the best cat kibble and treats and enjoying the most love and attention two cats could ever dream of. I never thought that I would be sharing my life with one cat; now I had two.

Through all of the stress, busy days and changes, the cats remained a constant. I discovered a great joy in taking care of their basic needs. Cleaning up after them, feeding them and administering ear drops without getting my arms completely shredded! They also ministered to me, coming to find and entertain me when I was worried or depressed. Taking a bath, I would look over to see the pink tips of two ears peaking over the edge of the tub, followed by two green eyes and finally the triangle nose and whiskers. Abby would stand there on his hind feet, peering at the fascinating water and then at me, as if demanding an explanation.

One of the biggest stresses of my life was trying to balance work and school. Though I found the courses interesting, I did not fit into the university scene. I could not imagine going to school for years and years as a professional academic or finally graduating from university only to discover that I still did not truly know what I wanted to "do" for my life's work. I expressed my concerns to an academic advisor, who suggested that I take some time to consider what, in my day-to-day life, made me happy.

One evening, as I sat stroking Abby, who was laid out on his side, eyes closed, purring like a finely tuned engine, I thought about what that advisor had said. What made me happy? I suddenly realized something. This made me happy! Taking care of these furry beasts and there basic needs was the work that I was meant to do. It dawned on me, what peace I found in performing these humble and simple tasks.

I quickly began doing some research and found a college nearby that offered a course in animal health. I was fortunate to be able to volunteer at the local animal shelter and veterinary clinic to gain valuable experience. I immediately found a job at a pet resort, doing exactly what I was meant to do.

The other day, someone commented on how lucky I was to do what I love every day. This made me think. Sometimes, the satisfaction we seek in life does not come from a high salary or powerful position. I am very lucky that an abandoned kitten stumbled into my life to show me the importance and value of the simple things in this world.

~Kimberley Ward

The Tail of Little Guy

Our perfect companions never have fewer than four feet.
~Colette

"There's a hurt kitty in the field," my husband said solemnly. "I think it's going to die."

It was Canada Day, July 1st and I was in the midst of preparing a barbecue for friends. I really didn't need this right now. Not that I hate animals. In fact, I'm queen of the strays. Aside from one, the German Shepherd, Kali, all our animals have come from desperate situations. But I just did not need one more vet bill. Sensing I might be swaying, Kali whined and looked up at me.

"What's wrong with her?" I asked.

"Well Kali found it. She thinks it's our responsibility to care for it now. Finders, keepers I suppose."

"And how are we supposed to pay for another stray?" I sighed, not looking up from cutting vegetables for the salad.

Kali barked and made the "let's go find the kitty" motion towards the door. But I was adamant. I had too many strays already. We were a two-cat one-dog two-rabbit family. Several chickens and one bad-tempered cockatiel rounded off the mixture. That was enough, even for the country.

My husband hung the leash on the hook and went inside the living room. I made tea while pondering what to do next. Obviously we had to do something.

"How bad?" I asked as I brought in the tea.

"The back legs look broken. Or maybe the spine. It's also really weak, probably been without water."

We looked at each other and I sighed. "Well, we'll take it some water and see how it is."

Together we strolled down, dish in hand. But the place the cat had been was empty except for a mark in the tall grass where he had lain. "Well, he must have gone somewhere," I said as we looked around.

"But he couldn't walk!" my husband contended. "He can't have gone far."

We searched and searched through the tall grass and by the creek that runs through our property. An hour later we found him. He had crawled 150 feet over a bridge and up to our shed. He had crawled after a dog and a strange man, not away from them, and had settled inside the shade of the entrance. He managed a whispered meow of thanks as we put down the water and he struggled to stand up. This cat was a fighter and I knew we had to save him.

Putting the food for the celebration back in the fridge, we made some hurried phone calls and left a note for the friends who we hadn't reached. They would understand, for anyone who knows us knows how crazy we are for our animals. The barbecue could wait for another day.

Canada Day is a national holiday—so finding a vet willing to come in even for the call-in price wasn't easy. And what if the cat belonged to someone else? The only option was to take him to the SPCA and drop him in as a walk-in case. Surely they would take care of him. We finally found a place willing to accept him forty-five minutes away.

I sat in the back with the cat on the way up. His breathing was tortured and every now and then he seemed to fade. His emaciated body was a mass of matted fur, burrs and dried mud. There were maggots on his open wounds. "Hang on," I whispered. "Hang on, little guy."

At the center they examined him. He was too far gone to be considered adoptable, but as it is law, they kept him alive and fed for three days and waited for someone to claim him. I phoned in often, checking on his progress. Surely someone would call and claim him. He was such a sweet, determined little cat.

But no one called. The vet care to save him was going to cost hundreds of dollars. The SPCA only allotted a maximum of $150 for each animal. I didn't blame them. It was all they could afford and this cat had already used up his funds. A few hours before he was to be put down humanely, I made the decision. Somehow we would have to find the money. I couldn't give up on him and I couldn't see him being put down after he struggled so hard to survive.

Our wonderful vet in Sooke took on the responsibility of helping us care for him.

Even with rehydration and food the cat was still in rough shape. He weighed just over six pounds and his fur came off in your hands, a sign of malnutrition. Maggots had eaten away at his back end. His spine was broken near his tail. His tail hung lifeless and limp. "This," the vet said, "will have to go." Luckily his legs were intact and the determined sparkle was coming back in his face. He defiantly swiped a paw at the vet when he got too close to his wounds. "How do we proceed?" I gulped. "We'll have to see after the surgery," the vet said, "but he sure is a fighter, isn't he?"

The tail came off in an operation; also something else came off, which cured him of being a future father and wanderer. We went in the next day to pick him up. "Stick him in a box, keep him quiet. His spine may knit," the vet said. We took him home and set him up in an upstairs bedroom with glass doors. The other cats and dog kept interested vigils over the next month as the little guy recuperated, ate tuna, had antibiotics forced on him with a syringe, and got stronger. Kali especially took great interest in her charge.

In three days he was up and walking. In four days he had managed to break out of his cage and was atop the furniture when we went in to feed him. At three weeks he managed to fire himself at breakneck speed out the room and down the stairs to meet the other members of his new family face to face.

That was three years ago. Nowadays we call Canada Day

"founding day" and usually have a party with our animal-loving friends. Both Little Guy and Kali get a special treat to share with their family friends and Kali gets a hero cheer for finding Little Guy. Yes, it is my country's birthday but this experience gave us something more important to celebrate—a tailless cat who taught us to never give up fighting, and a German Shepherd who wouldn't let us shirk our responsibilities.

~Nancy Bennett

The Purrfect Guest

The cat is above all things, a dramatist.
~Margaret Benson

There is a "family" of cats living beneath a cement culvert that's nestled in among the palm trees and lush landscape in our neighborhood in Florida. I don't think the older cats are related, but the kittens that appear now and then are the result, I imagine, of romantic moonlit nights. Some of the residents have tried to adopt these homeless creatures but no matter what we do, other cats eventually take their place. The word is out in the feline underground — this is prime housing and vacancies don't last long.

There is one black-and-tan fellow whom I have dubbed Spike, for the interesting way his "bangs" stand straight up. Spike has taken a shine to the second-floor landing at the top of the stairs leading to my front door where the sun is warm and the view is good. I believe everyone needs something to live for and Spike lives to frighten me. He seems to take perverse pleasure in waiting until I'm halfway up the stairs before relinquishing his spot. He leaps through the air — nearly grazing me as he flies by — pole vaults over the railing and hits the ground at a run. Despite the fact that I can admit that his landings are a thing of beauty, the adrenaline surge I get every time he dives past is taking years off my life.

It doesn't happen often in southwest Florida, but we get the occasional night when below-freezing temperatures drift in on the jet stream, bringing a damp cold that goes straight to the bones. My first personal encounter with Spike happened on just such a night.

I had worked late and the winter sun had already begun to slide into the Gulf, leaving murky shadows and biting winds. I climbed the stairs quickly, intent on escaping the cold, but stopped short when I noticed my homeless friend sitting beside my front door. I stepped back, prepared for him to bolt past me. I actually pointed toward the steps and said, "Well?"

Spike made no attempt to move as he watched me through world-weary eyes. I realized he was shivering. I stepped carefully around him, pulled the door open and asked if he wanted to come inside. To my surprise, he did!

I was laying down the rules before the door had been firmly closed. I don't pretend to understand these mysterious creatures but I hoped we could arrive at a tentative truce for the evening.

I asked my guest to stay in the foyer. I couldn't imagine what might live in the fur of a homeless gentleman like Spike. "I have a friend who allows her cat to walk all over the kitchen counters and dining room table," I explained to Spike. "I can't have that, okay? Just stay off anything that is used for food and we'll get along fine. Deal?" His calm expression gave nothing away but I had the eerie feeling that he understood.

Spike turned out to be the perfect houseguest. I borrowed some cat food from a neighbor so he could have a suitable dinner. He ate every bite with lip-smacking appreciation. I took an old blanket from the closet and made him a cozy bed in the foyer. As far as I could tell, he stayed in the foyer, and we both enjoyed a cozy night's sleep in our little burrows, safe from the freezing temperatures.

Spike was waiting patiently to go outside when I awoke the following morning. I opened the door and he scurried away without a goodbye. When I returned from work that evening there was no sign of Spike, but there was a dead field mouse by my door. My cat-loving neighbor insists that was Spike's way of saying thank you.

I wish I could say Spike has stopped dive-bombing me on my way to the front door. He hasn't. If it's possible, he comes even closer as he passes. It could be the old guy is getting arthritis or his eyesight is failing but I like to think it's because we have become friends. He hasn't asked to come inside again, because any time Spike might have spent as a domestic cat is a distant memory. It's the star-filled sky and the smell of hibiscus that call to him now.

I've thought a lot about Spike since we shared one unremarkable winter night but I believe he has the perfect philosophy of life. Here are the rules of life from a wise, old homeless cat:

1) Ask for help when you need it.
2) Accept help when it's offered.
3) Take only what you need.
4) Respect the "Rules of the House."
5) Send a thank you note. (Or a dead mouse.)
6) Be open to new friends.
7) Be true to who you are.
8) If you find something that gives you joy—like sailing by a woman on her way upstairs—do if with all your heart.

It would be a better world if we followed Spike's rules of life. Yes, I think he has it exactly right!

~Vicki Kitchner

Courage in a Small and Furry Package

Fall seven times, stand up eight.
~Japanese Proverb

I got the call one day after school. My father had seen a little black and white kitten at the animal hospital where he used to work as a veterinarian before he started his own practice. It turned out the kitten and her mother were being fostered for the county animal shelter by a veterinarian technician. The mother cat had received a modified live virus distemper vaccine while pregnant. The vaccine infected the developing kittens. Only three were born live: one died later, one was suffering and had to be euthanized, and one was Penelope.

Penelope was about six weeks old when we took her, over my mother's protests that five cats were plenty. She couldn't be returned to the animal shelter, or she would be euthanized, and the woman fostering her couldn't have another cat. You see, Penelope was born with neurological damage that rendered her nearly unable to walk, or even to stand. Her hindquarters would randomly flip over her head, and she fell repeatedly. But she managed. She could always get where she wanted, even if it took her much longer than it would have taken a normal feline. She even had difficulty using the litter box, as she struggled to control her body long enough to do her business. Listening to her cry as she fought to hold still was heartbreaking, and more than once I steadied her. As she grew older, she learned to control her body. She was able to stand, and even to walk a dozen steps or more before falling.

Penelope was a comical cat. Watching her move, weaving from side to side, and seeing her jump up on beds and couches was always a surprise, since no one (including Penelope) knew where she would end up. It was not at all uncommon to see her smash into a wall or corner, or to miss her jump and land on the other side of a bed, rather than on top of it. We winced for her between our chuckles. The other cats didn't accept her, and never did. Only one tolerated her; the rest hissed and made it clear she was not welcome.

One would think that, in the face of all her adversity, Penelope would just give up and become a sullen, miserable cat. After all, she struggled to walk and jump, was almost always bruised from her crashes, and she was hated by her fellow felines. But she kept on going. She was a spunky, feisty, determined little cat. And she was little—she matured at about six pounds, by far the smallest of our six cats. She held her own with the other cats and pushed around the dogs, all of whom were in the hundred pound range; she lived her life to the fullest. We soon gave up trying to keep her inside when it became clear she wanted nothing more than to enjoy the outdoors at will. Penelope lived her life to the fullest.

One day, a little less than a year and a half after that telephone call from my dad, we realized Penelope was not acting like herself. However, her lethargy was not terribly serious, and she did seem to have improved over the few hours we were watching her, so we didn't worry too much. Two days later, I called home from college to check on her. My mom answered my question "How's Nellie doing?" with the words "I was hoping you wouldn't call."

Penelope had died a little earlier. I listened to the details while holding back sobs. She had a bruised lung, bleeding in her chest, and other injuries, which we suppose were the result of being hit by a car. Those six pounds of black and white fur spoke volumes about courage in the face of adversity. She never cried about the pain she surely suffered every day as a result of her frequent falls. She never stopped trying to do what she wanted. She was a once-in-a-lifetime cat, the kind who can teach you more about life and bravery in a short year or two than the average person learns in a lifetime. Penelope was proof that a willing soul can do anything if it just tries hard enough.

~Joanne Vukman

Practice Makes Purr-fect

There are two means of refuge from the misery of life—music and cats.
~Albert Schweitzer

In high school, I decided to learn to play the piano. It was a decision based primarily on dreams of playing music on stage, rather than an affinity for a particular type of music. Plus, I already knew how to read music, so I figured the piano would be a snap. After a few lessons with a local teacher, my dream of instant musical fame hit a snag—I loved to play, but I hated to practice. To non-musicians, playing and practicing might seem interchangeable, but the lack of an audience made it difficult for me to play for more than a few minutes. Bored and lonely, I would drift away from the piano after a few bars of music. My lifelong love affair with the piano might have ended after a few short weeks if not for the instruction of an unlikely teacher—the family cat.

Jonathan was a highly intelligent, inquisitive Siamese/tabby mix. The biggest cat of the litter, he was the alpha cat in the household of humans and he knew it. He meowed loudly and insistently when he wanted to be fed. He vigorously scratched the back of the sofa even after he was declawed, delighting in the game of chase that invariably ensued when he was caught. He loved to perch atop bookcases, windowsills, and the refrigerator—anywhere high enough that he could swat at people's heads when they walked by. While he would sometimes deign to sit on selected laps, he was not the cuddly, nurturing cat found in storybooks and pet food advertisements.

That's why I found it odd one day when he decided to jump up on the piano bench and sit quietly next to me as I played Pachelbel's Canon in D Major. The choice of music, as always, had been my teacher's; I shrugged in response whenever she tried to engage me in the selection process. From my view, one type of music wasn't much different than another. I played what I was told to play.

Jonathan's eyes followed my hands as I played, his dark tail quietly swishing back and forth like a metronome. The Pachelbel finished, I reached for a short piece with lots of staccato notes. It only took a couple of notes to see that this song had a different effect on my audience of one. Jonathan swiped at my hand with his paw and looked at me. Ow! I stopped and glared at him. I played a few more notes. Swat. Stop. Swat. Stop. Was he tired of my playing? Or did he just want to be fed? I put the music away, relieved to have an excuse to stop practicing.

The next time at the piano, Jonathan again jumped up beside me and again, he reacted the same way—waiting patiently during some songs and swatting his paw at me during others. Over the next few months, practice became fascinating. I couldn't wait to try out new songs and see how he felt about them. Classical was a good bet, as were church hymns, while themes from TV, movies, or musicals were hit and miss. Sometimes his tastes made me laugh. "Memories" from *Cats* was a winner, while "Linus and Lucy," the *Peanuts* theme, was not. As silly as it sounds, I tried to please him as much as possible. The increased practice time improved my playing immensely, at least on songs that were "cat approved." My teacher puzzled aloud over how some pieces progressed while others didn't, since the difficulty of the piece didn't seem to figure into the equation. When she chalked it up to me developing my own taste in music, I didn't correct her. It was too embarrassing to explain.

Jonathan and I might have continued like that for a while, with me bending my music to suit him, just as I curved my body around his when he took the prime middle spot in the middle of my bed at night. But then my teacher gave me a book of ragtime. For the first time, I found a type of music I truly loved. I enjoyed the odd rhythms and the pleasing clash of notes in Scott Joplin's "Maple Leaf Rag" and the other ragtime tunes. Jonathan hated it. He swatted repeatedly at my hands. Eventually, I had to shut him in the bedroom during those songs. I felt bad that I couldn't play just for him—what kind of musician deliberately plays songs that she knows her audience hates? But at the same time, I wasn't willing to let go of my newfound love. I had finally found something I was willing to fight for.

Luckily, Jonathan didn't seem to hold it against me—he'd still occasionally sit on my lap or rub his head against my leg when I finished practicing. I took courage from the idea that it was okay to express different opinions and still be respected. Rejection of your work was not rejection of you. It was one person's opinion. It wasn't until I was an adult working in creative careers such as writing and jewelry design that I truly appreciated this lesson. No matter what was said in a rejection letter from a publisher, editor, reader, or contest judge, it was much less painful than a swat of a paw from a curmudgeonly cat!

~Michelle Mach

The Gift of a Demanding Cat

Time spent with cats is never wasted.
~May Sarton

I knew I had found true love the first time my new kitten suffered through my bath time. Knowing how much Kate Kat liked to be near me, I placed a bed far enough from the old tub to allow her to see over the tall sides. Kate Kat would not stay that far away. She came right to the tub and stretched up as high as she could. Her whiskered face peered over the edge as two tiny gray paws sought purchase on the slick tub. Her little face slid sideways as she struggled to keep her tip-toe balance. Then she disappeared, only to appear again a moment later to repeat the process.

Afterwards, she happily followed me as I went about my routine. When I opened a new milk jug, I threw her the blue plastic ring that secured the lid. With a clatter of claws on tile, she batted her new toy like a hockey puck until it disappeared under the refrigerator.

She played fiercely, chasing strings and toy mice. When I came home from work, I could see she had been busy. Some days I had to search my sparsely furnished house for twenty minutes before finding my bathtub stopper. Other days, she TP'ed the house in my absence.

Kate Kat was also my sleeping companion. When she was tiny, I made sure she slept in front of me in case I rolled on my back as I slept. That evolved into her sleeping in the crook of my arm with her head out of the covers like mine. I couldn't have asked for a better companion than a warm furry partner who purred.

That is not to say that Kate Kat was always happy. When her little claws became too sharp, I trimmed them with nail clippers. She never struggled, but her yellow eyes glared at me the whole time. All was forgiven when she got a piece of cheese as a reward.

Kate Kat was also obedient for a cat. Whenever she did something she shouldn't, I only had to say "No!" She stopped, but not without a vocal "wow wow wow" that sounded like grumbling. Glaring and grumbling notwithstanding, Kate Kat was happy and loving.

Then, when she was two years old, a terrible thing happened. I got busier. Not only was there my full-time job and the house to keep up, but I found a friend who developed into a husband. This meant I did more socializing (with humans), more cooking, laundry and mending. It was harder to find time for Kate Kat.

My cat changed. She meowed demandingly. No longer was she satisfied with a new toy or having her food bowl filled. If she went out, she wanted right back in before I could get any work done. If she was inside, she cried to go outside. If I went to let her out, she turned and ran the other way.

Finally, I realized the problem. She wanted me to play with her, to pay attention to her as I had before. I spent months trying (futilely, of course) to explain that I was simply too busy. I had three loads of washing to hang out on the line, apples to peel and cook for applesauce, a casserole to prepare for a potluck, and a rug that needed vacuuming again where I tracked in leaves after hanging out clothes.

Kate Kat did not understand. Why should she? After encouraging a close relationship, I had changed the rules.

I tried to fit in some playtime with my cat. It was hard to focus. When she was a kitten, Kate Kat played hard. As an older cat, her play consisted mostly of watching me try to play with her. I resented the waste of time when I had so many more important things to do. In response, Kate Kat sulked and grumbled more than usual.

Eventually, Kate Kat's message seeped through my thoughts of schedules and chores. Clearly, Kate Kat did not love me unconditionally, or she would have accepted my preoccupation. She placed one condition on our relationship—that I return her affection.

I remembered that I loved animals, cats, and Kate Kat in particular. I had chosen to bring Kate Kat into my life because I wanted her warmth, purring, and companionship. On the other hand, I chose to bring a washing machine into my home because it was necessary for keeping clothes clean. I did not buy a washer for its comforting swishing sound or because I had a passion for laundry. Why then, was I giving laundry priority over my cat?

As I tried again to play with her, I noticed Kate Kat's reaction. True, she didn't leap at the string like a kitten, but her ears pricked forward. She watched attentively in the long moments between pounces. I had her interest. More importantly, she had mine.

From my new perspective, Kate Kat's demands seemed less selfish. By insisting her one condition was met, she ensured that I did what I had wanted to do in the first place. Without that one demand, I might have wasted too much of my life on things less important to me.

My demanding cat taught me to listen to my heart and reexamine my priorities. I was honored to return Kate Kat's one-conditional love.

~Susan Cooper

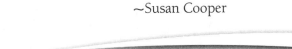

Business Lessons

*Do what you do so well that they will want to see it again
and bring their friends.*
~Walt Disney

I thought I knew everything about building a business. After all, I had spent an entire career teaching others how to be successful. So when I fulfilled a lifelong dream of owning a bookstore, it was quite humbling to realize that what I really needed to know about customer service, I learned from my cat.

I wanted the bookstore to have a warm, homey atmosphere where people felt comfortable browsing and spending time. Soft classical music in the background, the aroma of coffee brewing, stimulating book talk and, of course, a cat curled up in an overstuffed chair in the reading corner. I began my search for an adorable kitten who would grow along with our store.

It was February and I soon discovered that due to the cat mating cycle, kittens in February can be scarce. (Who would have dreamed there could ever be a kitten shortage?) Kittens were whisked from the shelters the day they arrived, and the local pet store had only one—a scrawny gray Maine Coon with a seeping eye infection. Not quite the mascot I had envisioned. Because this kitten was also going to be a February birthday gift to my daughter who worked with me, I reluctantly took him, along with a prescription for eye drops.

For days the kitten just slept.

"Great," I thought, as I lifted his eyelids three times a day to insert the drops. But as his infection cleared he showed signs of being the playful Maine Coon described in the cat books on our shelves.

The first thing we did was have a "Name the Cat" contest. Soon a huge jar was overflowing with names from customers and their children. Because the name of our store was Pages, the entry of Footnote seemed the most appropriate winning choice. Lesson #1: Participation creates a sense of community.

The day our neighboring merchant, the hardware store, had a sale on earthenware pots, I chose a little round one for my patio. I set it near the front door till I went home. Footnote approached it cautiously, sniffing and marking. Then he curled into it and blinked his big green eyes at me as if to say, "Thanks. It's a perfect fit." The pot never left the store.

As Footnote grew, the bowls did too. He climbed into each one to accommodate his growing stature. Often he was so curled up so you couldn't see his face, just a mass of gray fur. Other times he sat up in the bowl, near the front door, in a welcoming posture. Lesson #2: Customers like to be greeted with a friendly and familiar face.

Soon customers were bringing in their friends and family—even out-of-town guests—to see the "Cat in the Bowl."

Although they came in to see him, they usually left with books in hand and a promise to bring yet another friend. Lesson #3: A clever niche or conversation piece can attract customers.

Our used-book corner was in the back of the store. People brought in used books to trade. When we heard laughing and squealing from that corner, we knew Footnote was jumping in and out of their bags and boxes, often to the children's delight. Lesson #4: People like to be entertained.

At Friday Night Bedtime Stories, the children wore their pajamas and spread their blankets on the floor while I read to them. When they started giggling at parts of the story that weren't funny, I saw that Footnote had once again stolen the show by burrowing his way under their blankets and slithering from one child to another like a secret mole. Lesson #5: Making children happy opens parents' hearts—and wallets.

When mothers came in with baby carriages, Footnote would gently stretch up on his hind legs, put his paws on the front of the stroller and sniff the baby, often causing them to smile. If a baby or toddler accidentally pulled his furry tail, he patiently let them. Lesson #6: The customer is always right.

However, if an older child teased him, he often retaliated with a swat. Lesson #6a: The customer is always right, except when he's old enough to know better.

When we had book discussions, we gathered in a circle and ladies' purses were set on the floor beside their chairs. Footnote often sauntered from reader to reader, choosing the spot he would grace with his presence. Because he could not resist the curiosity of an open purse, (or open anything) we soon heard him digging and pawing. When his head resurfaced, he had a five-dollar bill in his mouth, which he proceeded to walk away with. He passed on several ones as he dug his way to the five. A cat of discriminating taste. Lesson #7: Laughter is a great ice breaker and bond.

One of Footnote's favorite lounging spots was the center aisle of the store where he would lay on his back, all four feet spread wide in the air, causing customers to walk around him. It's been said cats do that only when they have ultimate trust in their surroundings. Lesson #8: Trust creates customer loyalty, as the following incident proved.

One summer evening, a customer popped in to browse while taking a walk through our strip mall. She didn't have her purse with her, but wished she had when she saw a new release she had been waiting for. I knew she wanted to start reading it immediately so I encouraged her to just take the book and pay for it the next day. I was confident she would return. (We were, after all, the neighborhood store where everyone knows your name). She brought the money in the next evening, by which time she had told countless people what a great store we were. What better advertising than word-of-meow, I mean mouth.

As lease payments increased and big chain stores were encroaching, we decided to close this chapter of our lives. We shed many tears with customers (by now dear friends) who told us how much they would miss our store—and Footnote.

The bookstore was the only home Footnote had known, other than trips home with us on Christmas Day to play in discarded wrapping paper. Because we were open seven days a week, he probably had more attention than any household pet. When the last book was sold and we locked the door for the last time, my daughter took Footnote home with her.

Today, some fourteen years since we closed our doors, I still run into former customers in our community.

Often the children who came to bedtime stories (now in high school or college) are with their parents. I hear the mother say, "Do you remember how you loved going to Pages bookstore to see the cat in the bowl?"

A lasting lesson: Footnote left footprints on many hearts.

~Vy Armour

A Path from India

Kittens are angels with whiskers.
~Author Unknown

"Please don't cry. We both know... I'm not what... you neeeeeeed," I sang into the shrubbery, employing the highest-pitched whisper I could manage. "And I... will always love you."

Presently, a young couple walked by, eyeing me queerly. I jumped to my feet, emitted a little cough, and offered a weak smile. Then, blushing in a shade of crimson, I chuckled and attempted to mask my moment of absurdity with a brief explanation. "The things we won't do for our pets, huh?" Fortunately, my fluffy little tabby chose that moment to dash from the bushes and run back to our apartment, proving my sanity to the still doubtful couple.

After giving my jeans a few necessary pats, I escaped the thick dust cloud it produced and followed her inside. I slammed and bolted the door behind me.

"Well, India," I began in a tone that clarified my mood, "if you think I'm going to sing Whitney Houston songs to the bushes every time you go missing, you'll soon lose your outdoor privileges, young lady!" Whether she adored my singing voice or intensely despised it, I was never sure. It was, however, the only tactic I'd yet found that would bring her running back to me from her little adventures.

After enduring my scolding, she cautiously dropped her worn old mouse toy at my feet and looked up at me, waiting for a reaction.

"And if you think I'm gonna play with you now..." I went on, stooping to pick up her play toy, "you can just forget it."

Suddenly the toy squirmed in my hand and I let out a scream. I nearly dropped it before I realized it wasn't a toy at all. In fact, I couldn't tell what it was, only that it was alive. Still at my feet, my half-blind kitty bobbed her head up and down, scanning the pink, furless object lying in my hand.

While she nodded her head up and down, I shook mine from side to side, trying to think of my next move. I clasped the chilled mystery animal tightly in my hands to keep it warm.

India looked at me as if she had presented me with a karmic gift. Somehow that prompted my thoughts to drift back to memories of the previous year, and how I had come into possession of my precious feline friend. I had learned that my grandfather's callous neighbor owned a cat that had just given birth to a litter of kittens. The unthinkable tales of how this old man had rid himself of previous unwanted litters was common knowledge in the neighborhood. I realized that these helpless, unwanted kittens didn't have much time. I put a quick catnapping plan into action and rescued the kittens and their mother from a horrible fate.

I was able to find homes for all of them but one, the runt of the litter. She was born with a neurological disorder that affected her eyesight. As a result, she was always scanning objects like a barcode reader in order to see them. I finally managed to adopt her out to a nice couple, but they soon returned her, asserting in less than politically correct terms that she was developmentally challenged.

"Just because she's a little cross-eyed and habitually drools," I argued, "it doesn't make her a special needs kitty." To me she was just plain special, so I decided to keep India for myself. Every day she brought me more and more joy, but on this day... she had brought me a problem.

Being the young, naïve college student that I was, I didn't know where to find help for India's little treasure. I got a nursing kit from the pet store, but didn't really expect the animal to survive.

To my surprise, I was able to nurse the small creature back to health and soon identified it as a tree squirrel. India must have stumbled upon her little friend by chance, because she lacked the visual perception and balance to climb a tree. I knew little about wildlife at the time, but was determined to successfully raise the newborn squirrel alongside my young kitty. It wasn't long before the two became inseparable, taking long naps together, living up playtime, and even sharing shelled peas.

The experience of raising Nigel, the orphaned squirrel, had piqued my interest in wildlife rescue. Before long I found myself engrossed in classes about wildlife rehabilitation and I started to bring home other small critters for care and release. India never once showed an interest in harming any of the unique animals recovering in our home, and at times she even let me know when an animal was in distress. She would meow and scratch on the door until I investigated the matter. Consequently, I was often able to avoid a crisis.

For years it was just my sweet, little devoted cat and myself. We moved a dozen times and faced every problem head on as it came. Whether I lost a small animal or a close relative, India always sensed my pain and would quietly crawl into my lap and cheer me with her soothing purrs. It seemed that our modest animal rescue adventures were just as enjoyable for her as they were for me. What started off as a newborn squirrel grew into a daily ritual of answering calls about wildlife, or taking in injured or abandoned critters from shelters, veterinary offices, or the general public.

Eventually I obtained a state wildlife rehabilitation license and began teaching classes.

India is an old lady now, but she continues to be there for me when I'm in need of a hug. "Don't worry, you're still my little girl," I always assure her. Then, like a kitten, she licks my face, kneads her paws into my chest and drools all over me. I no longer have to lure her out of the bushes with sappy love songs, but I do offer her an occasional vocal treat, which seems to perk her up when she needs it.

Fortunately, my little heroine hasn't presented me with any additional reanimated chew toys! However, it is because of her that I have journeyed on this unique and rewarding path of wildlife rescue. She started out as a "special" kind of cat, but she became more special to me than I could have ever imagined. I hold her directly responsible for saving the hundreds of compromised lives who have come under my care since she presented me with that hairless, newborn squirrel. Since then, we have both crossed paths with an extensive variety of animals, ranging from tiny field mice to large elk.

It's amazing what we can learn from our best friends, even when they are your cat. If there was one thing that my adoring feline taught me, besides humility, it is not to discriminate. It didn't take long for me to realize that if a cat could love a squirrel, I could love anything.

~Mitzi L. Boles

What I Learned from the Cat

Learning to Laugh

Everything I know I learned from my cat:
When you're hungry, eat.
When you're tired, nap in a sunbeam.
When you go to the vet's, pee on your owner.

~Gary Smith

Sympathy for Rodent-kind

Cats were put into the world to disprove the dogma
that all things were created to serve man.
~Paul Gray

Our cat, Holly, is a loveable, silky gray creature, who has turned looking cute into a fine art. As she sprawls in the sun or winds herself around your legs, purring for England, it's hard to imagine her being anything other than affectionate and cuddly. But don't let appearances deceive you; our beloved feline is a natural born hunter, the terror of the local rodent population.

In many ways this should please us. After all, the most practical purpose that cats serve is to catch rats and mice; throughout the centuries cats have been raised specifically with this task in mind. And yes, there is a part of us that is proud to own a feline with such awesome seek-and-destroy capabilities; she's certainly no Garfield-esque fat cat. We like to think that, in her own way, she is contributing to the welfare of our local community by halting the spread of these disease-carrying pests.

But the thing is, as a household, we didn't have a rodent problem before we had a cat; now we do. I know it's meant to be a sign of devotion and we don't mind so much when she brings them home dead (though deceased mice aren't exactly top of my wish list) but it's fair to say that I'm less than thrilled when she presents them to us live.

The first time this happened I was on the phone when I heard the cat flap open and in trotted Holly, looking very pleased with herself, with a large juicy rat in her mouth. Before I had a chance to stop her she had ducked past me and raced up the stairs. I just had time to shout up the stairs to my wife, "Holly's brought a rat in. I don't know if it's dead or alive" before a scream from the bedroom confirmed that it was definitely the latter.

Half a minute later, I was treated to the sight of a small brown rat-shaped ball of fur shooting past me on the way back down the stairs, hotly pursued by a gray feline streak of lightning. The ball of fur found refuge behind the radiator in our kitchen while the streak of lightning attempted to dislodge it by insinuating its paws round the back of the heating device.

By this time my wife had recovered slightly and decided to aid Holly's efforts by pouring a bottle of water down the back of the radiator to dislodge the rat. It clung on, looking like the proverbial drowned rodent but we eventually managed to get it to release its grip by poking it with a stick. It fell to the floor and there followed a merry dance round the kitchen as we attempted to catch it in an ice cream container. For creatures with such short legs, rats can certainly move fast!

Eventually it sought refuge underneath our cooker. We tried poking it to encourage it to come out but only succeeded in getting it to climb up inside the cooker. At a loss as to what else to do, we turned the cooker on. Some minutes later, we heard a scuttling sound and then a "thump" as the rat dropped back onto the kitchen floor. Again we poked underneath the cooker; again it climbed back inside.

This remained the pattern for the next hour or so: wait for the rat to get hot enough to drop down and then try to poke it out with a stick, which inevitably resulted in it climbing back up again. We were actually due to visit some friends of ours that evening, but neither of us was prepared to leave the house with a rat on the loose so we phoned our friends and explained the problem, promising to get there as soon as the situation was resolved.

So we sat there, trousers tucked into socks, stick and ice cream tub in hand, waiting for the rat to show itself. The cat had by this time lost interest and had begun to wonder whether it should find another rodent playmate to liven up the atmosphere. We gave it some very dirty looks indeed.

Eventually we got weary of waiting and rolled the cooker upside down. A frightened looking rat leapt out. Holly's interest was suddenly reawakened and she darted forward. The rat fled in the opposite direction, straight into my ice cream tub. I trapped it and carried it out of the house. As I left, I could hear my wife giving the cat a real earful for what she'd just put us through. I have to say that I agreed with her. While it had been an experience, chasing a live rat around our kitchen wasn't something I particularly relished doing again. And by this time it was far too late to go and visit the friends we had been planning to see.

I did actually feel quite sorry for the rat. After all, it hadn't asked to be in our house. It had been rudely carried in, screamed at, chased, drenched with water, poked with a stick and slowly roasted, before being stuck in a pot and taken out into the freezing cold again. Quite a heavy evening all in all. I think it agreed with me. When I reached a point far enough from our house, I put down the plastic container and let the rat out. It looked up at me as if to say "Is it over? Is that gray monster gone?" Once it had ascertained that there were indeed no cats about, it slowly dragged itself into the dark safety of a gutter, incredibly slowly given the way it had just zipped round our kitchen. "I'm heading for bed. I'm beat. What a night!"

I still don't want them running round my house but, while I am proud of our cat's hunting prowess and appreciate that she wants to show her devotion to us, that night has given me a certain amount of sympathy for her victims.

By the way, the telling off didn't work. To date, she has brought us a further fifty-three rodents. Holly must be really devoted to us.

~Tim Crooks

Never High-Five Your Cat

Cats as a class, have never completely got over the snootiness caused by that fact that in Ancient Egypt they were worshipped as gods.
~P.G. Wodehouse

When a little black cat decided to become part of our family, there was a certain period of adjustment. Not being pet owners, we were absolutely clueless on the care and keeping of felines. You'll be happy to learn that Toonsie turned out to be an excellent teacher and my husband and I are now very well trained. For those of you contemplating adopting a kitten, I'd like to share with you a few pearls of wisdom that we picked up.

10. Never High-Five Your Cat
    There may be moments when you wish to congratulate your cat for a task well done. Try to avoid the traditional high-five—or low-five, for that matter—as they tend to flex their claws on impact, leaving your palm with tiny triangular flags of skin. It's your cat's little way of reminding you who's in charge. Not that you need reminding—that was firmly established in the first five minutes of making her acquaintance.

9. Avoid a Midnight Swim in the Dark

Now of course we know that cats don't swim. Most of them hate water and consider anyone who immerses themselves in liquid to be a total idiot. Still, if your cat is used to watching you take a daytime dip, she'll keep her eye on you, but leave you to enjoy your swim. Not so if you decide to take that dip in the dark. Avoid this at all costs unless you wish to have your cat clinging to your screen like a very loud decorative ornament. You see, you think you're alone in the dark, but your cat can see all the nocturnal creatures out there and will continuously scream a warning at her rather obtuse parents.

8. Napping One Hour Prior to Your Cat's Supper Is a No-No
    You know how you stick a toothpick into a baking cake to see if it's done? Well, Toonsie will stick one sharp claw into you to see if you're still alive and able to feed her dinner. She may not be hungry yet, but prefers the peace of mind that food service will run smoothly at the first rumble of her tummy. She will continue this test every ten minutes just to be on the safe side. Not only will you not have slept, but you'll probably have thrown your back out from the landing you took every time she used you as a human pin cushion and you flew into the air.

7. Decorate Your House to Match Your Cat
    This may seem like a silly hipster affectation, but trust me, it's not. If the color of your cat matches the color of your rug, sofa, bedspread, any and all comfy spots where she will choose to sleep, it will save endless hours of vacuuming in the long run. Fortunately for us, everything in our house was already black before Toonsie arrived. If down the road we ever get a tabby,

for instance, I'd definitely redecorate in beige. It's just easier.

6. Remember that Cats Like to Read
    Cats like to keep abreast of current events, so should you open a newspaper, be prepared for your cat to jump on top of it and snuggle in for the long run. Feel free to read around her, but she will not be budged from her sweet spot. Even if you buy your cat her own paper, she will still prefer to read along with you. Just enjoy it.

5. Cats Are Natural Helpers
    I can't tell you how many times Toonsie got involved in construction projects around the house. She helped the TV man install a satellite dish on the roof. She assisted the cable guy with wires in the attic. The phone man couldn't have wired the phone in the basement drop ceiling without her. I even watched her follow my husband step for step between the pool filter and skimmer, sticking her nose in to inspect the process right along with him. Of course Toonsie was the most helpful when my husband demolished the bathroom down to the studs in order to remodel it. She never missed an opportunity to get into the floor or ceiling to do an inspection.

4. Never Think You Can Outsmart Your Cat
    Like world champion chess players, cats plot their game plan several moves in advance. Whether you are trying to get in or out of the door, climb a stepladder or a flight of stairs, your cat will find a way past you. Just because your cat is sleeping on the other side of the house doesn't mean she is unaware of your actions. Try sitting down for dinner while she's sleeping. Your

stealth cat will be sitting between you instantly without the sound of even one paw step. You may not know where she is, but she knows where you are. Get used to it.

3. Keep to a Schedule and NEVER Take a Vacation
    There's an urban myth that cats are independent creatures who are aloof and can fend for themselves if left with enough food and fresh water. Not true. To arrive home so much as one hour later than her supper time will result in a very angry cat. She will sit with her back to you and let you know that you are no longer on speaking terms. We needed to take a business trip that would only keep us away one full day. Toonsie was fed breakfast on day one, brunch on day three, and was left big dishes of all her favorite dry foods and canned foods on timers. When we arrived home, not one morsel was touched and she was royally pissed. She stared at us accusingly, stamped her paws when she walked, and refused to come near us. You've never been stung until you've been snubbed by a cat.

2. Always Buy Extra Sushi
    Believe me, it's just easier. When placing your sushi order, decide what you can eat and then just order a few extra pieces of sashimi—cats watch their carbs. Toonsie can eat sushi faster than you can cut it into pieces and put it on her plate, and it's probably the only food she will overeat if we don't control her portions. It's a culinary treat that gets to be pretty pricey since she prefers it from a good Japanese restaurant as opposed to the supermarket. Why do we do it? The look in her eyes that tells us, "Raw fish, you two are smarter than I thought," is reward enough for us.

1. Thank Your Lucky Stars Every Day

   You've never been loved until you've been loved by a cat. They become an addiction. Toonsie gives us endless hours of entertainment and affection. From waking us for breakfast at sunrise until she gets her goodnight kiss, Toonsie never lets us forget that we're happier people for having her in our lives.

   ~Lynn Maddalena Menna

All for the Love of Precious

God helps those who persevere.
~The Qur'an

It was the flight from hell. You would think I would read the signs. "Go back." "Don't go." But I didn't pay any attention to them. I was in a hurry.

How could I have missed the first sign? On the morning of my departure, my car wouldn't start because the battery was dead. I never had problems with my car, but that day I did. I don't know anything about cars. My solution is to call AAA. Fortunately, my husband was still home and jumpstarted the car. It was just after 8:00 A.M.

Okay. I was just a few minutes late. I needed to stop by the designated spot where I was to pick up my best friend's cat named Precious. My dear friend Barbara had moved to Washington, DC earlier in the year and left her cat with another friend until she was settled. When Barbara heard I was heading to Philadelphia for a presentation, she asked me if I would bring her cat on the airplane. She would pick up the cat at the airport. What was I to say? Of course, I would. It was, after all, a non-stop flight.

So there I was meeting Ed who was the caretaker's husband. Ed was waiting for me patiently. He had Precious—so far so good. As I looked at Precious, I realized she would barely fit in the carrier that was designed for traveling cats. She must have weighed twenty-five pounds, maybe even thirty pounds!! She wasn't too happy even though she had been sedated a half hour earlier.

It was then Ed dropped the bombshell and the second sign. He forgot to bring the note from the vet saying that Precious was cleared for air travel. Oh great. Now what?

I quickly came up with Plan B. (Hindsight says I should have just cancelled the whole thing, but I always find solutions.) I told Ed to go home and get the note. I would head for the airport and he would meet me with the note at the airport counter.

I called Barbara on the way to let her know the situation. She had already left and was on her way to Philadelphia. There was no turning back.

After I parked my car in the long-term parking lot I began to think about how I was going to manage this huge cat in the bag plus my own carry-on suitcase. I'm sure if anyone was watching me, they must have howled. Poor Precious was howling—not mewing. She was not happy. I kept on wondering when the drugs were going to kick in.

When I got to the ticket counter, out of breath from carrying a thirty-pound cat, I found out that I didn't need the letter. Just then Ed showed up with his letter. Whoops, no one told me. Ed didn't seem to be too upset about making a sixty-mile roundtrip for nothing. I know I would have been.

Given the struggle I had getting Precious from my car to the ticket counter, I had to check my bag. I then proceeded to the security line. I handed over my ID, put my purse on the X-ray screener and now what about the cat? I couldn't believe what was next. The security people wanted me to take the cat out of the bag!! Didn't they know this cat wasn't too happy? Alright fine. So I took the cat out of the bag. She had gotten even heavier. Then I buzzed. Now I needed to be hand-searched. Could I put Precious back in the bag? No, she needed to be searched as well. I was thinking "good luck" as I struggled with a squirming, heavy, drugged cat. Once they determined the cat wasn't concealing any weapons, I was allowed to put the cat back in the bag. It was my shoes that beeped. Okay. Took the shoes off.

When the person at the gate asked if anyone needed any assistance in boarding, I thought about raising my hand. I reminded myself that Barbara would be very happy to see her Precious.

Thirty minutes into the flight, the pilot came on with the third sign. Apparently, the nose gear of the plane wouldn't go back up and we were turning around and heading back to Kansas City. Oh no, this couldn't be. Precious and I had to get off the plane, find out which plane I needed to get on, and go through security again. Yes, I had to take the cat out of the bag again, but this time I took my shoes off.

I called Barbara and informed her of the situation. I also called my parents, who were picking me up at the airport and informed them. My updated information included that I was no longer on a non-stop flight. I would be heading to South Carolina and then take a connecting flight to Philadelphia. I was due to arrive three hours later. Oh great. How was Precious going to handle the situation? The bag didn't come with cat litter. Fortunately, before I left the house, I had placed in the cat bag an opened Huggies Pull-Ups diaper that I took from my toddler's supply. I hoped this would take care of Precious's needs.

The plane arrived in South Carolina around 2:00 P.M. and I headed for the connecting flight. Of course my plane landed on Concourse A and the connecting flight was on Concourse C. As I carried my heavy precious cargo, I wondered if my arms would ever come back to their natural position.

When I arrived at the designated gate, I was informed of the fourth sign — the airline decided to switch airplanes. The plane that we were to go on was previously headed for Germany. Since it was fueled for a cross-Atlantic flight, they had to de-fuel the plane since it would be too heavy to land in Philadelphia. Do you know it takes about three times longer to de-fuel a plane than to fuel a plane? It was about 5:00 P.M., and we were about to board when an electrical storm arrived at the airport. All flights were grounded.

As I looked at my fellow passengers, I wondered who had it worse. Me, with a thirty-pound cat, or the mother trying to manage a very cranky three-year-old? At least mine was in a bag and somewhat sedated.

It was about 7:00 P.M. before we were allowed to board the plane. All this time I was keeping my parents and my waiting friend informed of our status. Once I was sitting in the plane and we were in the air, I thought it would just be a couple more hours and this trip would be over. So I thought.

Mother Nature decided to follow us and show me the fifth sign. We couldn't land until the storm had passed Philadelphia. We started to circle. We even flew above Washington, DC where Precious was headed. I thought about the scene from the children's movie *Dumbo* where the stork drops off all the babies for their animal moms, but I decided that Precious was even heavier than baby Dumbo and she wouldn't float down as easily. Bad idea.

By the time we landed in Philadelphia, it was 9:30 P.M. Of course, the Jetway wouldn't line up to the airplane properly. It took another thirty minutes before we were able to get off the plane. As these two weary travelers worked their way out of the concourse, I saw an anxious Barbara on the other side of the security partition. When she saw us, her face lit up in a way that made it all worth it. I handed the cat in the bag to Barbara. My arm and back muscles were cramping, but my face was smiling.

I waited for my parents outside baggage claim. It was 10:30 P.M. It had been a very long day, but I did it for the love of a friend. And for the love of Precious.

~Mahnaz Shabbir

35

Swiss Cat

People that don't like cats haven't met the right one yet.
~*Deborah A. Edwards*

No cats! I was determined, not just for all the usual reasons, but also for this unusual fact: this would be a cat that spoke German. Instead of "Here, Kitty Kitty Kitty" there would be "Komm, Puss Puss Puss!" Every "No" would be "Nein" and I could only imagine the difficulty of a visit to the vet. I told my wife and children we could not do it.

Adapting to life in a foreign country is never easy and it had been a struggle for me. After graduation from Harvard Divinity School, my wife and I decided to leave my native Massachusetts and take up life in her country, Switzerland. I had learned some German, but was still faced with a formidable linguistic challenge, not just at the local supermarket but in the largest church in the city of Zurich where I took over as co-pastor. There were enough problems, and adding one more burden to my life would be too much.

But children have large, soulful eyes and persuasive talent. After years of holding the line, I finally gave in to their tears—we would give the cat a try and see how it went. I had no way of knowing that the cat would one day provide a great moment of laughter in a tense situation.

The troubles I had feared all came to pass, of course. There was cat hair, a stinky litter box, and clawed furniture. In addition, as luck would have it, the cat and I were left alone during the day as the children and their mother, who is a teacher, all left for school. My office, which was connected to the minister's home, became a curious place for the Swiss cat, and she would often enter the office while I was there, meowing for attention or asking to be petted. Slowly, I came to resent her less, and I practiced some new German words on her. She never corrected me, so I figured I was doing okay. She also would follow me into the church next door, where she would wander through the premises, sometimes finding a spot to nap. When she was lost, she meowed loudly enough to be heard throughout the church.

My work progressed well, although it was challenging. As I conducted one of my first weddings, almost everyone present was nervous: the wedding couple, the parents, and me. The tension grew when the big moment came—the wedding vows. I turned to the groom and asked him in German, "Do you take this woman to be your wedded wife? If so, say, 'I do.'" Overcome with emotion, the young man paused and struggled to regain his composure. There was a moment of awkward silence in the centuries-old stone church, and, as everyone watched and waited, rather than "I do," a "Meow!" could be heard echoing through the sanctuary. Our cat! She must have sneaked into the church earlier and gotten lost. I was very embarrassed, but noticed that the laughter had eased the tension everyone was feeling.

From that day on, I started looking at our cat differently. I focused less on those things about her that irritated me and more on those which I found pleasant: her cute antics, her company on lonely days, and the fact that she had actually helped me when I needed it. And I came to realize that it is not unlike all of our relationships; if we can pay more attention to those things we like about those we share our lives with, rather than what we dislike, we can live together a little bit better.

So it is definite: the cat stays. Today when I call, "Komm, Puss Puss Puss!" she comes, and I am thankful for all she has taught me.

~Arthur Bowler

Prince Rilian

To bathe a cat takes brute force, perseverance, courage of conviction —
and a cat. The last ingredient is usually hardest to come by.
~Stephen Baker

I couldn't help but spoil him. Who wouldn't adore this little bundle of cuddly cuteness? He was my little prince, named after Prince Rilian in *The Chronicles of Narnia*. By day he slept placidly in my sweater pocket as I typed away at my keyboard, emerging occasionally to pounce on my cursor. By night he chased dust balls, scampered about, and sharpened his feline hunting skills. After a few sleepless nights, I decided to give him his own room.

I supplied him with food, water, bed, toys, and scratching post in the downstairs bathroom. Each morning I would feed and pet him as he purred and rubbed against my legs. Sometimes I would have to throw away shredded rolls of toilet paper before I scooped out the litter box. How I despaired of digging out clumps of waste each morning!

He grew large enough to put his forepaws on the lid as I dumped it into the toilet. He even watched intently as the water swirled around and disappeared.

"He understands," I thought. "What a smart cat."

That gave me an idea. What if I could get him to go directly into the toilet? Then I wouldn't have to worry about the kitty litter at all. Wouldn't my friends be impressed!

"Are you feeling okay?" my husband asked, when he found me duct-taping garbage bags over the toilet bowl.

"Don't worry," I said. "I know what I'm doing."

Even Rilian watched as I put the seat down over the bags and poured kitty litter over the top.

"See, look at him!" I assured my husband. "He's so smart. He'll have it figured out in no time."

As soon as I scooted the little footstool in front of the toilet he hopped up to scratch around. I gazed in amazement as he immediately used his new "litter box." Not only had I discovered the latest craze in pet training, but a sure-fire way to save me work. I proudly displayed a sign outside the bathroom door: "Prince Rilian's Throne Room."

I planned to decrease the amount of kitty litter gradually so he would eventually only use the plastic. When it had been devoid of litter for two days, he was still hitting my intended target. "All I have to do now," I thought, "is remove the plastic. Voila! My talented little kitty will go directly into the toilet!"

It took six hours, but I finally succeeded in scraping off all the duct tape. As I finished, he sat curled in the corner, intently watching.

"Hey, Kitty," I said. "You want to try it out?"

He hopped onto the seat, per usual, but seemed distressed.

"Don't worry, you'll get the hang of it," I assured him.

The next morning, I hoped to see proof of my success. I smugly thought, "There might even be a way to get him to flush."

Then I saw it: a big, stinky pile of cat poop right in the sink! I'm sure the whole neighborhood heard my cry of disgust. I held Rilian in one arm, while I used the scoop to deliver his "present" to the toilet, and let him watch me put it in.

"See, it goes in there. You have to poop in the toilet." He watched once again as it disappeared in a swirl of water. "At least he knew he wasn't supposed to go on the floor," I mused.

My husband noticed me scouring the sink with several cleaners and suggested a litter box might be easier.

"No way," I insisted. "He's a very, very smart cat. He can do it!" I wasn't about to give up so easily.

He just needed a chance, that's all. In fact, all that day it seemed he had understood and used the toilet properly. I didn't catch him in the act or see anything unusual on the floor or in the sink. Maybe, just maybe.

That is, until the next morning when I went in to cuddle him. He wasn't cuddly; his feet were wet and he smelled horrible.

After a short investigation, I found his new privy. "What on earth! No, not in the bathtub," I groaned.

Six cleaners, four hours, and fifteen bandages later, I had the bathtub and the cat scrubbed shiny clean. I figured since he tried to climb my arm so many times to get out of the bath, he wouldn't want to get in there ever again.

Wrong. That was now his potty of choice. It didn't matter how many baths he got, or how many explanations I gave him. He simply would not use the toilet. That's when it hit me: it would be easier to scoop out the litter box!

~Lynetta L. Smith

Kitten Capers

An ordinary kitten will ask more questions than any five-year-old.
~Carl Van Vechten

I got a kitty recently. A cuddly bundle of joy and delight who is always endeavoring to figure out the world around her. She is constantly reminding me of the awkward but endearing quality of learning, and of the play and bizarreness of the world.

Yesterday she put her head in a small backpack sitting on a chair. Sticking her face in the outside pocket, she sniffed around to discover leftover cucumber slices from my picnic lunch. At first with interest, and then with vigor, she was stuffing her head and then her whole upper body into the pocket to make sure she hadn't missed anything.

But before long, having that curiosity satisfied, she sat up ready to move on to another adventure. In one zesty move she jumped off the chair—hooking one of her little back legs on the backpack strap on the way down. Suddenly, what she thought was a harmless inanimate object with some boring human food was a fierce and attacking animal, right on her tail! Onto the floor and around and around the LIVE and wild backpack was chasing her.

I watched. First I worried that her little legs would be injured in her fight for life with the luggage. Then I felt the mild concern of seeing a terrified expression on someone you love, even in the face of something you know to be harmless. And then came humor—this kitten was doing battle with an inanimate object. How many times had I done battle with things that were completely harmless to me? Expending much energy and great fright defending myself from "a backpack," so to speak.

It got funnier and funnier as the scene went on—a terrifying backpack of all things. Man, the world can be strange! Slashing around on the wood floor in a fury, she managed to free herself from the horrific monster before too long. However, her bold curiosity of moments before was gone. She slunk away from the terrible scene and hid under the nearby wood stove, collecting herself.

I don't even remember the moment when she discovered it was just a stupid backpack—the same uninteresting one with the dying cucumber slices she had seen and tried to leave behind only moments ago. Though I know it wasn't long afterward.

I just remember sitting there laughing. Laughing at the funny situations that life deals us and at the weird ways we forget and then rediscover the illusion. Laughing at seeing myself battle luggage on the kitchen floor. Attaching to things that I could be rid of—perhaps just for the drama of it all.

Sometimes the most random moments bring a clarity that can't be ignored, making the game so obvious—all you can do is sit back and laugh.

~Aimée Cartier

Mothers, Daughters, and Cats

A cat can be trusted to purr when she is pleased,
which is more than can be said for human beings.
~William Ralph Inge

My mother phones. "Puss Puss is constipated."

I stifle a groan. Puss Puss, an overweight tabby, is Mother's constant companion. I rescued her from the SPCA and gave her to my mother for a Mother's Day gift seven years ago. Puss Puss repaid me by immediately worming her way into my mother's heart, driving me farther down her list of loved ones. I can live with being displaced by grandchildren, but by a cat?

"Give her some of that laxative, Felaxin, like you always do," I respond, not seeing why this health update rates a phone call.

"I can't," she says. "I finished the last tube yesterday and the vet doesn't have any more. It's backordered because the manufacturer is missing an ingredient." Her voice lowers. "Puss Puss won't take any other brand, will you Puss Puss? Such a good girl."

The last is directed to the cat. Good cat nothing. A good cat would take what she's given, regardless of brand, rather than keep her legs crossed in protest. Still, the cat adores my mother and keeps her from getting lonely.

With a promise to help locate some of this wonder drug, I assure my mother the cat will be her old self in a day or two. I hang up and call my vet. He doesn't carry this particular brand, but the receptionist gives me the name of someone who might have it. No luck.

I start calling clinics in my area. Nothing. I try ones farther away. Fifteen calls later, I get the same story every time. Either they don't stock it or they're out of it and it's on backorder.

By now, my frustration level has reached the stratosphere, but I am not giving up until I find the stuff, even if I have to call every vet in the phone book. My finger continues down the page. On my twentieth call, I hear the words I've been waiting for, "Yes, we have Felaxin."

It's like finding the Holy Grail. "Could you reserve three tubes for me?" I ask. "I promise I'll be there before 5:00 P.M. to pick them up." The receptionist agrees. I'm tempted to call my mother with the good news, but decide to wait until it's a done deal and I have the tubes in my hand.

One bus, a subway train, and a fifteen-minute walk later I arrive, breathless because I ran the last two blocks. It's 4:45 P.M., and I'm terrified they've given the Felaxin away to another desperate cat owner. I take a few deep breaths to calm myself and ask for my prize.

The receptionist hands me the three tubes as if it's nothing, as if everybody carries this magic elixir. I take them reverently. As she's filling out the bill, I glance at their product shelves and see another six or seven tubes. I daringly ask for a fourth tube.

"No problem," she says.

Thirty-eight dollars later I leave.

Now comes the other tricky part. I live in Toronto. My mother and Puss Puss—the joy of her life—live in Montreal. Having attained my prize, I have to get it to Montreal as quickly as possible before the poor cat explodes.

Canada Post comes to the rescue with its next-day delivery service. For a minute, I'm tempted to send the package via Outer Mongolia, but I relent. I pay, knowing my time and effort will be greatly appreciated, if not by the cat, certainly by my mother who will be thanking me for weeks.

I'm already envisioning a really big birthday present as an appropriate show of gratitude.

I can't wait to get home and tell her the good news. The moment I'm in the door, I head for the telephone. "You and Puss Puss are in luck," I crow. "I found a vet who had a large stock of Felaxin. I picked up, not one," here I pause for the grand finale, "but four tubes. You'll have them by 5:00 P.M. tomorrow."

With that, I sink back in my chair, expecting to hear words of praise. Instead, she says, "You mean they had more than four tubes?"

A sinking feeling fills my stomach. "Yes," I say.

"So why didn't you buy them all? Go back tomorrow and get the rest of their stock."

I slump down, hand clenched around the receiver so tight my knuckles are turning white. Gone are the visions of a huge birthday present. Instead, I think about the time spent calling various vets, the two hours of travelling, the Visa bill, the post office bill, and the phone bill. I say—nothing.

This is the woman who carried me for nine months, gave birth to me, changed my diapers, and did the million other things that mothers do for their children. Still, I want to kill her.

I count to ten twice, then a third time for good measure. I tell myself to cut her some slack. She's worried about the cat. Once Puss Puss is fine, I'm sure she'll be more appreciative.

I mumble something and hang up. And you know what? I go back—because she's my mother and she loves her cat. But if she expects a Mother's Day present this year, she's crazy. This is it.

~Harriet Cooper

Halfway House for Wayward Cats

Psychologists now recognize that the need in some people to have a dozen cats is really a sublimated desire to have two dozen cats.
~Robert Brault, robertbrault.com

I'm afraid I've noticed an alarming development. My house, which I've always thought of as an average, two-story tract home on the end of a quiet cul-de-sac, is really a halfway house for wayward cats. Now, while this may sound farfetched to you, let me just say it sure explains a lot of things, like why, for instance, when we moved in we had one cat, a few months later we had two, and now we are up to nine cats. NINE.

I must admit, if anyone had ever told me that I shouldn't keep the garage door open because a pregnant stray cat might wander in and gave birth to six kittens, I would've thought they were dipping into the cooking wine. However, I've come to accept that this is just the type of thing that happens to people who live in a House for Wayward Cats.

But I still don't understand why this particular cat chose my garage. There are much cleaner and quieter places it could've gone, like, say, back alleys and freeway underpasses. My friend Linda said that there's an old saying that cats choose their owners. This can only mean that 1) I must possess profound inner qualities I didn't know

I had or 2) I'm now the new owner of a cat that is a really, really bad judge of character.

Of course there are other explanations, depending on whom you ask. My friend Nicole, who's a religious person, thinks there is some deep and meaningful reason it chose me. My friend Julie thinks cats instinctively pick caring, responsible people to adopt them. But my theory is that I'm the only person on the block stupid enough to keep my garage door up.

Oh, it's not that I don't like cats. I do. But, frankly, my relationship with them has always been the more superficial "here-kitty-kitty nice-kitty-kitty" type rather than the "let-me-hold-your-paw-while-you-take-a-deep-breath-and-push" kind. If you know what I mean.

Needless to say, watching the birth process was a priceless, educational experience for my children. I could tell they were in awe of it by the way they greeted the birth of each kitten by shouting, "Ugh! Gross!" and covering their eyes.

One thing I've learned about owning nine cats is that your life suddenly becomes much quieter because most people will avoid you. Now, don't get me wrong. At first you will be the most popular person in the neighborhood, with people dropping by at all hours just to see the kittens. But after they reach adoptable age you will be lucky if someone makes polite conversation. And, on top of that, no matter whom you talk to, they will always ALWAYS find a way to work in a reason why they can't adopt a kitten. Take, for example, the last phone conversation I had with my friend Barbara, who I've known for over thirty years.

"Hi, Barb it's me."

"Oh, hi. Say, did I ever tell you that I have a terrible allergy to cats?"

"Well, uh, no."

"Yeah, it's bad. I can't even so much as look at kitten without sneezing."

"But..."

"In fact, I feel one coming on now. Gotta go. Bye."

The other thing I've learned is that there are a lot of people out there who take cats seriously. Very seriously. Sort of the way some people take sports teams or mutual funds very seriously. And these well-meaning people will give you more advice than you ever thought possible. They will tell you to weigh each kitten five times a day on a postage scale, feed it warm milk by hand from a miniature bottle, and various other little things that you'd never ever do, not even for your firstborn child. But don't let that fool you. When it comes time to give the kittens away, they too will become allergic to cats.

Nevertheless, between you and me, I'm not going to let that stop me. No Siree. I'm not going to end up in my dotage like one of those ladies who lives alone with a bazillion cats. I'm going to take control of the local feline population and show them that my house isn't a harbor for any stray cat that wanders in. And, on top of that, I'm not going to rest until I find a good home for each kitten. All of them.

Well, okay, except for maybe the fluffy orange one. And possibly the gray one with the cute pink nose. And, oh yeah, the black striped tabby. I mean, you just can't find colors like those anywhere, you know.

~Debbie Farmer

The Cat Delivers the Goods

A cat has absolute emotional honesty: human beings, for one reason or another, may hide their feelings, but a cat does not.
~Ernest Hemingway

Don't ever join a church just because it is close to your home. That is definitely not a criterion to use. My family and I made that mistake several years ago, hoping to avoid long drives elsewhere. We avoided the drives all right, but found ourselves involved in a situation we had to get out of.

We made our decision to leave. Soon the pastor telephoned and asked to come for a visit. When he arrived, we showed him into the living room. My wife, the pastor, and I all sat on an L-shaped sofa, the pastor in the middle. It was soon clear he wanted to convince us that we were wrong in our decision.

As we talked, our adult male cat, a wonderful gray-and-white that had been with us for ten years, walked into the room. Fluffy always was on his best behavior when guests were around. In fact, he was always on good behavior, never getting on the furniture or bothering anyone.

This particular day Fluffy slowly approached the sofa, rubbing my wife's leg on his way past as he always did. Staying close by the edge of the sofa, he proceeded to the spot where the pastor sat. In one quick moment, while we continued with our discussion and barely noticed the cat, Fluffy stopped over the foot of the pastor and proceeded to relieve himself right on top of the pastor's shoe.

The gasps from the three of us were clearly audible. For a moment all our mouths were open but no words were spoken. Never had Fluffy done that before, nor did he ever do that again. My wife and I quickly moved to clean up the mess. The pastor tried only a few more words and then departed.

I still smile about that day when God used our cat to make a point in a language that could not be ignored, a day when I also learned very graphically that God has a sense of humor.

~John Newlin

Yoga Cat

I have noticed that what cats most appreciate in a human being
is not the ability to produce food which they take for granted,
but his or her entertainment value.
~Author Unknown

I took up yoga two years ago, around the same time we got our cat. Having read that owning a cat and practicing yoga were both fail-safe methods to soothe troubled nerves, I envisioned a life filled with peace and inner reflection. Now two years wiser, I know that people who own cats do yoga simply to release the stress in their lives that exists because they own a cat.

My cat mocks me while I do yoga. As I sit on my padded blue mat, tangled up in a pose the human body, or at least my body, was not meant to perform, she'll sit beside me and perform the same pose flawlessly.

"Now, raise your right leg, keeping your left leg fully extended," coos my video yoga instructor. "Balance on your sitting bones, and raise the leg over your head."

Puffing and grunting, I try to extend my leg. Without breaking a sweat, the cat plops herself down beside me and raises her right leg over her head, making sure her back leg remains fully extended. I look over at her. She looks back and, pointedly, bends down and licks herself, without lowering the leg.

I find this insulting.

I decide I need more personalized instruction, and sign up at our local Y, paying $75 to have a certified yoga instructor twist me into painful and humiliating poses. But the cat is not there, executing a better version of "Downward Facing Dog" than me, so it's bearable.

"You're doing very well," says my instructor.

"Thank you," I say. "I'm trying to impress my cat." The instructor backs away, and avoids me for the rest of the class. But I don't mind. I am raising and extending my legs at an advanced rate. I can't wait to show the cat.

I return home and pull out my mat. The cat looks pleased. It's been a few days since she's humiliated me.

"Ha! That's only what you think is going to happen," I say. "Watch this!" I proceed to execute a flawless "Dead Bug" pose. The cat looks amused.

"That's not all," I say. "I can also do this!" I move into Downward Facing Dog, remembering to breathe, as my instructor said.

The cat ambles over, takes a seat next to my head, and stares at me. My arms begin to tremble, but I refuse to give up the pose. The cat continues to stare, glancing significantly at my now shaking torso. I am no longer breathing properly. In fact, I think I am close to hyperventilating. The cat begins to purr.

I can't go any further. I collapse onto the mat. I'm pretty sure I've strained something. I can't locate exactly where at the moment, because my entire body is trembling.

Now that I'm on the floor, the cat yawns and stretches, fully extending her front legs and arching her back. She holds the pose. And holds it. And holds it. And darn it all, she's breathing. Releasing the pose, she takes a deep cleansing breath. Her final word on the subject is to claw at my yoga mat before exiting the room.

The phone rings. It's my yoga instructor.

"I was wondering if you wanted to sign up for our next series of classes," she said. "You were making such good progress."

I think about the physical anguish and sweat of the yoga class. Then I ponder the money spent to experience this pain. I tell the instructor I will not be returning to class. If it's pain I'm after, I can get that at home for free.

I'll just do yoga with my cat.

~Dena Harris

What I Learned from the Cat

Learning to Accept Help

*Too often we underestimate the power of a touch, a smile,
a kind word, a listening ear, an honest compliment,
or the smallest act of caring, all of which have the potential
to turn a life around.*

~Leo Buscaglia

The Gentleman Caller Cat

The cat is the only animal which accepts the comforts
but rejects the bondage of domesticity.
~Georges Louis Leclerc de Buffon

In 1998, I moved into my first home. It was an incredibly exciting day despite the relentless summer heat and the long string of crazy snafus that are typical of moving days. When I purchased the house nestled on a quiet cul-de-sac, I thought I would be the only tenant, save for the three felines I called friends. The move was not even finished when I discovered that was definitely not the case.

Taking a break, I collapsed on the stairs of the small deck that served as my new front porch and gulped water. To my surprise, a thick-chested tomcat sauntered out from under the deck. Looking at my sweat-drenched form, he announced quite loudly that watching me haul all of those boxes had made him hungry. When could he expect dinner to be served? I already had three furry mouths to feed; a fourth was not on the agenda.

He pled his case while eyeing me warily and keeping his distance. This brown tabby tomcat clearly meant business. I acquiesced, but when I stood to do his bidding, he scrambled under the deck with the breathtaking quickness displayed by ferals who do not grow up around people.

When I reappeared on the deck with a bowl of dry food and started down the stairs, the tomcat hissed at me, then growled. He moved back under the deck and cried at me until I set the bowl down on the front walk beside the deck and backed away. Studying me like a cop sizing up a suspect, my visitor edged over and began munching cautiously. His eyes never wavered from me more than a few seconds. I kept my distance and, after setting out a bowl of water, left him to his meal.

We quickly fell into a pattern of him squawking at me most mornings until I proffered a bit of food. Our relationship was tenuous. We were fine when I was quietly sitting or far enough away to pose no threat. When in close proximity, we were both cautious of each other's next move. I named my boarder Toby and we continued the dance of uncertain friendship for a bit.

Then one day, he was gone and I dearly missed him. A couple of months later he sauntered back into my life. My home became Toby's bed and breakfast; he occupied his "room" beneath the deck when not away on adventures.

During his visits, we continued the odd dance. I slowly positioned his food bowl closer and closer to the front door until, after a couple of years, he was eating on the edge of the deck. It took nearly five years before we'd grown to trust each other enough for him to approach my outstretched fingers. After sniffing them, he lurched forward, causing me to quickly withdraw my hand, my heart thumping a million miles an hour.

Toby gave me a quizzical look like he thought I was nuts. After repeating this scenario several times, I realized he was not being aggressive, he was head-butting my hand—a sign of affection, albeit an odd one.

When a fire burned my home, I was away from the place for nearly six months while it was rebuilt. A few weeks after I returned, I was greeted one morning by Toby's familiar guttural greeting. If you have ever encountered an old friend after a long time apart and within a few minutes joked and laughed just like you were never parted, then you know what our reunion was like. Toby and I slipped back into that familiar pattern of a meal every morning when he summoned me to the front porch.

One afternoon, I returned from work, and Toby greeted me with a loud and persistent request for dinner. I reminded Toby that he ate in the morning. He objected and we argued for awhile—suffice it to say he wore me down. When I set the plate down and backed away, Toby swaggered over to the dish, sniffed it, then ambled to a spot about a foot and a half away and settled down.

"I don't get it," I chided my old friend. "You asked me for food and when I give it to you, you just sniff it and go sit down? You're getting awfully picky in your old age, aren't you?" While Toby meowed me a lengthy explanation, I could not figure out why he would do such a thing unless he just had no appreciation for my menu selection.

That's when I spotted a tiny gray-whiskered nose skittishly nearing the plate of food. Silently I watched. Another tiny muzzle appeared, then another and another. Stunned I watched as a mother and five kittens scarfed up the food, and then scampered back under the deck for safety.

"Well, well, well." I was enthralled. Mama was a striking bicolor shorthair cat—deep Russian blue coloring contrasting with a dramatic white tummy, feet and a blaze up her nose. The kittens were even more dazzling. Their fur was long and silky and their coloring unique in its patterns. With vivid blue eyes that crossed in varying degrees, the kittens clearly had some Siamese in their lineage. I would come to discover they were Snowshoe kittens, each more beautiful than the next.

My relationship with Toby changed that day, perhaps because of my newfound respect for this husky tomcat, who begged for food to feed a mother and her kittens, then settled nearby to protect them while they ate. Our friendship grew until I was finally able to pet his forehead with the tips of my fingers. One morning not too long after his rescue of the kittens, I went out on the deck and called for the tomcat. Toby didn't respond for a bit.

When I finally heard that grumbling meow, I spotted him limping through the ivy. He was covered in blood and appeared to be in terrible pain. I was not at all sure Toby would let me tend to him. That day I promised the old guy that if he would let me take him to the vet, he could retire to a life of luxury in the house. Battle-scarred and one-eyed now, he lives mostly in a bedroom suite where he even allows me to stroke the soft white fur on his belly when he's in the right mood—a feat that took nearly a decade to achieve. Though he no longer comes and goes as he once did, my gentleman caller Toby dotes on his kittens who cuddle around him. He remains a quirky and protective friend.

Developing a friendship with Toby over such a long time taught me that trust is a precious and tenuous thing. Trust, or the lack thereof, defines the relationships that we have, whether they are positive, uplifting connections or filled with uncertainty and pain. Toby taught me that trust is something that takes time to grow, but it is truly worth the effort.

~Nancy Sullivan

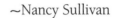

Unexpected Blessings

There is something about the presence of a cat...
that seems to take the bite out of being alone.
~Louis J. Camuti

"My doctor says I need a pet for therapy. Do you happen to have a white kitten?" This phone call changed my life. I'd been aware of service dogs, but therapy cats? That idea had never occurred to me.

Mary was an elderly lady living alone in a senior apartment complex. She had no family nearby and few friends. Her doctor, concerned for her health, suggested a pet for her to care for. She hoped this would give Mary a reason to get up each day. When the call came into the shelter, we did have one white kitten. He had been brought in with three siblings. Infested with parasites, the others didn't survive. This little, white, mitten-pawed kitten had a fighting spirit and grew stronger each day. He was too young to leave the shelter yet, but the decision was made to save him for Mary. Every day brought phone calls asking about her kitten's progress. Learning that Mary was on a very limited income, supplies were gathered by the staff to help with the kitten's needs. Soon, it was time for the kitten to leave the shelter. Delivered to Mary's apartment, they began their new life together. Progress reports came into us each day and I decided it was time to meet Mary.

After being buzzed into her apartment building, I walked to Mary's door. She only opened it a crack and I wondered why, until

I looked down and saw a tiny white face peeking out. He didn't act like any kitten I'd ever met. Don't they usually hide from strangers? Bending down, I scooped up the fluffy kitten, now named Cosmo. Cosmo didn't wiggle or struggle to get away, he studied my face and must have decided I was okay. From that day on, Mary, Cosmo and I became great friends.

One of Mary's biggest concerns was what would happen to Cosmo if she couldn't care for him. I reassured her that Cosmo would always have a home with me. Shortly after this conversation, Mary's health took a turn for the worse and she was in and out of the hospital and nursing home. During her stays, Cosmo was her day brightener. He was allowed into the transitional care unit of the hospital and each nursing home she was admitted to. As I pushed Mary down the hall in her wheelchair, Cosmo might sit in her lap or walk wearing his harness and leash. We were a mini-parade! Patients called out from their rooms asking for a visit. Staff members stopped us in the hall. Everyone wanted to pet Cosmo and talk to him. Mary was the center of attention too—she wasn't lonely anymore. I started to realize the impact Cosmo had on each person he met. Soon, calls came in from other area nursing homes requesting visits from Cosmo.

We've had many memorable experiences since starting our work. At one nursing home, a staff member told us about a resident who loved cats and would enjoy spending time with Cosmo. This lady was non-verbal and had some type of neurological problem. As I placed Cosmo in her lap, her eyes lit up and she appeared to pet him with her claw-like hand. Instead of petting him, she ripped a clump of his fur out. I was horrified, but Cosmo sat quietly. He didn't hiss, scratch, bite, or try to run away. He waited for me to rescue him. It was as if he knew that this lady didn't mean to hurt him.

One of our favorite nursing home residents had been receiving visits from Cosmo for over a year when she was hospitalized and died. On our first time back after her death, I tried to avoid her hallway since Cosmo had always led me straight to her room. Agitated, he pulled out of his harness and ran for her room. Chasing after him, I caught up to him in her doorway. Cosmo stood still looking for his friend. When he didn't see her, he walked around the room, touching each piece of furniture with his nose and cheek. He looked into the closet and bathroom and then he lay down in the middle of her floor and let out a pitiful meow. Who says animals don't grieve?

In another nursing home, a resident who we had visited for several months was lying in bed with her husband and daughter at her side. I'd never heard this lady speak, but she seemed to enjoy spending time with Cosmo, so I put him in bed so that she could feel his soft fur. When it was time to go, I picked him up and started out of the room. Hearing a soft sound, I turned around. Her daughter looked at us and said, "I think she just said goodbye." I'm not sure who was more surprised.

Eventually, Cosmo joined Stein Hospice as their first Delta Society registered therapy pet. Many people think that hospice is a depressing place. Cosmo and I don't agree. We've made many new friends there. Patients, family, visitors and staff all look forward to spending time with Cosmo. As we walk onto the unit, we might meet a student doctor who scoops Cosmo up and takes him to visit a patient. EMTs may be coming down the hall delivering a patient to the unit; they wave and call out "Cosmo." Children run up to us and want to walk with him or spend time laying on the floor beside him. Friends and family cuddle and pet him and tell us about their pets at home and how much they miss them. Each patient is different and all enrich our lives. Some sit quietly in a chair with Cosmo at their feet. Others are in bed and ask that he lay next to them. Others ask me to hold Cosmo so that they can comfortably reach and pet him.

One of our special patients had been on the unit for several weeks. He looked forward to spending time with Cosmo and always had a smile for us. As we were walking towards his room one day, his nurse stopped us and said that he was having a bad day. She asked us not to visit that day. As we passed his room, this man waved at us and motioned for us to come in. After checking with a nurse, we were allowed in. This man was having a lot of difficulty breathing, but that didn't stop him from smiling, petting and talking to Cosmo.

A local celebrity, Cosmo takes all the attention in stride. His greatest pleasure continues to be meeting people and making each life better, one at a time.

Who could have imagined that a tiny, shelter kitten who almost didn't live could be a blessing to so many people.

Who could have guessed that pet therapy would become our mission and my blessing from God?

Unexpected blessings—they're often God's best.

~Janet Freehling

My Little Helper

When I play with my cat, who knows if
I am not a pastime to her more than she is to me?
~Michel de Montaigne, Essays, 1580

After we brought our first baby, Adelle, home from the hospital, we had many conversations about giving our very friendly cat, Mitchell, away. A cat and a newborn baby—would this work? I didn't think Mitchell would be good for the baby, but I couldn't give him away after he gave me six years of unconditional love and affection. Mitchell was family.

Time passed and Mitchell stayed away from the baby. He watched from afar. He didn't snuggle as much as he used to. I was impressed that Mitchell respected the fact that I was a new mother.

My husband and I spent hours trying to teach Adelle how to crawl when she was seven months old. She just wasn't interested, and this made me feel like a failure.

One afternoon, when Adelle and I had playtime on the floor, Mitchell joined us. This was the first time he had tried to get close to the baby. Adelle's eyes glowed just looking at that cat. I'm sure she thought, "Wow, my new toy." Mitchell lay close to her, and Adelle tried to play with the cat as gently as you can expect for a baby. Mitchell wasn't bothered at all. He lay close for about an hour. The next few days, the same thing happened.

On the fourth day, Mitchell lay close to Adelle for only about five minutes until he moved two feet away. You could see that Adelle wasn't happy with this. Her new friend was so far away. You could see her frustration. That was it, the motivation that she needed. She crawled for the first time. She crawled to the cat, which in turn, moved two feet away again. Adelle laughed out loud at this new game. And it took her a little while, but she crawled to Mitchell again. I sat in amazement. This game continued for about a month. They played until Adelle was fast and could get anywhere she wanted to go.

Finally Mitchell seemed to be finished with this game. I thought it was just Adelle's time to crawl. I have to tell you, I still didn't think Mitchell had anything to do with Adelle achieving her milestone.

Mitchell started to lie on the couch with his tail hanging down. Adelle crawled everywhere looking for Mitchell. Finally she looked up. And that was the day she learned to cruise. She reached for his tail, put her hands on that couch, and stood up. Mitchell was helping me as a parent. Teaching my child to crawl, to walk even. Mitchell sensed my frustration, and like any regular member of the family, he decided to help out.

To think that I thought about giving her teacher, her friend, and my helper away. To think, I thought Mitchell wouldn't be good for the baby.

~Genevieve Read

Unexpected Miracles

Kittens can happen to anyone.
~Paul Gallico

I had failed as a "cat parent." My little cat Maisey, when she was just a smidgen over a year old, was going to be a mother. At first we weren't sure. Perhaps we were leaving a bit too much milk in her saucer and too many scraps of deli meat in her food dish. Perhaps that was the reason for her suddenly ballooning mid-section.

But my husband and I soon noticed that it wasn't just her size that was changing, it was her attitude. She no longer wanted to bat at the shoelace my four-year-old son Elijah dangled for her. It seemed as if she hardly wanted to move at all. Once a playful, romping, kitten, Maisey now took four or five lethargic steps and then flopped down like a beached whale and went to sleep. When I picked her up to nuzzle her under my chin like she always loved, she would let out the faintest most pitiful, human-like groan. I remembered similar groans escaping my own lips when I was nine months pregnant. And it became painfully clear that sooner or later, she was going to lactate.

But the most incriminating fact remained—I had let her out. More than once. Without a supervisor. Without a leash. Without being spayed. I can hear Bob Barker's chastisement now.

Yes, I had failed as a cat parent. And people let me know it, too.

"Didn't you know that she was in heat?" asked a friend of mine who volunteered at the Humane Society. "She was bound to get pregnant, with all the cats in the neighborhood."

I called the Humane Society to check on their policy of accepting kittens.

"You didn't get her spayed, huh?"

"No, I know I should have but I never got around to it...."

"Well, I guess it's too late now."

There was no mistaking the "tsk tsk" in her voice.

And there was no stopping the inevitable. I did some research on the Internet and learned that cats liked privacy when their time came. So we prepared a box for Maisey, lined with soft towels and old blankets on which she could labor, and placed it in our basement bathroom. I even plugged in a nightlight so the atmosphere would be soft and soothing instead of glaringly bright or pitch black. And then we began to watch her like a time bomb.

My Internet research had also informed me that many cats, right before they go into labor, become ultra affectionate. They purr, they cuddle, they want to be held. It was a Sunday afternoon when suddenly our cat, who had wanted nothing to do with us for the last four weeks, appeared and sprang on my lap and purred with such vigor that I knew it was time.

My husband and I lead her to the basement birthing box. When the panting began we knew she meant business. We turned the lights off, made sure the nightlight was on and prepared to leave her alone. We had no sooner put a foot on the basement steps when she began to meow, long and mournful. She was right at our heels. We led her back to her box but she refused.

"She wants to stay with us," my husband said.

"But that's not what the Internet said she'd want."

He shot me a look. I hadn't wanted the back rubs that all my pregnancy books obsessed about while I was in labor.

I carried her labor box upstairs to our kitchen and set it in the corner. She crawled inside. I walked to the living room to tell Elijah what was happening. She followed me. I returned to the kitchen and knelt down beside the box. She went back inside.

"I think I'll stay with her for a while," I called to my husband as I eased myself down on the tile floor. The minute I stuck a toenail beyond the kitchen, Maisey left her box and yowled. She didn't want to labor alone. Not that I could blame her.

She did not labor for long. Her panting changed and I knew it would be soon. My husband knelt down beside me. My son crawled in my lap as I sat on the kitchen floor. We spotted the first little head, and then the body, and her first-born was out.

"It looks like a rat," my son said as we watched Maisey instinctively clean her offspring. The bath was cut short by the emergence of kitten number two.

"Isn't that amazing?" I marveled to my son.

It was impossible not to get caught up in the moment. To realize that's how creatures come into the world, to ponder the design of it all, to marvel at the God-given instincts with which animals are equipped. Planned or unplanned, the birth of anything is amazing.

"Is that what it was like when I was born?" my son asked.

"Sort of. Except you weren't quite as hairy. And I didn't lick you clean, the nurse gave you a bath."

We witnessed number three emerge, then four and then five. I began to get nervous. But it was clear from Maisey's expression that she was done, as her scrawny, sightless offspring began to nurse. I reached my hand into the box and scratched her behind her ears. Her purring grew louder and she only gazed at me when I touched each of her kittens with my index finger. "Good job, Maisey," I cooed. "Good job."

We hadn't planned on having five, furry kittens that all needed good homes, but sharing the miracle of new life with my son is a memory I'll never forget.

~Rachel Allord

Reprinted by permission of Off the Mark
and Mark Parisi ©1994

Kitties to the Rescue

Cats are mysterious kind of folk—
there is more passing in their minds than we are aware of.
~Sir Walter Scott

I am allergic to cats. Sneezing, runny nose, and itchy, watery eyes are just a few of the annoyances I deal with as a result of the allergy. However, I have loved cats all my life and a runny nose is not going to stop me from keeping them around. Every morning, I pop a wide variety of pills, both prescription and herbal remedies, to help keep my sinuses clear. When I first met my husband, who is also allergic to cats, I explained to him that he too would learn to pop the pills every morning or, sadly, our relationship could go no further. Quickly understanding the seriousness of the situation, he complied and we have been together ever since.

The only rule my cats, Fuzz and Tony, have in the house because of the allergy is that they are not allowed in the bedroom. That is the "cat-free" zone. This way, I always sleep in peace without having to worry about inhaling cat hair in the middle of the night and being jarred awake when the sneezing fit commences. They have never been happy about the rule, but they have at least built a routine around it. Once we go to bed, Fuzz and Tony head for the downstairs couch and call it a night as well. And when we wake up in the morning, they are right outside the door to greet us, anxiously waiting to be petted.

Several years ago, before I met my husband, an unusual break in this routine jolted me out of bed in the middle of the night. At around two o'clock in the morning, I was awoken by the sounds of howling and scratching at the bedroom door. Half asleep, I wondered if perhaps a small forest creature had made its way into the house and was now trying to gnaw its way through my bedroom door. As I wiped the sleep from my eyes, it became apparent to me that it was Fuzz and Tony making all of that horrible noise and pawing at the door. The howling noises I heard were long, drawn out, panicked meows, almost like a baby crying for help.

My first instinct was to try to ignore the racket and go back to sleep. However, when I thought about it for a minute, I knew that something had to be very wrong for my cats to be acting this way. They had never woken me up before and they certainly had never made such frightening sounds before either. So, I dragged myself out of bed and stumbled towards the bedroom door.

Once I opened the door and Fuzz and Tony leapt upwards, pawing at my legs, that was when it hit me. The smell of gas was over-powering—it burned the inside of my nose and made my eyes water. I immediately rushed around the house, opening every window and all of the doors. Then I grabbed the cats, ran outside and tossed them in the backseat of my car to get them away from the fumes.

Once I was able to get the gas shut off, I joined my two little heroes in the car and gave them both big hugs. If not for Fuzz and Tony's persistence, I can only imagine what might have happened that night. Perhaps it was just a survival instinct for them to wake me so I could get them out of the house or maybe it was loyalty that led them to my door. Either way, they probably saved my life that night. I will always cherish the relationship I have with my cats, sneezing and all.

~Jennifer Zambri-Dickerson

An Unexpected Guardian Angel

Who hath a better friend than a cat?
~William Hardwin

Something was wrong with Percy. Panting, his dilated eyes darted back and forth. He paced up and down over my stomach and rib cage. Over and over again. I put my book down and lifted the sixteen-pound mass of fur, muscle, and fat off my stomach again and set him on the floor beside my bed.

Yes, I was irritated. It was Sunday afternoon—my one day to get some rest. I wanted to read, just for a little while. But Percy wouldn't have it. Seconds later, he jumped up on the bed and resumed his routine.

What was with this cat? In spite of being beaten and abandoned, Percy had always been laid back with me. For ten years, he had been the only man in my life—healing my own broken heart. He loved to snuggle. On days like this, he'd curl up on my lap or find that special crook in my knee and settle down for a nap while I read.

But not today. I glanced out the window. Not a thunderstorm in sight. I wasn't surprised. Spring in central California usually didn't include rain. The sun shone brightly outside. There wasn't a cloud in the sky. All was silent. Well, except for Percy, who continued to mew and pace up and down across my stomach.

I threw the book across the bed, hoping to distract him. The pages flipped, and I knew I had lost my spot. My anger began to boil, and I swore I felt the slightest hint of a headache forming. That was it. Sitting up, I planned to lock him out of my inner sanctum, but just as I reached for him, I felt it—the now all-too-familiar flutter in my stomach.

Oh no. Not today.

Panicked, my mind raced through all the emergency procedures. My roommate had left for some afternoon errands. I wasn't sure where my cell phone was. The front door was locked and only a few trusted friends had extra keys—in case this happened again. It was amazing, but I had never been alone when one started. But today, my greatest fear was happening. I was alone.

I pushed myself off the bed, grabbed the glass of water on the nightstand and tried to walk to the kitchen to get my medicine. Normally, I kept a dose or two in my purse, just in case of such emergencies, but even my purse was nowhere to be seen.

My legs trembled as I stumbled into the hallway. It was coming fast. I gasped for air, and my vision blurred. I reached for the door frame but missed. The glass slipped out of my hand and rolled down the hallway ahead of me. Water sprinkled the carpet where I was about to fall.

When my legs finally crumbled underneath me, I prayed. "No, God, please. Please help me." But it was too late. The seizure had already taken control. My medicine was still too far away and no one was around to help. My shoulder scraped against the wall and bounced slightly as I hit the floor.

I never remember much once they start. Since I had been diagnosed with epilepsy six years earlier, I had been so careful to avoid the normal triggers and heed any warning signs. Some days, the unsettling auras began hours before an episode. I always had enough time to take my medicine or call one of my friends who lived nearby. What had I missed?

The world suddenly became a dream. My arms and legs shook. Tears streamed down my face. "No. Please, no." I heard myself pleading, but even my own words seemed muffled as I floated in and out of consciousness.

My breath stayed locked in my throat. Only gasps escaped.

Somewhere in the dream, a weight moved onto my chest. After what seemed like hours, but probably only a few minutes, the tremors stilled. Just before sleep finally came, my hand fell on the mound of fur that had climbed up on top of me.

I never know how long I'm out unless someone tells me. Sometimes the sleep only lasts a few minutes. Other times, close to an hour. As I slip in and out of consciousness, I normally hear the strange voices of people around me, sometimes the touch of someone's hand. But this time, all I heard was a steady rumbling—the guttural purring of a cat.

Some time later, I woke up, confused. Where was I? What had happened? I lay in the hallway, looking up at the burnt out light bulb screwed into the ceiling. My head spun, and my shoulder hurt. My fingers brushed against something damp on the carpet as my eyes saw the empty glass just a few feet away. The memory of what had just happened seemed far away, but I knew it hadn't been a dream.

As the fog in my brain lifted, I turned and was nose-to-nose with my big fat cat, still laying across my chest and purring loudly. Stretching, he pushed his paw up against my left cheek. He leaned forward and sniffed my nose, staring at me with his green eyes, as if to ask, "Are you okay?"

As Percy rubbed his head gently around my chin, I dragged a weak arm to my side and buried my fingers in his fur. I don't know what it is about the rumble of a cat's purr that is so calming, but it worked. My breathing steadied. My arms and legs relaxed as I closed my eyes to rest. I was never alone after all.

It would be a while before I could stand, but Percy stayed with me until I was able to sit up. Even then, he refused to leave my side the rest of the day. He followed me into the kitchen and watched me take my medication. I spent the remainder of the afternoon on the couch, recuperating. Although he didn't crawl on my stomach, Percy was never far away. He curled up on the chair across the room and slept, but I suspect he kept one eye on me the whole time.

~Carolyn R. Bennett

To Everything There Is a Season

It always gives me a shiver when I see a cat seeing what I can't see.
~Eleanor Farjeon

After months of pleading, my husband had finally agreed I could have a cat.

And Cody was definitely mine from day one. He was in my lap, between my feet, on the arm of my chair, on the side of my tub and even once from a miscalculated jump, in the tub with me. For twelve years he followed every step I took.

When you are that close it's amazing what you can learn about an animal that cannot talk. I learned that he loved to drink warm water that dripped from the faucet. He was a lefty. He loved to be combed but not brushed. He preferred to sit on my right side. And when he got mad at me for any reason, such as clipping his nails, he would park himself in front of me where I could clearly see him and turn his back to me ignoring any pleas for forgiveness. His favorite food was chicken. He never drank water that was not dripping or running. But he always had to have a fresh bowl of water on the right side of his food dish. He knew the word "milk" even when you spelled it and went running full speed to the refrigerator anytime it was mentioned.

He had a claustrophobic aversion to closed doors. He wanted all inside doors open at all times even though he had no desire to be on the other side of them. He dearly loved milk and ice cream together—vanilla but not chocolate. And he could apparently tell time. On more than one occasion when our power went out, he would come to my side of the bed, lock his claws into the sheet, and "pop" the sheet until I woke up. And was the sole reason that we were never late to work.

From the very beginning we noticed something strange about his eating habits—he never put his head in a bowl and ate from the bowl like other cats. Instead he picked up his dry food with his left paw and raked it over the edge into his water bowl, swished it around, and then fished it out and ate it off his left paw. If his bowls got mixed up and the water was on the left he would push and shove until he turned it over trying to get it where it belonged. He couldn't or wouldn't eat canned cat food because when he placed it in the water bowl, it sank to the bottom and disintegrated and he couldn't get it back out.

For twelve years it was our nightly routine to spend a half hour before bed in my bedroom recliner. I would read and my faithful friend kept me company on the right arm of my chair. He used to fall asleep there every night, at which point all four paws would dangle off the sides and his head would be hanging down over the end. Although it looked uncomfortable, for twelve years it remained our way of winding down the day. Wherever I sat, if he wasn't in my lap, he was on my right on the arm of the couch or chair I was in. We were close and we knew each other very well, which is why when he started nudging and pawing at me I couldn't help but notice behavior that was out of character for him. Cody hadn't been himself since just before Christmas and at first I attributed it to a ploy for additional attention and just passed it off.

All through December he got slower and slower. He slept more and ate less and seemed to be having difficulty getting around. In mid-January he took a turn for the worse. My friend kept urging me to "do what is best for Cody and let him die in dignity." I knew she meant well and though I tried, I could never make peace with that decision. I couldn't look in those big gold eyes and convince myself that was best for Cody. He wasn't himself but he never seemed to be in pain. He got slower and his breathing seemed labored at times, but he still followed my every step. I justified my aversion to euthanasia by thinking about how I valued the older people that were in my life. Their breathing was sometimes labored, they had slowed down, their memory wasn't what it used to be—but they still had a purpose and a place in my life. I simply couldn't do it. And so he lived. And he continued with his strange new behavior of nudging me in one spot... for attention.

And though I did notice that it was always the same side, since he sat primarily on my right I assumed it was just convenient. However, after three months of him pushing his head up against me and just leaving it there, he began to do something else strange. He began to place his paw on that same spot and just hold it there even if he had to lock his claws into my clothes for support. Finally, one night out of sheer exasperation at carefully removing his claws from my new sweater for the fourth time, I just blurted out to my husband, "Do you suppose Cody knows something about this spot that I don't?" And that is when he looked up from the TV and said, "Isn't that the same place where you have that unusual dark spot?" I said, "Yes, as a matter of fact it is and maybe I should go and have the doctor look at it after all."

I had noticed an odd looking mole more than a year before and had been watching it for any changes; since none had occurred I had pretty much forgotten about it until now. However, I began to think back and realized that Cody had been gravitating to only this one place for the past few months, so I decided to make an appointment with a dermatologist just to be on the safe side.

I made an appointment to have that "mole" removed. Nine days later, my beloved Cody-cat died peacefully in his sleep in a little bed I'd made him in my closet while I sat quietly at his left side.

My one last gift to him—to allow him the peace and comfort of dying in his own home with the one he loved at his side. And his one last gift to me—a biopsy confirming malignant melanoma in the earliest possible stage, caught early only because of his persistent nudging in the last days of his life.

~Andrea Peebles

Chelsea

A mother is one to whom you hurry when you are troubled.
~Emily Dickinson

Home from college for the weekend, Sunday afternoon found me wandering, reluctant to break away to my new place at school. Nothing appealed to me at the record store, so I entered the pet shop next door, inexplicably drawn past the fish, hamsters and birds to a small cage holding a Siamese kitten.

Her fur was delicate, like the silvery fuzz on top of a dandelion. She perched like a tiny statue, inches from the front of the cage. Icy blue eyes diffidently surveyed the small, dusty store.

I had never owned a cat; my only pets had been a Doberman Pinscher and a Great Dane, both, like me, taken care of by my parents. But, leaving home for the first time made me understand the concept of loneliness in a new way. It made me crave the unassuming and undemanding comfort of a pet. Visions of friendly greetings and warm, affectionate cuddles had me forking over ten dollars and accepting a cardboard carry-box holding the newly christened Chelsea.

The box lasted exactly ten minutes. I drove the remaining eighty minutes of the trip back to college with small, sharp claws embedded in my shoulder and Chelsea's glass-breaking yowls reverberating in my ears. Also reverberating in my ears was the voice of my mother on the cell phone, detailing the stupidity of the acquisition, which only served to strengthen my resolve.

Chelsea grew up in a college town; she came of age among humans doing approximately the same thing, only with less grace. She was standoffish, challenging, mean and beautiful—developing the glossy, dark brown markings of her breed in counterpoint to her silvery undercoat.

Shortly after graduation, Chelsea and I left home for real. I married my high school sweetheart and settled on a military base in South Georgia. It was bleak. I found the small town to be provincial, narrow-minded and smelly, and life on a Navy base was very different from my sheltered upbringing. I felt as if I was being bombarded with changes from every angle, losing my family, my identity as a student and my comfortable surroundings.

Chelsea was about to experience a much different metamorphosis. For three weeks she stood by the door and meowed incessantly, immediately climbing on anyone who ventured near the door. I awoke every night to the scratch/thump/slide of this deranged animal jumping up and trying to turn the doorknob, her frustration growing on each attempt.

Finally, I had had enough. One steamy afternoon, I flung open the door and pitched her out onto the grass, slamming the door behind her. For five minutes I was thrilled by the silence. My relationship to the cat had never been idyllic—I considered her to be a supreme pain, and she had never viewed me as anything but a facilitator for the opening of cans. Early attempts at affection had resulted in bloody scratches and deep puncture wounds, and we had learned to exist in a peculiar harmony of disinterest, happily ignoring one another. I should have been overjoyed that she was gone. But I wasn't. Worry set in, and I spent the next two hours walking the neighborhood, calling her name. She returned the next day with no fanfare and after that roamed freely.

A Naval Petty Officer, my husband went to sea for three months at a time. I would bundle Chelsea into the car, and we would show up on my mother's doorstep, where I could bury myself in the quiet normalcy of my childhood home, and Chelsea could terrorize an entirely new set of butterflies and neighborhood dogs. The distance between my mother and I would fall away as we talked and laughed and got to know one another as adults for the first time.

When I got the call heralding my husband's return, I would reluctantly head home for a short period of married life. During these times, the distance between Mother and I would again grow; the intervals between phone calls stretching out while I played house. I felt as though I was living between land and water, constantly shifting realities, alternating between being a strong, independent wife and a protected child.

After two years of marriage, my husband stopped going to sea. The strain of living in the same house full-time took its toll until one day I realized that we had not spoken for a week. By the time we decided to try to fix the relationship, it was gone. We were too tired to speak civilly, much less argue, and nothing remained but resignation. I packed up my life and left—Chelsea and I were headed home for good.

We settled at Mother's house. All my family wanted to do was make me feel better; all I wanted to do was feel worse. The grim reality of what I had done with my life wouldn't allow me to accept comfort from those who cared the most about me. Where before, being at home had brought my mother and I closer, this time was different. I didn't want to see disappointment when she looked at me, so I hid and healed in my own way.

Soon I decided that I had to begin again, so I got up, got dressed, got a lawyer, got a job, got an apartment and got a roommate with a convenient allergy. Mother agreed to keep Chelsea, and I was free of all of the entanglements of my previous life. Almost. At least twice a week, I would get The Call from Mother. The Call always started out the same: "Guess what your cat did?"

My emotional state wouldn't allow me to talk about my divorce or accept advice, and Mother had trouble dealing with the fact that she could not make everything better for me, but Chelsea was common ground. Talking about her adventures took the place of retelling my own. Where I could not talk about my former life and feelings, I could easily talk and laugh about the cat's antics.

The stories were myriad: Chelsea managed to climb onto and then fall off a windowsill fourteen feet above the ground. She ate a chipmunk that my mother had been hand-feeding for six months. She hissed at every person who approached her, and clawed and bit anyone stupid enough not to heed her warnings. Chelsea bridged the gap between Mother and me; through her, we began to tentatively find our way back to each other.

Chelsea's story, and her life, ended suddenly. She'd been missing for four days, and Mother had a bad feeling about it. Mother was right. Chelsea's body rested in a ravine about ten feet below the side of the road. Her neck was broken, her beautiful fur muddied. Her eyes were open, staring at the flies that swarmed her body. Dad climbed down and retrieved her, and she was buried in our unofficial pet cemetery in the woods. My mother and I stood together and cried.

My relationship with Chelsea was never easy. She gave me scars that still linger, and an abiding desire to stick with dogs in the future. She also gave me my mom back, and that was worth every scratch.

~Stacy Leslie

Lessons from My Cat

Cats seem to go on the principle that
it never does any harm to ask for what you want.
~Joseph Wood Krutch

O ur housecat, a pretty calico, has a sweet nature. Patient with our human foibles, she nonetheless lets us know what she wants.

Hers is not a demanding nature. However, when we fail to attend to her needs in a timely manner, she gently steers us in the proper direction.

One of her favorite activities is to look out the patio doors. Blinds incased between double-paned doors prevent her from simply pushing them aside. Instead, she scratches at the doors to inform me of her wishes.

I take my cue and open the blinds.

When I've neglected to fill her water bowl early in the morning, she nips at my leg, then nudges me in the direction of her bowl.

She doesn't pout or sulk; rather, she states her wishes in the best way she can. Rarely do I misunderstand what she is telling me.

One day I found myself envying her simple, uncomplicated existence.

How many times had I expected my husband or my children to anticipate my wants without my ever giving voice to them? How many times had I been disappointed that they couldn't understand when I needed a hug, a compliment, a chocolate bar?

After a pleasant afternoon with my husband, I wanted to stop somewhere nice (translation: somewhere where crayons weren't served alongside the meal) and have dinner.

He ignored my hints.

"Couldn't you see that I wanted to go out to dinner?" I asked when he pulled into our driveway. To my horror, I noticed a whiny note had crept into my voice.

"Why didn't you say so? I can't read your mind," he answered in exasperation.

His admonition gave me pause. Had I expected him to read my mind? Why hadn't I expressed my desire more clearly? I realized I had fallen into the female trap of "If you loved me, you could read my mind."

Now, I emulate my feline friend. No longer do I "pussyfoot" around my needs. I state them with clarity and directness.

I look at my cat and know she approves.

~Jane M. Choate

One Cat Too Many

I have studied many philosophers and many cats.
The wisdom of cats is infinitely superior.
~Hippolyte Taine

I always considered myself a dog person, but when I married Liz I knew that her beloved cat, Benny, was part of the deal. Benny was friendly, for a cat, I conceded, drawing upon my preconceived opinion that cats were not particularly friendly as a whole. Before marrying Liz, I used to quip that a household with one cat already had one cat too many.

Although Benny was easy to tolerate, I never paid much attention to him. He, too, seemed to only tolerate me. He was much more amicable toward visiting family members and guests than he was toward me. Often he would approach a visitor with one of his toys, obviously hoping for a friendly game. Benny liked to fetch and play tug of war. I used to tease Liz that Benny thought he was a dog. When people commented that Benny showed little interest in me, Liz would explain that he was an exceptionally perceptive cat, and that he knew I wasn't particularly fond of him. I laughed at her ridiculous assumptions regarding the intelligence and cognitive abilities of her cat.

Benny and I put up with one another with admirable grace and a hint of begrudged respect until our son, Anthony, was born. Anthony cried a lot, and no amount of comforting seemed to help. Our pediatrician told us that newborns sometimes have a hard time adjusting from the dark, quiet, warm, secure comfort of the womb into a busy, noisy, lighted world. He advised us to swaddle the baby and hold him and comfort him when he cried. Liz's mother suggested that the baby had colic and we would have to patiently ride it out.

Fatigued from lack of sleep and burdened with constant worry, my nerves were raw and my patience was thin. Benny acted strangely toward the baby and my tolerance of the cat quickly changed into distrust. Often, when the baby slept, Benny would stand by the bassinet and watch him for long periods of time. Sometimes he would mewl softly in a guttural way which I found alarming. "Can't you make him shut up before he wakes the baby?" I would snap at Liz. "If not, put him in the bathroom and close the door. The baby needs his sleep and we need what little rest we can get."

When the baby cried, Benny's behavior was even odder and more frightening. He would pace the floor and wail, often looking up at us with wide, imploring eyes. "He is jealous of the baby," I warned Liz. "We can't trust Benny around the baby." I figured that Benny was upset by all the attention the baby was getting. When my grandmother, quoting an assortment of old wives' tales, warned us that Benny might actually harm the baby, my mistrust of the cat grew deeper.

"The baby's crying bothers Benny because he is concerned about him," Liz insisted. "He isn't jealous, and he would never hurt Anthony. Haven't you noticed how he looks at us as if he expects us to do something?"

"Yeah," I said sarcastically. "He expects us to get rid of the baby. I say we get rid of the damn cat."

Most newborn babies wake up with soft whimpers that escalate into cries if their needs aren't met quickly. Anthony woke up screaming. Often, when we rushed to pick him up, Benny was already at the bassinet, staring intently at the distressed infant. As the weeks passed, Benny seemed to grow more agitated around the baby. He began to flick his tail angrily as we tended to the crying infant. The cat's wails became deeper, almost mournful. "Do you see that?" I said to Liz. "Benny is mad, not concerned. He doesn't like the baby. If you keep that cat you're going to end up regretting it."

Liz, who was cradling the baby in her arms, looked at Benny, biting her lower lip. As if he could read her mind, Benny crossed the room, jumped up in Liz's lap and began nuzzling the baby's cheek. "See," she said triumphantly. "Benny likes the baby. He would never hurt him."

"Then you explain his behavior," I said. I was amazed at Liz's inability to perceive the danger her cat posed for our baby.

Blinking fast, Liz looked at me. "You might think I'm crazy, but I think Benny knows there is something wrong with the baby. I think he is trying to tell us that it isn't merely adjusting to life outside the womb, or colic, that is bothering Anthony."

I scoffed. "So you think the damn cat knows more than the pediatrician."

Near tears, Liz protested. "No. The doctor sees dozens of babies a day, and I'm sure his explanations for constant crying are reasonable. I have no doubt he is right most of the time. But Anthony isn't getting any better. I want to take him back to the doctor. I want tests to be made, if for no other reason than to put our minds at ease."

I grunted. "I think you're right. If nothing is found to be wrong, we might have to endure a few more weeks of little sleep, but at least we can have peace of mind knowing that Anthony really is going to be fine soon."

The tests revealed a blockage in the baby's lower intestines. Immediate surgery was in order. While Anthony was in the hospital Liz stayed by his crib day and night. I had to work, so I went home at night to feed Benny and to get a little sleep. Benny spent a lot of time staring into the empty bassinet. I had to admit that the cat appeared to miss the baby, although I wasn't ready to admit that he had saved Anthony's life, as Liz proclaimed.

When we brought the baby home, Benny ran up to us, crying joyfully. Liz stooped down so the cat could get a good look at the baby. Purring, Benny nuzzled the top of the baby's head. Liz looked up at me, and I nodded in surrender. I could no longer justify feeling that Benny posed a threat to the baby.

In the days that followed I noticed that Benny no longer wailed and paced the floor when the baby cried. Although he often peered into the bassinet at the sleeping baby, he no longer stood sentinel for long periods of time. I gained a new respect, even a fondness for the cat. As if sensing this change in my attitude toward him, Benny began, on occasion, to drop one of his toys at my feet, trying to entice me to play with him. One evening he jumped up in my lap, seeking affection. "What is this?" Liz exclaimed, laughing.

I shrugged. "Like you said, Benny is a very precocious cat. He knows that I know that he saved our baby's life."

Our pets often try to tell us things that they instinctively know or sense. Benny taught me to pay attention to their efforts. The next time Benny has something to say, I'll listen.

~Joe Atwater

Chapter
6

What I Learned from the Cat

Learning to Play

Play is the beginning of knowledge.

~Unknown Author

52

The Legacy of the Sun Spot

If there is one spot of sun spilling onto the floor, a cat will find it and soak it up.
~J.A. McIntosh

Once upon a time my husband and I were still fresh and new in our marriage. We had not yet been blessed with children, but we did have a puppy (testing our fortitude for parenthood some day) and two cats. Our lives were busy with work and our evenings and weekends were focused on turning our house into a home.

It was on a Sunday when I first discovered the magic of the sun spot. Alan and I were diligently working on renovations and in passing through the house we noticed our two cats sprawled on the floor, eyes squinted shut, with a look of pure ecstasy on their faces. A halo of sunlight surrounded both of our feline companions. This was a not a rare occurrence in our household—wherever the sun spot was, that is where the two would be found. "It must be nice," Alan chuckled, and I nodded in agreement. We continued working and it became a joke between the two of us about sunning ourselves with the cats. What a simple life it would be.

On one of my passes through the house I took notice once again of the cats stretched out across the floor, absorbing every ounce of the glorious sunlight streaming through the window. The warmth of the sun beckoned to me—the sunbeams danced for joy, inviting me to be their partner, hear the surreptitious music of life that only a select few dared to listen to. Come! And I did. I placed myself right there next to the cats on the floor, mingling with the sun spot.

The sun spot cast a magical spell over me as my "to do" list faded away, replaced by the contentment of just being. I knew it was inevitable that my husband would search out his wayward wife sooner or later. It happened sooner. "What are you doing?" he laughed. "Meow," I purred sheepishly. It didn't take much convincing for him to join me in my newfound, sun-filled paradise. That afternoon the two of us laughed and talked, made plans for our future, and finally drifted off to sleep holding each other under a canopy of brilliant sunlight that eventually faded to twilight.

For years Alan and I shared this secret. We would take moments out of our busy day to search out the sun spot. Then the children came along and our sunlit rendezvous became less frequent until it was just a sweet, treasured memory that I placed on a shelf. That is, until another Sunday afternoon that came to pass. I was trying to convince my three-year-old daughter of the benefits of taking a nap, something that she had recently started to boycott. While chasing her, I noticed something that brought a smile to my face. I caught up with my prodigal child, pulled her close and whispered in her ear about a magical place... the sun spot. The two of us excitedly collected pillows so we could cuddle together on the enchanted, sun-filled landing. My cat stretched and yawned as she gave up her place of honor drenched in luminous light.

The two of us giggled at first, but then we became silent as we both were engulfed by the sun's radiance. The moment was as warm and tender as a hug and kiss—we were both glowing, body and soul. Daddy soon came upon us and laughed, "What are you two doing?" But he winked a knowing wink and joined us. There the three of us lay, arms entwined, enjoying the splendor of the sun spot. I knew then that I would keep the legacy of the sun spot alive. This sweet, simple joy, an unexpected gift from my cats, would be lovingly passed along to my children... and maybe one day the magic would be shared with their children as well.

~Kimberly J. Garrow

Beginning Again

There is no more intrepid explorer than a kitten.
~Jules Champfleury

New beginnings are like getting ready for an exciting trip to a place you've never been. Or like falling in love without a parachute. There is always the promise of adventure and none of the security of knowing the outcome.

When my twelve-year-old cat had a stroke and died, my grown children suggested I get a kitten. I was uncertain whether I was ready for this new beginning. No matter how tempting the journey, for the first time in all my years of loving pets, I wasn't certain that I should continue bringing animals into my life.

Though I still had my five-year-old dog, another twelve-year-old cat, and a parakeet living in a cage in the kitchen, it occurred to me that perhaps I was being selfish at my age, adding another animal to my family. When I'd adopted a pet in my thirties, I was confident that I would outlive him. But now, at more than twice that age, my certainty had disappeared. Chances were the animal would outlive me. And then what? I had never thought of the future in these terms before, and did not enjoy thinking like this now.

There were other reasons for not introducing a new pet into the house. I told myself, "Be reasonable. Be practical. There are benefits to keeping the pet population down. Less work emptying kitty litter. Less money spent for pet food. Fewer trips to the veterinarian. When the one cat remaining is gone, that will be the end of it. No more cats. Eventually no more pets. And then you will have more freedom."

I knew it was good advice, but the house took on shadows I never noticed before. And a stillness that seemed ominous. There had always been two and sometimes three or four inside cats. Now, the one remaining cat, who had daily groomed the other, slept with her paws wrapped around a stuffed animal. Something was missing from her life and she knew it. The dog, who had been a loving companion to his deceased cat friend, appeared listless. Bored. His nap times increased. And so did mine.

Yes, it was easier now. Too easy. I lay in bed one day, persuading myself to remain there another hour and another. In fact, when I piled up all the sad stories I could think of and all the pets I had bid goodbye, I thought it would be quite easy to remain in bed the entire day. After all, what did the outside world offer? Trouble, that's what. If I didn't go out, why even bother to get dressed? Who would know anyway, if I walked the dog in my long coat?

"You need a kitten," my daughter told me one day as she frowned in my direction, sensing my mood. "This place needs some excitement."

That's how Sunny came to live here. A tiny thing rescued from the woods, he arrived in my daughter's arms, rehabilitated, cleaned, de-fleaed, and inoculated. "He's perfect for you," she said. I had not yet reached that conclusion. Neither had Sunny.

It took only a second for him to step onto the living room rug, but in that moment, silence rushed from my home—exiting through the front door—and chaos entered without warning.

The dog ran after the kitten. The older cat hissed and spit. The two ganged up on the new kid in town. What ingratitude, I thought. Here I'd been concerned that they were lonely, in deep depression, and they were rejecting my solution.

"I'm too old for this," I said at one point in the evening, as I tried to catch the kitten that had hidden in the basement.

"I'm too old for this," I repeated after four trips to the basement, two stiff knees kneeling on the kitchen floor, two attempts to scramble beneath the bed to retrieve a frightened Sunny hiding from the dog that was on guard duty.

Exhausted and certain I had made a mistake, I pleaded, "Take him back. I'm too old for this," as soon as my daughter entered the house the next day.

At that moment, I meant it. I believed it.

I stood in the kitchen, tears in my eyes. I was crying not only for the cat in my mind already gone, but for the part of me that had vanished also. My enthusiasm to try something new. The belief that I could. The energy to do it.

I wanted everyone who told me I was young enough, to be here, running after this kitten. I wanted them to be with me at five in the morning when Sunny arose and decided to attack my feet beneath the covers and then woke up all the other animals in the house. I wanted them here when he explored the lampshade until he knocked over the lamp, or decided everything on the kitchen table needed reorganizing, removing all napkins, spoons, glasses filled with water, and of course any tempting food on the plates that begged to be shared.

But I knew I could not blame it all on Sunny. It was just too difficult to begin again. To love again. To take on the responsibility again. I was frightened because I did not know if I had it in me. I didn't want to find out.

While I agonized over his future, Sunny had settled in a basket and was enjoying a nap. The sun settled on his beige fur. The old cat had left her stuffed animals to sit by the basket, suddenly interested in the new member of our family. The dog, exhausted from kitten guard duty, had settled in the same sunny spot, sharing it. It was as if they understood things had changed. Nothing would ever be the same. Something had left and something else had entered. Now they would have to adjust. I understood the message in their eyes. We could do it together, accept the change, and perhaps even enjoy the challenge of beginning again—if I let myself.

The next morning, Sunny investigated the kitchen with renewed interest. Something was different and he noticed it immediately; it was raining for the first time since he had come to live with me. The raindrops splattered on the roof and made tantalizing sounds. He looked up as he explored each room. As if he expected whatever he heard to eventually come down and introduce itself. They were just raindrops falling. But their sound was new to him. And suddenly, through his eyes, the falling rain became refreshingly wondrous for me, too.

I hurried to get dressed. Sunny started his adventures early, and I didn't want to miss any of them.

~Harriet May Savitz

Eat, Sleep, Play

Who among us hasn't envied a cat's ability to ignore the cares of daily life and to relax completely?

~Karen Brademeyer

It had been a rough few years, alright. I had nursed my mother through a long illness, and immediately after her death I was thrust back into the position of caregiver for my father as the stress of his grief caused his own health to fail. Working, caring for my home, and caring for my parents had me living life like a person running on a treadmill that had no "off" setting. To accommodate all my responsibilities I borrowed time wherever I could, barely sleeping and skipping meals just to gain a few extra hours for my already too full days. I had become nervous and tired. My hands shook. And just when I thought things were bad enough, I lost my job along with several other co-workers.

I came home early that afternoon, toting whatever personal belongings I could salvage from my desk in a plastic shopping bag. My faithful little tuxedo cat, Chuck, blinked his sleepy eyes and greeted me by rubbing against my ankles as I walked through my front door. He was always serene, without a worry in the world. Just seeing him made me feel better. I tickled his chin and gathered the courage to phone my husband, Bill, and give him my latest bit of news.

"Don't worry about it," he told me in his comforting way, and assured me that we would sort out the situation together later that evening.

True to his word, Bill and I sat down after dinner on our living room sofa with Chuck nestled between us and discussed my options. Well aware of my level of exhaustion, Bill suggested that I take this time between jobs to relax, returning to the workforce refreshed by my little impromptu "vacation." So, it was agreed, and that was my simple plan.

In the days that followed, however, I found that my simple plan was not so simple in its execution. Worn into the rut of years of bad habits, I still ate on the run, fought through my fatigue, and couldn't find the peace to sit still long enough to read even one paragraph of the bestseller I promised myself I would enjoy "if I ever had the time." Still spinning from my years of overwork and anxiety, I paced the floors day after day.

One morning, frustrated, I flopped onto the sofa and clicked on the television as Chuck snored nearby in his wicker basket bed. Nothing disturbed him, not even his harried owner. His life was a simple one. He ate when he was hungry, slept when he was tired, and never missed an opportunity to play with his favorite toy mouse or tug at a piece of loose string. As I watched him lying peacefully, I silently wished I could be more like him.

That's when the mental light bulb went off over my head. "That's it!" I cried out loud. "I'll follow Chuck's example." He listened to nature and followed his instincts, while I still continued my old, unhealthy routines.

It wasn't easy at first, but with Chuck as my guide I soon learned to savor my meals, to lie down when I was tired, and to allow myself the luxury of a few hobbies. Friends and family soon noticed the change in me and commented that the strained look I had worn for so long had left my face. I also noticed that my shaky hands were now magically still. One afternoon, I gathered myself and sat down at my piano. It had been years since I had played and I wondered if I still even had the touch. I laid my hands on the keys and a melody resounded through the air while Chuck sat at my feet as if to say, "Good job." And not only did I finish reading that bestseller, I went on to return to college after a twenty-year hiatus and finally earned my degree.

I still feel harried from time to time. We all do. Yet now, I need only take one look at my feline mentor, Chuck, whenever I need a simple reminder to slow down and focus on three very necessary activities of life: eat, sleep, and play.

~Monica A. Andermann

A Feline Wonder

*I love cats because I love my home
and after a while they become its visible soul.*
~Jean Cocteau

It took a homeless cat to restore our sense of wonder.

My husband, Bill, and I weren't aware that wonder had vanished. It slipped quietly into the periphery of our lives, waiting to be noticed, while we focused on circumstances that gripped our attention: Bill's diagnosis with mantle cell lymphoma (MCL), extensive chemotherapy, and stem cell transplant; my reoccurrence and treatment of a tumor disorder; my hectic job as a school social worker, and my decision to accept early retirement. When our beloved tuxedo cat, Gilligan, died from an incurable blood disease, we were in the dumps along with Tiffy, his lifelong pal and our only remaining cat. Even though we believed in the power of prayer and positive thoughts, our joy and awe of daily life had dimmed.

Then we met Teddy.

We were hooked the instant we saw him in the cat condo at the local animal shelter. He was a stunning cat with his large frame, ash-gray coat, camel-colored belly, and bold black stripes. Teddy jumped into Bill's lap the moment he sat down. He gazed at Bill with his beaming eyes. He snuggled up against him, laid his massive paws on his arm, buried his big round face, and started to purr. He swished his tail to and fro like a parent lulling a baby to sleep. Later we played with the other cats in the condo, but Teddy won our hearts with his vim and vigor. He batted toys with unbridled enthusiasm while he reveled in our attention.

We worried about Tiffy. She was the smallest and most sensitive of all the cats we'd had. She showed spunk, but she was easily upset. Would she like Teddy? Would she adjust? While we pondered these questions, Teddy cocked his head, engaged us with his adoring look, and seemed to say, "Just leave her to me."

Did we have the same kind of fearless faith?

Our worry was needless. To our surprise, Tiffy and Teddy made a striking pair who quickly became inseparable. Her black and brown fur blended with his, while her gleaming white provided contrast. Although he was twice as big as she, and almost ten years younger, he drew out her playful side. With his gentle manner he gave her loving pats, licked her face, and abided by her wishes. We chuckled at the friendly romps and tussles of this giant and his petite pal.

Teddy inspected his new home with gleeful delight and unlimited curiosity. Everything was worthy of his notice and his attention. He savored each moment by capturing it through his curious eyes and his expressive face before he pounced on all potential items for learning and play. Big, floppy snowflakes outside our living room window became bugs to catch. Stray pieces of paper turned into balls to bat. A cardboard box doubled as a hideaway. He entertained us with varied positions—on his back, on his tummy, roll over, twist around, paws stretched, paws tucked in, feet and tail hanging off the bed, and rolled up tightly like a ball of yarn. Teddy's antics helped us to remember that life was full of simple joys and unexpected blessings that were ready and waiting for us to notice them. We caught ourselves smiling often. By watching him, life's wonder inched back into our lives.

Teddy's arrival opened a whole new world of hope and possibility. He reminded us that each day brought many delights if we stopped, paid attention, tuned into others, tried something new, and lived the day with unrefined gusto. From Teddy we learned once more to rejoice for the gifts of each day.

Now our home was filled with wonder, the pitter-patter of paws, meowing voices, and sounds of laughter. All because a charming homeless cat knew we needed him. How did Teddy know? Why did he pick us? A small ridge on the end of Teddy's chin, which resembled a goatee, gave his face a wise appearance. Looking back, we're convinced that he used his wisdom and intuition when he latched onto us at the shelter. We have no doubt that God sent us a furry angel of wonder who could teach us to celebrate life's joys, no matter what we faced.

~Ronda Armstrong

Baxter's Mission

There are few things in life more heartwarming
than to be welcomed by a cat.
~Tay Hohoff

Baxter, a rather large gray tabby cat, was raised with a puppy, and now lives with three dogs. He truly thinks he is part (if not all) dog too, hence his nickname "puppy-cat." He takes walks with us, plays fetch, and even joins the dogs in panting, if it suits him. And unlike any cat I have ever had, he is a social creature. He will greet anyone he comes across, and knows no fear of dogs, cats, or humans. I've had several calls from people saying, "Your cat is here visiting." Though he always stays in our neighborhood, Baxter's social antics are really starting to drive me crazy! He'll help one neighbor walk his Bassett Hound, and help another neighbor walk their baby stroller. Everyone knows Baxter better than they know me!

One day, I spied Baxter out our front kitchen window. He was making a beeline across the street for an elderly lady walking her older Golden Retriever. I had seen her and her dog a few times before, but I did not know their names, or even what street they lived on. I watched open-mouthed as he ran right up to them, and started rubbing around their ankles. Baxter then proceeded to plop down on the sidewalk in front of them and roll over onto his back to have his belly scratched. This was ridiculous! Now he was preventing people from taking their walks.

That was it. I dried off my hands and went outside to get my overly social cat. The lady saw me walk over and smiled warmly. She had obliged Baxter and was scratching his fully-exposed tummy. The dignified Golden was white around the muzzle, and sat patiently, waiting to continue his walk.

"I'm so sorry," I apologized. "Baxter just really likes people and dogs."

"That's okay," she replied. "He's just saying hello. Our cat looked just like him, and we lost him about a month ago. It's getting harder for us to go on our walks, and seeing Baxter really makes our day."

I didn't know what to say. I told her I was sorry for the loss of her cat, and pointed out our house with an open invitation for her to visit any time. After some small talk, they left to finish their walk, and a purring Baxter and I went inside.

The incident really made me think about Baxter and his social life. What I'd been rolling my eyes and complaining about was something people really enjoyed, and it even made their days a little brighter. I thought about all of the people he visited and all the calls I'd had. Everyone looked forward to their walk or visit with Baxter. Even more, he seemed to innately know which people's souls need uplifting. I am truly convinced that Baxter is an angel with fur whose mission during his lifetime is to find people who need an extra smile or an extra laugh and provide it for them. I am in awe of the lesson I've learned from him — take the extra second to smile and say hello to someone, regardless of who they are.

I still see the elderly lady and her dog when they take their walks. They seem to get a little slower every day, and Baxter never fails to run over and greet them. Baxter is on his mission, and now I just smile and let them enjoy their visit.

~Kristin L. Wilson

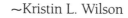

The Bandit Who Stole Our Hearts

A meow massages the heart.
~Stuart McMillan

Moving Day began hot, blisteringly hot, but nothing was going to keep us from our new home. Many boxes were stacked in the garage, along with some rolled-up area carpets. As we took turns bringing the boxes into the house, Jeffrey came running in, breathless and overjoyed. "Guess what, Mommy? Guess what? We have a cat in our garage! Come look! Quick!"

Sure enough, there was a large black cat, with white on all four paws, and the tiniest of white spots on the tip of his nose, roaming through the garage. He was definitely inspecting our belongings, jumping from one stack of boxes to the next, and walking along the rolled-up carpets as a gymnast on a balance beam would do. He stopped to check out all the open boxes, and having been satisfied with his preliminary look-see, decided he would go inside and make sure things were satisfactory there, too.

He sat near the door that led into the family room, turned his head and looked at us, with every expectation that we would let him in. He waited patiently while we figured that out. Which we did, eventually. It wouldn't be the last time that we would do this large cat's will.

Bandit, we found out from our new neighbors, was this cat's

name. He was a well-known character, known up and down the street as a real schmoozer, always on hand to take that last bit of cat food (or people food, for that matter) off your hands.

At a neighborhood Christmas party we found no fewer than four families who admitted that they succumbed to Bandit's wiles, and were feeding him on a regular basis. But, as far as we could tell, it was our house he preferred to shelter him from inclement weather.

He was a street-smart cat who never lost his ability to love a little boy. Despite the not-always-so gentleness of a three-year-old, Bandit never got angry or upset. I never saw him hiss or even bare a claw despite being put into baskets, lullabied to sleep and cradled lovingly, but sometimes uncomfortably, in a little boy's arms, a little boy whose normally gentle ways with animals were sometimes lost in his exuberance to play with his brand-new friend. Bandit somehow knew this, and was content to be placed in a shirt-sized gift box one Christmas Day, which was then moved from place to place, until the proper spot was found for the lullabies and loving pats on the head to begin, which continued until Bandit fell asleep.

I didn't know much about cats back then, but I knew that this was a rare blend of outside-cat toughness and inside-cat gentleness. He was a true gentle giant of a cat.

Jeffrey and Bandit grew up together and became fast friends. In fact, whenever there was a storm coming, we could rely on the fact that Bandit would spend it with us, sometimes allowing us to keep him indoors overnight during hurricanes and snowstorms. It seemed as though he took comfort from being with us—Jeffrey, in particular.

Jeffrey, in return, seemed to always enjoy Bandit's company. He grew to be both confident and gentle with animals, especially cats. This was the direct result of his close friendship with his pal, Bandit.

Bandit is gone now, and is sorely missed. He had lived a long life, but it wasn't long enough to suit us. I think he knew how much he meant to us. But I wonder if he could ever know how much he influenced a small boy. From the moment they met, Jeffrey loved cats.

Bandit, through his own good nature and gentle treatment of a little boy, taught our son to be kind and gentle with animals.

Thank you, Bandit.

~Donna Lowich

Bargains and Boundaries

One is never sure, watching two cats washing each other,
whether it's affection, the taste, or a trial run for the jugular.
~Helen Thomson

Dusty reigned as pet monarch for five years in our home. Then one day my eleven-year-old son Jeff announced, "I want a pet of my own."

"You have Dusty," I said.

"He's the family pet," Jeff countered.

"We don't need another pet."

"You bought Kelsey some fish."

"Your sister has two goldfish. You want some? I'll get you some."

"I don't want fish. I want a kitten."

"Dusty wouldn't like having another cat in the house. He thinks our house is his own private kingdom," I explained.

"He needs a friend."

"We'll see," I said.

Jeff knew that "we'll see" usually meant "no way," but he never surrendered without a fight. That's one reason my husband and I often call him "Relentless."

Over the next few weeks, Jeff persisted in his plea for a new cat: "It will teach me responsibility."

"You never even feed Dusty."

"Dusty likes Kelsey better."

"Why would a new cat be any different?"

"He could sleep in my room at night. I'd feel safe. You wouldn't have to leave the bathroom light on... we'd save energy." Relentless.

Eventually he wore me down. "Look," I said, "I'll make a bargain with you. We'll go to the vet's office on the next pet adoption day. If there's a kitten that has already had its shots and been neutered, we'll take it."

I knew the odds of finding a neutered kitten at the vet's were slim to none, but Jeff didn't know that. He stopped begging. I had two weeks of peace, until the Sunday that we headed to the vet's office after church. I felt confident that we'd go home empty-handed. Jeff wanted a kitten, and I figured that all the cuddly young felines would have been adopted earlier in the day. Most likely, only the older or special needs cats would be left.

As soon as we entered the office, I sensed defeat—too many meows and not enough adoring listeners. Jeff immediately spied a large cage filled with furry balls of six- to eight-week-old kittens. I reminded him of our bargain. (Kittens aren't neutered until they are at least three months old.)

He shuffled to another cage and read the sign—a five-year-old special needs cat. Then he rounded the corner and stopped. In a cage by itself was a black and white kitten, his nose pressed against the wire door, his meow pitiful and... relentless.

I read the sign—Four-month-old male, neutered. Jeff grinned at me and asked the vet's assistant to open the cage. Jeff picked the kitten up, and it curled against his chest. He said, "I'm calling him Rex. Now he can be king of the house."

I sighed. Jeff's eyes glistened with triumph. "You promised," he said. I surrendered.

Dragging myself over to the reception desk, I signed the papers and paid the $50 adoption fee. On the way home, Jeff gloated and said, "I knew there'd be a kitten for me. I just knew it." I said nothing, still stunned by his victory.

Dusty must have smelled Rex the minute we opened the back door. I heard the familiar rhythmic thumping as he lumbered down the stairs. He spotted Rex, fluffed his fur, arched his back, and hissed.

Rex cowered in Jeff's arms. Now it was my turn to hiss. I shot Jeff an I-told-you-Dusty-would-be-mad look, clenched my jaw and said, "Take Rex to your room and shut the door."

As soon as Rex and Jeff were gone, Dusty turned and looked at me. I interpreted the unblinking stare to mean, "How dare you?"

Over the next few days, our household throbbed with tension. Whenever Rex entered a room where Dusty lounged, Dusty hissed. Rex ran. Gradually, the hissing subsided, but Dusty still fluffed his fur and strutted out of the room. They ate separately. They slept separately. Dusty spent an inordinate amount of time out in the yard.

Then one evening, as Rex reclined on the kitchen floor grooming himself, I heard the kitty door in the garage slam. I opened the back door to let Dusty enter. Too late I noticed that he carried a mouse in his jaws. He walked over to Rex and dropped the mouse in front of him. Rex bent his head and sniffed the dazed rodent.

"Dusty!" I scolded. "Pick up the mouse!" He acknowledged the sound of my voice with an indifferent glance and strolled to the other side of the kitchen. "Dusty!" I said more firmly, "Get your mouse." The mouse struggled to its feet. Both cats just stared at it — as if neither of them knew what it was or what their reaction should be.

Dusty's eyes tracked the mouse as it crawled feebly across the floor. Rex watched it, too, but quickly lost interest. He lowered his head and began to lick his leg.

A tense minute passed. Dusty then walked over and picked up the mouse. He dropped it at Rex's feet again and returned to the other side of the room.

Suddenly I understood Dusty's odd behavior. He was teaching a class — Mouse Catching 101. My horror turned to fascination.

This time Rex stretched his paw toward the mouse tentatively. As his prey crept away, Rex followed. Then he began to nudge it with his nose. Finally, he grabbed the mouse in his jaws and carried it off to a corner.

Dusty turned and walked out of the room. I shook my head in disbelief. Even though Rex had invaded Dusty's world without his knowledge and certainly without his approval, Dusty instinctively embraced his responsibilities as a mentor for the younger cat. Like a noble monarch, Dusty had bowed to duty, putting his personal preferences aside for the good of his subject.

Over time, our two cats have established a peaceful co-existence. Dusty preserves both his dignity and preeminence by remaining aloof. When Rex invades Dusty's private quarters—like Kelsey's room or the top of the sofa—Dusty reminds him of the boundaries with a regal hiss. If Rex attempts to snatch a morsel from the royal dish, a low growl sends him scurrying out of the king's presence.

Sometimes, though, Dusty grants Rex an audience. Rex then approaches Dusty respectfully and nudges his Sovereign with his forehead. Dusty dutifully turns to clean Rex's ears. Then he licks the tough spots—between the eyes and between the ears. Rex returns the favor.

The feline harmony in our home is maintained by mutual respect, distinct boundaries, and reasonable bargains. Both cats make allowances for the tough spots. It works for Dusty and Rex. It works for mothers and sons, too.

~Denise K. Loock

Reprinted by permission of Off the Mark
and Mark Parisi ©1998

A Special Offering

The manner of giving is worth more than the gift.
~Pierre Corneille

I walked into my bedroom after work and sighed as I spotted the white Q-Tip on my blue and yellow comforter. "Why does she keep doing this?" I asked myself. This was the third day in a row. I picked up the Q-Tip and tossed it into the hallway. It barely touched the floor before twelve pounds of gray and white fur pounced on it.

My cat, Buscemi, loves Q-Tips. It doesn't matter where she is in the house, as soon as she hears the squeak of the hallway closet door she is instantly beside me. I'll peer into her large green eyes and they will sparkle as I produce a Q-Tip. She is instantly under my spell. As long as I am holding it the mesmerized cat will follow me anywhere.

"Get ready!" I'll tell her. She'll quickly find a doorway entrance and flatten herself low to the floor. I'll flick the Q-Tip into the air and she will do a very ungraceful leap for it often looking like an uncoordinated cheerleader. She'll land with a thud and race off with her prize.

Often I'll hear her in the kitchen splashing around in her bowl of water. She likes to watch the Q-Tip floating around. Then I get the job of retrieving the swollen Q-Tip and throwing it away followed by mopping up the wet floor. Occasionally, she likes to let the Q-Tip "escape" under the stove or refrigerator and then she'll desperately try to get it back. If she is unsuccessful, she'll lay on the floor sprawled out with one paw under the appliance staring at me with those beautiful green eyes. If I'm not in the room she will meow until I come to her. Then I have to hunt down a metal coat hanger that can be twisted into a hook to reach the darkest corner underneath the appliance where the Q-Tip has unfortunately rolled.

This is all to please a cat that keeps leaving Q-Tips on my bed.

The next morning I filled up her food bowl with the remainder of the cat food. "This will have to last you until I get home from work," I told her as she stared at the pitiful amount.

At work I pondered with a co-worker over the Q-Tips' sudden appearances on my bed. Her cat also likes to play with them, but it never leaves them anywhere special.

On my way home from work I stopped at a nearby store and bought another bag of cat food. Once home I filled up Buscemi's gleaming white bowl. She must have licked it clean while I was at work. "Drama Queen," I called her as she rubbed up against my legs purring.

I headed back to the bedroom to retrieve the Q-Tip I knew would be waiting for me on the bed. "Why?" I wondered as I dropped it in the hallway next to another one that was already laying there. I went downstairs to put clothes in the washer and forgot about the Q-Tips. At some point I heard Buscemi playing in the hallway with them and then all was silent.

I was walking in the kitchen to put dish towels away when something odd caught my eye. In Buscemi's near empty food dish were two Q-Tips! I smiled, as I instantly understood what she was trying to say.

Cats that have access to the outdoors often leave dead mice, birds or rabbits on the porch for their owner as an offering. Buscemi is a house cat so Q-Tips are her prey. What I had perceived as an annoyance was her way of giving me a tribute or saying thanks; my "tip."

~Valerie Benko

From Pianos to Purrs

Cats come and go without ever leaving.
~Martha Curtis

For twenty years, my husband's workshop had been filled with the antique musical instruments that he restored. "Listen to this," Carl would say, as he cranked a vintage cob organ or pumped a 1920s player piano roll. Music floated about the workbench and the room was alive with purpose.

Then, unexpectedly, Carl died. His friends completed his unfinished projects and, one by one, the instruments left. After I gave the extra piano strings, bolts of felt and other supplies to these helpful friends, I was left with an empty workshop. Now the walls enclosed only memories.

I stood in the silent, empty room with tears dripping down my cheeks. What should I do with this space? Could I make Carl's shop a happy place again? How would I rebuild my life?

An image of Willie flashed into my mind. Carl and I had found the old Beagle plodding across a busy highway. We brought him home, advertised that we'd found him, and called him Willie. Because of our cat and elderly dog, we kept him in the workshop. Each morning, we laughed when we found him asleep on the floor, underneath the soft blanket we'd provided as a bed. After eight days Willie was reunited with his worried owners.

From my involvement with animal rescue groups, I knew there was a need for foster homes for rescued animals, so I decided to turn the piano workshop into a foster home for cats. Despite my happy memories of Willie, cats made more sense in my current situation. Because of weakness from post-polio syndrome, I can't handle a large dog, and most abandoned and rescued dogs are big.

Two days after I contacted Pasado's Safe Haven and offered to take a foster cat, Edgar arrived. I had never seen such a terrified animal. A black cat with big yellow eyes, Edgar had been at Pasado's sanctuary for two weeks. Despite the efforts of volunteers, he hid all the time and didn't eat. Edgar was afraid of everything and everyone.

When he was let out of the carrier, Edgar squeezed underneath Carl's workbench.

For three days, I spent hours lying on my stomach beside the workbench, talking softly and trying to coax him out. I put dried salmon and other treats next to him. He came out at night to eat and use the litter box, but he scurried back to his hiding place whenever I entered the room. It took two weeks before he remained where I could see him and many more days before he let me pet him.

Gradually, Edgar overcame his fear. He began to play with his toys. He let me pick him up. The first time he purred, I felt like cheering. Slowly he learned to trust other people and eventually my friends could hold Edgar and pet him. Edgar explored every inch of that workshop and I often found him perched high atop a cabinet. Once again, Carl's room was filled with life and laughter.

Of course I fell completely in love with Edgar and considered adopting him but that would have defeated my purpose. Anyone who volunteers to help animals knows that you can't keep them all. It was more important to find a loving permanent home for Edgar, and then use Carl's workshop to foster another needy cat.

When Pasado's held a cat adopt-a-thon at a local pet store, I took Edgar and spent the day talking to prospective adopters. A wonderful woman came in looking for a cat and Edgar turned out to be exactly what she wanted. She filled out the adoption application, Pasado's did a home visit, and a few days later she arrived to take Edgar home. After all my bragging about how friendly he was, Edgar hid under the workbench that day! I had to drag him out and stuff him into the carrier. However, he quickly adjusted to his loving new home and I get frequent updates and photos of him.

Edgar had been here for six months, so I missed him greatly. That night I cleaned his room, washed out the litter pan, and put away the toys. (His favorites had gone to his new home with him.)

The next morning, a neighbor knocked on my door. "A kitten followed me home from my walk," she said. "I have no idea where it lives. I tried to shoo it away but it kept coming. Can you take care of it?"

I turned the cat room heat back on, and Charlie moved in. I posted FOUND KITTEN signs around the neighborhood, and made numerous phone calls. A scan by my vet showed no microchip. He estimated that Charlie was four months old. Charlie stayed only a few days because when my friend, Mark, picked him up, Charlie put his front paws around Mark's neck in a hug, and Mark instantly decided he needed a pet! Animals are often dumped in my rural neighborhood; Mark says that Charlie is afraid of cardboard boxes.

Two tiny kittens, so small that they had to be fed with doll bottles, were my next charges. One of my granddaughters had a wonderful time feeding those fuzzy little kittens, who found a new home together.

The most recent foster cat, Gus, was a chunky gold-colored tabby with a kink in the end of his tail, who came to me as a stray. I had him neutered, vaccinated, wormed, and tested for feline leukemia. Gus purred constantly and loved to be petted. He was with me for nearly four months and it was hard to see him leave, even though he went to a wonderful family.

The cat room has been vacuumed, the litter box scrubbed, and the blankets washed. I sent the scratching post with Gus because his new family didn't have one. I'll buy one today so that I'm ready for the next foster cat.

Each of my foster cats arrived as an unwanted animal. Each is now a cherished companion who adds joy and laughter to his or her family. During their transformation from unwanted stray to beloved pet, the cats helped me as much as I helped them. I still miss Carl but his workshop is no longer a sad, empty space. It's now known as the cat room, complete with a "Strays Welcome" sign. When the room is occupied, it contains mouse-on-a-string games, and purring lap-sit sessions. An eager cat watches out the window when I come home, and hurries to rub against my legs as I enter the room. Even when I'm between cats, there is a sense of anticipation and the knowledge that the emptiness is only temporary and that soon the room will once again come alive with love and purpose.

~Peg Kehret

Pyramid of Friends

Way down deep, we're all motivated by the same urges.
Cats have the courage to live by them.
~Jim Davis

I sat on my deck. Smoke from the barbecue drifted into the air. As the steaks cooked, I put my feet on an adjacent chair, picked up my book, and quietly read. It was another peaceful spring evening in Nova Scotia.

In the corner of my vision, I sensed movement. It was a large white cat. His long white coat was a stark contrast to the green and brown of the awakening world of spring.

I watched the cat. He approached my flowerbed, sniffed at the newly turned soil, and began to dig. "Hey!" I jumped from my chair, "Get out of there." The cat ran so fast it was nothing but a white blur as it fled.

A couple of days later, I was on my deck again. The cat appeared. I chased it away again. This continued through spring and into summer. Every time I sat on my deck, the cat would appear, and I would chase it away.

One evening, as I sat, I heard a "Meow!" There was the white cat standing a few feet from me. It had come around the house from the other direction. Its blue eyes showed no fear as it looked at me. I looked back and admired its courage. I put my hand down, "Here, Kitty." The cat rushed to my hand and rubbed its head against it. A few minutes later, it was in my lap, purring softly. The cat had worn me down.

I couldn't chase him anymore.

I saw the direction it went when it left my lap. It was always in the direction of a new neighbor. One evening I saw my neighbor in his yard. I walked up the hill and introduced myself. His name was Ron. As we talked, the white cat appeared. "Ron, is that your cat?"

"That's Matey. I got him a few months ago. I noticed he goes down the hill to your property almost every evening. I hope he isn't bothering you."

"Not at all, Ron. In fact, he has become a friend." Ron and I became friends too.

For several years we lived as neighbors, sharing Matey's love between us.

A few years after meeting, I had to move for a new job. My family stayed behind to sell the house. While I was away for three months, my wife had a mouse problem. Ron sent Matey to help. Matey stayed in our home for a couple of nights. The mouse problem was solved. Ron also cut a Christmas tree, got it in our house, and on the stand for my wife that year.

Four years and two moves later, we crossed the border to the USA and into Ohio. My barbecue was on my patio. I sat, cooked a steak, and read a book. Across the field, I saw a black cat. It glanced in my direction and continued on.

One night, I went outside for a breath of fresh air. The black cat appeared.

It walked in my direction, came within thirty feet, stopped, rolled onto its back, and meowed. I approached it. It fled. A few nights later, it was there again. The routine was repeated—it ran away. The cat became a challenge.

I would look for it every evening. It would hear me, wander in my direction, and run away when I got close.

One night I sat on the curb and talked to it. It grew brave and came within reach. I rubbed its head. A friendship was formed. I would step outside and make a noise. The cat would hear and come to me, rub against my legs, and allow me to pet it.

My wife thought I was nuts. I talked about the black cat all the time. I told her how wonderful it was, but she didn't believe me. She thought I was just going out to avoid chores.

I knew the cat's home was a house next to our housing complex. I saw the owner gardening one day and walked over to introduce myself. "Hi! I'm Mike. I live in the townhouse complex. Do you have a black cat?"

"I'm Don. It's nice to meet you, Mike. Yes, I have a black cat. His name is Bob."

We shook hands.

"Bob and I are friends," I said.

"Really?"

"Yes! He comes over to my townhouse whenever I am outside."

"Bob's a friendly fellow. He likes attention."

"I've noticed. He is always coming to me. He's a wonderful cat."

A week later, I was outside, and Bob came to visit. He rubbed against my legs. I took a chance, reached down and picked him up. I held him to my chest. He reached out, put a paw on each of my shoulders, and rubbed his face against mine, one cheek after the other.

A love was formed.

My wife came outside, "Mike, what are you doing?"

"Hon, meet Bob."

She fell in love with my friend. "I thought you were kidding." She rubbed Bob's head. Bob pushed his head into her palm. "He's beautiful," she said. Bob won another friend.

Don and I became great friends through Bob. Ron and I became great friends through Matey—two friends became four. No matter where I work or live, I make new friends. Through those new friends, I met more. Two friends become four. Four friends became eight. The chain of friends grows.

Have you heard of pyramid sales? I have. I don't like them. This is different. This is pyramid friendship. Two persistent cats taught me a new concept—make friends, meet more through them, and meet even more. They taught me to allow my pyramid of friends to grow.

~Michael T. Smith

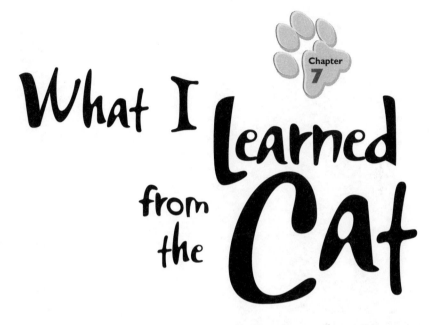

What I Learned from the Cat

Chapter 7

Learning What's Important

Only a few things are really important.

~Marie Dressler

Real Treasures

Even if you have just destroyed a Ming Vase, purr.
Usually all will be forgiven.
~Lenny Rubenstein

"What are you going to buy?" my friend asked as we stood gazing around the Southwest shop in Sedona, Arizona.

"That Talavera bowl, definitely. Those bright colors will look great in my kitchen." I was all about the right look.

I purchased the large, hand-painted bowl and then fretted about getting it home on the plane in one piece. I had the clerk double-wrap it.

It traveled without incident, and once home, I placed the bowl on the island in my kitchen. It made a perfect, striking centerpiece.

One day Barney, a gray tiger stripe, took a wild leap onto the island, slid three feet across it and then plummeted off the end, taking my beautiful bowl with him. Barney landed on his feet, unscathed. The bowl broke into shards of clay.

"I'm sorry," my husband said coming into the room at the sound of the commotion. "I know how much you liked it."

"It's only a bowl," I muttered, trying to keep my frustration in check as I swept up the pieces.

For over twenty years, my husband and I have rescued and adopted stray cats. The lessons I've learned and insights I've gained from them have been numerous and often taught or revealed by more than one cat.

Letting go of material possessions was one of the harder lessons for me to grasp.

Determined to have it all—the rescued cats I loved and a tastefully decorated house, I continued my pursuit of attractive and distinctive home accessories. I wanted the expensive objects, the unusual art, and a treasure trove of material things to make me feel good.

"Look at this," I said to my friend as I ran my hand over the silk and velvet comforter at the department store. "What rich colors."

"Very exotic," she said.

"Wouldn't it be wonderful to snuggle beneath it on a cold winter night?"

She agreed it would.

"I want it," I said, my desire based on taste, not practicality.

I smiled every time I walked by the bedroom and saw that comforter on the bed. The cats liked it, too.

Scratch, scratch. The sound came from the bedroom. I rushed in to find Keku, a white shorthair, digging her claws into my lovely comforter.

"No, no, no," I scolded, picking her up. "We don't scratch the bedspread," I said, placing her in front of one of the many scratching posts in the house. She looked at the post, looked at me, then turned and sauntered away.

A few months later, the comforter had become a shredded, snagged rag. Poco, a male tiger stripe, Calypso, a female calico, and others had taken up where Keku left off. Something about that comforter drew them. Possibly my attachment to it. With a heavy heart, I removed it.

I moaned and, sometimes, even wept through the years as one after another prized item ended up in the trash, the recycle bin, or the ragbag.

It took me a while to understand what the cats were patiently teaching me: Living beings are more important and more valuable than any inanimate object.

On a recent shopping trip, I admired a lamp with glass beads dangling from the silk shade.

"Get it," my friend said. "It's on sale."

I pursed my lips. I sighed. I thought of the cats and of glass beads all over the floor. Those colorful, swinging balls would be too enticing for them to resist.

"No." I shook my head. "I'm good with the lamp I already have." And to my surprise and delight, I was.

I've learned to pare down and live with less than perfect décor. The antique-gold drapes get a few more snags a year but are there to stay for a while. Clear packing tape works great to hold ravaged corners of the sofa and chairs together. It also helps discourage returning culprits to that scratching spot. I've packed away my remaining collector's pieces of china and glass.

I've come to think of our lifestyle as shabby chic. Do I miss the shopping sprees, buying that one-of-a-kind, can't-live-without-it item? Sometimes. But what I would miss more is not seeing Sage's sea green eyes when I walk in the door, not hearing Tansy's rumbling purr that reverberates all the way down the hall. I'd miss Priscilla's repeated nudge under my chin in the mornings before I climb from bed, and Crystal's paw snagging me as I walk by, an incentive to stop and rub her head.

I can admire a piece of ceramic art, but I can't snuggle with a chunk of cold clay. An expensive comforter might warm me on the outside, but stroking a cat's downy fur comforts my soul. Beauty abounds in my house, not because of glass or clay, wood or silk, but because of the affection, companionship, furry warmth, and gentle love of the cats who share it.

I might have been rescuing them through the years, but they were rescuing me, too. My life is simpler, my values more focused. I can now shrug my shoulders and say, "It was just a bowl, picture, vase, bedspread..." because the real treasures in my life are alive and breathing.

~Teresa Hoy

Withstanding Winter's Woes

Don't worry about a thing, cause every little thing gonna be all right.
~Bob Marley

Though I've always seen myself as a "glass half full" person, this winter I've nearly changed my mind. I'm sad to say that I've temporarily set aside positive thinking, forgotten how to make an affirmation or a wish upon a star... and have even rubbed a cynical thumb across my unicorn key chain, which I usually stroke like a good luck charm.

Give me a crisis, and I can cope. But give me an avalanche of crises, and I get too smothered to function. For instance, this winter my son survived three rounds of layoffs at the metropolitan newspaper where he's a copy chief, but a fourth round is pending, and things look bleak. My husband, diagnosed with end-stage renal failure, held up well throughout the holidays, but his remaining energy seems to be dwindling more rapidly than either of us ever anticipated. And my own good health has suffered a series of small setbacks, colds and coughs that I can't shake, accompanied by vague aches and pains that interfere with solid sleep and managing housekeeping chores.

I just feel stuck. Spring can't come too soon, but even Punxsutawney Phil saw his shadow on Groundhog Day, guaranteeing six more weeks of gloom.

So when I look out my kitchen window this morning, and spy

Chico, a black ball of fluff silhouetted against the gray sky and snow-covered pastures, I am astonished. Once again she is perched on top of the birdhouse, scanning the sky.

Now, let me set the scene a little more clearly. It's early February here in Northeast Washington... which my California friends allude to as Southern Alaska. We've crept above freezing exactly three days this winter. There's still a two-foot chunk of ice on my roof. And I can't recall seeing a bird other than a wild turkey anywhere near the yard since last November.

But if Chico expects a tasty snack to fly down to her, maybe one will. I've learned a lot about Chico and her expectations. She's the only cat I've ever known who dedicates herself to the principles of the Law of Attraction. This means that if you believe good things are going to happen to you, then they simply will. And for Chico, they often do.

Chico, and her siblings, Groucho and Harpo, were a freebie litter at The Flour Mill, an animal equipment and supply store in town. I had gone to the shop looking for a kitten, but couldn't settle on just one. I leaned towards Groucho, the tuxedo cat, and then towards Harpo, the marmalade. Chico, wholly black with emerald eyes, just sat and stared at me as if I'd be crazy to leave her behind.

Billed by the Mill as "barn cats," the trio belied that tag, taking to our house, particularly to the quilt on our bed, like babes to toyland. But from the onset, Chico demonstrated her difference from her siblings, her independence and daring. While the others hop into my lap, seeking affection, Chico prefers to curl up to Natty, our shaggy Great Pyrenees mix. The others rarely venture out in winter. Chico races the dogs to the door. Always up for adventure, hunting mice and birds is her obsession.

This afternoon I glance out the kitchen window again. Chico's back atop the birdhouse, but this time she's no longer alone in the yard. Dozens of English sparrows cavort in the adjacent tree, nibbling on the seeds. Chico watches them closely, swatting out a lazy paw whenever one flies near. She nearly loses her balance once or twice, but always digs her claws into the birdhouse roof just in time.

A little later she hops up on the windowsill outside our dining room window and yowls for my attention. Apparently today was not the best of hunting days because when I let her in she heads for the bathroom where she settles for a tamer meal of kitty kibble from her lavender dish.

I return to my computer and check my e-mail... at least there's no bad news from my son. I hear my husband upstairs and it sounds as if he's getting up to come down for an afternoon visit, still well enough to manage the stairs. The ache in my hip has subsided enough that I think I'm up to mopping the kitchen and hallway.

Chico ambles in and nudges Natty, licking her whiskers, satisfied and content.

Her message gets through to me. Maybe good things don't have to happen every day. Maybe it's enough just to be content simply because bad things didn't happen either.

And then I remember. Sometimes lowering your expectations is a part of the Law of Attraction. It doesn't always have to be great expectations. Like Chico, I simply could expect something that is readily available.

Hmmm. Birds in the trees once again. Spring can't be too far off. I manage a smile and go upstairs to greet my husband, trailed by Chico. Even though it's afternoon, I greet him, singing the verse from Bob Marley's "Three Little Birds" — "Rise up this mornin', smiled with the risin' sun."

My husband sits on the edge of the bed, smiling back. Chico jumps up next to him, waiting for a pat. She gets it.

So do I.

~Terri Elders

A Lesson in Ugly

Beauty is not in the face; beauty is a light in the heart.
~Kahlil Gibran

One of my earliest memories is being all dressed up to have my picture taken. I remember Mother bathing me, putting lotion on my hair and curling it around her finger as she blew on it. I twisted and squirmed and she patiently told me a story as she worked on my hair.

"This will make you pretty," she explained. "You're going to have your picture taken and you want to look pretty, don't you?"

I was a child in the late 40s and early 50s, and that was the time when ladies wore hats and gloves and nylon hose. Men wore three-piece suits, hats, and carried handkerchiefs. Whether it was to church, shopping, or to a special event, everyone dressed their best. There was no jeans, sweatshirts, tennis shoes, or baggy anything.

We lived in an antebellum house in Palestine, Texas, on a large two-acre lot. For some reason, we attracted the discarded and homeless pets of the area. If it was a stray, it ended up in our yard. In the evening Grandpa would fill a half dozen tin pie plates with leftovers and some cheap cat food and take them out into the backyard. He would bang a couple of plates together, yell "kitty, kitty, kitty." After he went back into the house, a dozen feral cats would creep out from the bushes, the sheds, and the storage building and chow down. Sometimes there was even a stray dog or two. If they were tame, Grandpa would try and find homes for them.

It was 1950 and just after Christmas when I came in from school, changed clothes, and grabbed a sandwich before heading across the hall to see my grandparents. I was surprised to see my grandmother sitting alone sipping coffee.

"Where's Grandpa?" I asked.

"Oh, he's in the basement working on an old stray cat that snuck in the basement window. The cat is badly burned, but you know your grandpa, he's determined to doctor that old cat up."

I headed for the cellar. In the past we had sewn up an old hen that had been attacked in the hen house, bandaged dozens of cuts, scrapes, and injuries of assorted cats, dogs, pigs, horses, and even a cow or two. Grandpa could not stand by and let any creature suffer.

Grandpa's back was to me and I couldn't see the cat that Grandma had mentioned. I saw a bottle of salve and one of Grandma's aloe vera plants sitting on the table, along with two large rolls of gauze and some adhesive tape. I thought the cat had probably blistered a foot or maybe his tail and hurried over to see if I could help.

As I reached his side and got a good look at his patient, I felt all the air sucked from my lungs. My gasp was loud and my grandfather looked at me and smiled a sad smile.

"Not very pretty, is he?" he said softly.

I couldn't answer. I had never seen anything so horrible. One side of the cat's face was totally devoid of hair and skin, his right ear was completely burned off and one eye was seared shut. There were large burns along his side and back, and his tail was missing. His legs and feet were blistered and raw, and the cat just lay in my grandfather's arms trembling.

"Is he going to die?" I whispered.

"Not if I can help it," Grandpa said with tears in his eyes.

"How did this happen?" I asked.

"He must have gotten cold and tried to get into the cellar. I figured he slipped when he got through the window and fell behind the furnace. I kept hearing this faint cry so I came down and found him. He had managed to climb out from behind the furnace."

"But, he is one of the wild ones, isn't he? How come he's letting you hold him?"

"He knows, my dear. He knows I wouldn't hurt him. He needs help. His pain is stronger than his fear."

"Grandpa, even if he lives, he's going to be so ugly," I commented as I looked at the damage the furnace had done.

"So what?" my grandpa said harshly. "Would you love me less if I were burned and ugly?"

"Of c-course not," I stammered.

"Are you sure?" he stared at me. He was smearing the burn cream from the jar over the cat's face and stubble of an ear. "You know, I was always told not to judge a book by the cover. Do you know what that means?"

I nodded. "It means sometimes a book is really good even if the cover isn't."

"That's right," he smiled. "It's important to look good because most people are too quick to judge by appearances. Still, it's even more important to take the time to get to know people and find out if the person is a good person, a kind person, and a person who might enrich your life. You mustn't associate with people who are mean, have no respect, and disregard the law, but those people usually have a reputation that is well known."

"Mother always wants me to look pretty," I argued. "All the most popular people at school are pretty."

"That's for now," he explained. "Now is what young people think about, but now isn't all there is to life. Animals don't care who's popular and who's not. All animals care about is staying warm in the winter, cool in the summer, food to keep them from being hungry, and friends to share their lives with. They don't ask for a lot and they only judge by actions, not looks."

Grandpa doctored the poor cat, smearing ointment on his burns, bandaging his wounds, and all the while murmuring soft comforting sounds. We spent an hour in the basement that day. We bandaged and wrapped and squeezed out the cooling sap of the aloe vera plant and applied it to the places that were the most severe.

Every day for the next month, Grandpa and I changed bandages, reapplied medication and hand-fed the injured cat. He did recover, but his injuries had taken their toll on his appearance. He lost the use of his right eye and it grew shut and his ear was little more than a bald stub. His fur never grew back over the burn scars on his face or his body.

What I discovered, what my grandfather had tried to tell me, was that the sparkle in his good eye, the soft purr from his scarred chest, and the gentle rub of his mangled head against my leg gave me a feeling that I had never experienced before. When I gathered Lucky, his new name, into my arms, I didn't see an ugly cat. I saw a cat full of love and appreciation, and happy to be alive.

It may sound fake, unbelievable, and mushy, but that cat changed my outlook. That cat, my grandfather, and the advice he gave me opened doors I didn't know existed. I started looking at my classmates differently. The beautiful people didn't stand out so much anymore and I discovered lots of new friends who made my years in school the best. I never made the most popular list, but I didn't care. I wasn't the prettiest, but that didn't matter. My friends, like Lucky, knew how to be friends, how to love, laugh, and appreciate life. None of them were ugly, nor beautiful, but I discovered that there is a fine line between the two and that fine line is deep inside.

I still like to look my best, but now I look deeper, beneath, inside. After all, that's where real beauty lies. Ugly is a word that defines a person's action, feelings, and lifestyle. As far as I'm concerned it had nothing to do with looks.

~Bobbie Shafer

Don't Forget the Shy One

You learn something every day if you pay attention.
~Ray LeBlond

We couldn't wait to get home. My husband and I had just returned from the breeder's, with our two American Shorthair kittens. They had the bold black and silver markings of classic silver tabbies. Although they looked very similar, we were soon to discover just how different they could be.

Asher was the larger of the two. He was very demonstrative and would come running the minute you sat down. He loved to be petted and played with, and let you know he expected lots of affection. Geordi was just the opposite. He was the quiet, curious cat. The kind of cat you would find with his tail sticking out of the cat food bag, after he had turned it over onto the floor. Although he loved to be petted too, he was not usually the initiator. He was much more likely to be into mischief. Asher was never far from people; Geordi was never far from trouble.

One day I was sitting on the floor of our apartment, playing with Asher, who, of course, came running the minute I sat down. He was still small and very cute, and was mewing and purring up a storm as I petted him. As he was rubbing against my knee, I was totally focused on him. He loved the affection and attention he was getting.

Suddenly, I remembered I had two kittens to play with. I wondered where Geordi was and began to look around the room for him. To my surprise, Geordi had been next to me the whole time. He was off to my right, just out of sight, lying quietly on the floor on his back, with his paws outstretched. His big golden eyes were fixed upon me, and the expression on his face seemed to say, "Aren't you going to pet me too?" To my shame, I almost missed him.

I was so focused on his affectionate brother that I neglected to look for him, my shy one. It was then that I had a funny thought. My husband and I had only been married for about a year. Although we were childless, we knew we would like to have children some day. I felt bad enough about forgetting a shy kitten, but what about missing a shy child? As I petted Geordi and gave him the affection he needed and rightly deserved, I made a mental note to myself. Don't forget the shy one.

God has a funny way of getting our attention and teaching us lessons we need to learn in life, even if He has to use kittens to do it. About seven years later, as I watched my two daughters play, I decided to sit on the floor and join them. My younger daughter immediately ran over, and plopped into my lap. She was my demonstrative child, and no one ever doubted when she was in need of affection. My older daughter was, of course, a different story. She was my shy one.

As I hugged my younger daughter, my thoughts went back to those two kittens, and how I had almost missed an opportunity to show affection to Geordi, the shy one. I realized I was about to make the same mistake. As I called my older daughter over to hug her too, I thanked God for His lesson. Don't forget the shy one. It was a lesson that has impacted my relationship with my daughter ever since. God used a small, shy kitten to show me how to appreciate both of my daughters, regardless of the difference in their personalities. It is a lesson I will never forget.

~Joanna G. Wright

Cats Are Cats

I think there's just one kind of folks. Folks.
~Harper Lee, To Kill a Mockingbird

Having been raised in Florida for half my life, I had been exposed to all races, colors and religions. When my family moved to Vermont, I barely noticed that most of the population was Caucasian like my family.

When my son, Shawn, was born in Vermont, it did not occur to me that he was being raised in an almost all white population since race had never been an issue with my family. So when I got a veterinarian technician job after college and we moved to central New York when he was three years old, I had not realized that he had never encountered a person who was not white.

When Shawn got home from pre-school his first day, he was very quiet. He seemed distressed but wouldn't tell me what was wrong at first. Finally he said very quietly that most of the kids at school were "funny." I asked him what he meant by funny and he told me, "They are brown and black, all different shades," and, "The teacher yelled at me when I tried to ask her about it." Then he started to cry.

I was flummoxed! How do you explain diversity to a three-year-old who has never encountered it before? I cuddled him in my arms and dried his tears while I thought for a moment.

Then I smiled and asked him to look around the room. Our seven cats lounged around, along the back of the couch, in a chair, curled in a corner. I asked him to look at the cats.

Cream-colored Diva with blue eyes and dark chocolate points accented by white boots, a gorgeous Snowshoe. Orange-striped Simon with dark amber eyes, a somber longhaired Turkish Van mix. Simon's short-haired sister, Brindle, a crazy tortoiseshell of black stripes over brown, tan and white patches, with multiple toes was our only polydactyl. Dapper tuxedo Sylvester in his black coat with white chest and paws. Fluffy Sassy, a Persian-cross with her snubbed nose and long brown-striped coat, a brown tiger. Black and white patches with a black mustache made Minx look like a clown. Solid blue-gray Ashley was an elegant girl.

I asked him to think about what he saw. After a few moments he said, "They are different colors." I could see the wheels turning in his mind as he thought about it. After a moment, he looked at me. "So people come in different colors too?" "Yes," I replied, "people come in different colors just like the cats, but we're all people just like they are all cats."

"Oh, okay." He gave me a perplexed look. "Why did my teacher get mad when I tried to ask her about it?"

"Well," I replied, "not everyone likes cats. There's no good reason for it and they usually don't like them because they don't know any better. Some people are like that about people who are different colors. It makes no sense but some people are like that. She probably thought you were having that problem and didn't realize you were just asking."

Shawn thought about that for a moment and then smiled at me. "I like cats," he said, "and people too. They're all pretty." He gave me a hug and then scooped up Brindle in his arms. A bright boy who likes everyone because of their differences, just like our cats.

~Tory S. Morgan

Roll with the Changes

The cat is the only animal without visible means of support
who still manages to find a living in the city.
~Carl van Vechten

We are such creatures of habit. We don't like change. This is true of humans and cats alike. If you have any doubts, just start rearranging the furniture and watch the cats freak out. Or start packing—you will quickly find yourself searching for the cat who has mysteriously disappeared, and will most likely be found huddling in the back of a cabinet or closet because whatever you have in mind, he wants no part of it!

When I first met Tuxford, he was living at a park in Burbank, California. A handsome tuxedo cat, he introduced himself one day when I was having lunch at a picnic bench. That day was the start of a beautiful friendship.

For the next year and a half, I went to the park every day. I took a can of cat food and a box of dry food. Sometimes I also took a brush. Often Tux would be waiting for me on the sidewalk; other times he would come scrambling over the wall at the back of the park when he heard my car.

Although I later learned that some folks called him Verdugo (because he lived in Verdugo Park), I named him Tuxford in honor of his striking black and white coat. Over time, I also discovered from various people that he had been living at the park for at least seven years! And although I wanted very much to take him home, my husband and five cats put their respective feet and paws down and told me NO WAY!

So I continued to care for him as best I could. I worried about him when the weather turned cold or wet, even though logic told me that after seven years he had obviously learned to take care of himself.

Tux was friendly but not too friendly. He would let me pet him but not pick him up. As I watched him with other people, I could see that he had a real talent for making friends... and yet nobody was taking that extra step and giving him a home.

Then came the day that he developed a large lump on his chin. Under duress, my husband helped me catch Tux and we carted him off to the vet. The lump turned out to be a salivary gland cyst, easily drained and nothing to worry about. What was much more disturbing was that the vet told us that Tuxford was at least fifteen years old!

I was no longer taking no for an answer. Tuxford was coming home with us.

But what would that mean? He had lived nearly half his life at the park—and I had no idea what his life was like before that! He was certainly friendly enough, but had he ever lived inside? Would he use a litter box? And what about the other cats? After all, in Tuxford's world, other cats were the enemy! Oh yeah, this was gonna be interesting... and not necessarily in a good way.

Whatever I had envisioned... whatever I could have imagined... I never guessed what would actually happen.

He used the litter box—and didn't even seem to mind sharing it with five other cats. He let me put a collar on him. He quickly learned that jumping on the counter and scratching the furniture weren't allowed and would result in loud yelling.

His interaction with the other cats—the thing I had worried about most—was also a non-issue. He shadowboxed with Murray, he gave Taz (our resident bully) a verbal dressing-down, and he swatted PC when she got too friendly (PC doesn't know she is fixed). But not even one real honest-to-goodness cat fight!

What was most surprising of all is that Tux never showed any interest in going outside—he avoided the door like the plague! How does a cat who has spent the last several years roaming free adapt to being restricted to a small one-bedroom apartment? Apparently, in Tuxford's case at least, quite well. And although it took him a few months, Tux eventually started doing two things he had never done at the park... he learned to cuddle and he learned to play!

A few months ago, I turned my entire life upside down. I ended my marriage and I moved halfway across the country (with all the cats). Although my choices were made for all the right reasons, it has not been easy. I have gone through depression and uncertainty. I have been scared and unsure of what to do next. I have never doubted my decisions, but I have not exactly run with the ball the way I had planned to do. In short, I have not adapted to my new circumstances with near the ease and grace that Tuxford did.

And there is a lot to be learned from that. If a cat can go from a homeless existence to being a perfect pet, I can certainly pick myself up off the proverbial floor and get my act together.

I have lived my life with cats. I have often admired them for their independence and ingenuity. But I think this might be the first time I have used one as a role model for my own behavior! But if I have to have a hero, I could do a lot worse than a cat who was smart enough to recognize a change in his fortune and adjust his attitude accordingly... he could have turned my house into a disaster (and my other cats into mincemeat) but he didn't. He looked around, saw what was good, and decided he could live with the bad. Can I do any less?

~Linda Sabourin

CATaclysmic Encounter

We often take for granted the very things that most deserve our gratitude.
~Cynthia Ozick

It had been another one of those hectic run-till-you-drop weeks. For what seemed the umpteenth time, I was on a bus heading away from my home in Jerusalem, well aware that, yet again, it would be hours until I'd return, exhausted, and hungry.

This time it was even worse than usual. I'd left ample time to make the right bus connections without the risk of running late, as I was on my way to an important appointment. Now here I was, stuck on a bus, which hadn't moved an inch for thirty-five minutes. All it takes is one traffic accident. The baby was crying, hungry, tired, and kvetchy from being forced to sit in one place for so long. A headache had settled itself comfortably in the back of my head. Conducting an orchestra composed mainly of drums, it beat a loud and steady rhythm in time with the baby's wails. Checking my watch every few minutes, I saw its hands moving inexorably forward to slip past the hour of my scheduled meeting.

Worst of all was my sense of déjà vu. Once again, I was feeling like a ballerina in a music box, my leg glued in place and spinning in an endless circle. All I seemed to do lately was run. I never caught up, no matter how organized I tried to be. Life had become a series of dashes, jogs, and sprints—to the bus, the store, the school, the doctor. I kept getting the feeling that I was rushing past something important but didn't have time in my schedule to stop and figure out what.

Finally, the bus was waved on, but was now stopping at every red light possible. Sitting at the edge of my seat and tapping my foot impatiently on the floor of the bus as if it would actually help, I happened to glance outside.

Questioning my own senses, I looked again. Everywhere I looked, I saw cats! They were pouring out of buildings, from under bushes, down trees, and out of garbage cans. They were all running as fast as they could, up a flight of stairs that led to a small garden behind an old apartment building. Fifteen... twenty... twenty-five street cats, all milling around, obviously awaiting something.

Then I saw him. An old man slowly made his way out of the building. He was painfully thin and doubled over in an arthritic crouch. His swollen knuckles clutched a plain, worn cane on which he leaned heavily. His feet, encased in slippers, shuffled along the path. His pants and jacket hung loosely over his gaunt frame. The pants were a little too long, the sleeves a bit too short. As he reached into his pocket, I noticed the numbers etched into his flesh, his constant reminder of a horror-filled youth. Extracting a small bag filled with food, he carefully balanced himself on his cane. To the felines mingling around his feet, this was their cue, as he proceeded to scatter the contents on the ground. Within seconds, it was all gone.

It was the look on his face which made this whole incident a special memory. As the cats finished their snack, they rubbed themselves against his legs and purred up at him. He stood there silently, pure contentment glowing on his features. An elderly cripple, enjoying the company of his feline friends and appreciating the simple pleasures in life.

When the light turned green, it was a different me moving forward. I leaned back in my seat and snuggled my baby. Taking the time to inhale his clean, fresh scent, I watched the clouds slowly drifting across the sky, and the leaves rustling in the gentle breeze.

~Michelle Borinstein

Rosie

I would maintain that thanks are the highest form of thought;
and that gratitude is happiness doubled by wonder.
~G.K. Chesterton

When I got married, two cats came with me; we were a package deal. After my husband and I had children, I started feeding my cats in our garage. This ensured that when my daughters were toddlers and started tasting what they found on the floor, their curious fingers stayed out of the cats' dishes. It was a practice I maintained even when my girls were older. When my daughters were two and four and a half, I noticed a stray cat sneaking into the garage to eat our cats' food. It seemed like every time I opened the garage door that cat would run in, grab a few bites, and before I could shoo him out, he would be gone in a blur of black and white.

One glorious Pacific Northwest summer day I left the garage door open as I gardened and my daughters played in the yard. A small breeze gently rustled the leaves in the trees. Birds sang and darted from branch to branch. The warm sun shone down from a blue sky dotted with small, puffy clouds. We decided to take advantage of the beautiful day and stay outside. When my daughters got hungry, I went inside to fix them a picnic snack.

On my way back through the garage I saw that cat. As usual, he ran. But this time, before he got halfway to the door he stopped and turned around and stared at me. Irritated, I stared back as we took measure of each other. My irritation quickly faded as I looked closely at him. His coat was rough and unkempt. His head looked much too big for his body. Understanding dawned. I realized this cat wasn't just a nuisance; this cat wasn't just hungry; this cat was starving. As my eyes met with his, I saw beseeching sadness. "Please, help me," he pleaded with his eyes. Those were my first and second lessons:

1) Know when to face your fears and take a stand.

2) Know when to ask for help.

After delivering the snacks to my daughters, I loaded up a paper plate with both dry and canned cat food. My daughters danced around excitedly as they watched the cat devour the food. They decided to name him Rosie. I said he was a boy cat and might not like being named Rosie. Amazed at the enormous amount of food he'd consumed, my little girls dubbed him with both a first and a last name — Rosie Cannacatfood. I made it clear to them, and myself, that we already had two cats and didn't have room for another. We would try to find a home for Rosie, but until then he would be our outside kitty. My daughters discovered where he'd been sleeping in the tall, dry grass in the ditch at the end of our front yard. From that vantage point Rosie had been able to keep an eye on our garage door and remain hidden. Our cats seemed to understand that Rosie was a part of our family and treated him with indifference... as long as he stayed out of their house.

Summer blended into fall with its incessant wind and rain. The covered area over our front porch where we kept firewood became Rosie's shelter and protected him from the turbulent weather. Fall was coming to a close and I still didn't have a home for Rosie. The weather was turning colder. With plywood from the garage I made a house for Rosie and placed it on top of the firewood with a warm, soft blanket inside. The roof was flat and the perfect place for Rosie's meals. Winter came suddenly with a frigid Arctic blast and snow. One clear, cold evening I took some rags and plastic bags to wrap and cover our outside faucets for protection from the freezing tempera-ture. Rosie followed along to keep me company. Our feet crunched on the glittering snow; our breath came out in white puffs. The clear sky was ablaze with stars.

I laid one plastic bag on the ground as I wrapped the first faucet. Rosie pounced on the empty bag, grabbed it in his mouth and started to shake it violently back and forth. They were the kind of bags I used to wrap and discard meat scraps before placing them in my garbage. Tears stung my eyes when I realized that he must have pulled those knotted bags out of my garbage in the past and struggled to tear the plastic to get at the scraps inside. I petted him and gently removed the bag from his mouth. "You don't have to do that anymore, Rosie," I said. Those were my third and fourth lessons:

3) Trust in others.

4) Never forget how to take care of yourself.

I worried about Rosie getting too cold. My husband had a weight bench in the garage. Every evening I would heat the five- and ten-pound round weights in my oven and place them between towels inside Rosie's house. He would quickly jump into his house to enjoy the warmth. I hung an old towel over the opening to keep the heat in. In the morning I heated a twenty-five-pound weight and placed it between towels on top of his house when I gave him his breakfast. On one of those crystal clear winter mornings Rosie sat on top of his heated towel and gave himself a thorough cleaning before settling down to look out at the day. Those were my fifth and sixth lessons:

5) Take pride in your appearance.

6) Take time to appreciate the beauty of nature around you.

Winter morphed into spring and spring into summer. We'd had Rosie for a year when he started to disappear for a day or two at a time. One day he didn't come back. I left his house out just in case. Fall came with the rain, then winter and still no Rosie. I put his house away and thought the worst. Soon it was spring and then summer.

Early one warm evening I was sitting on the porch reading to my daughters when some movement caught my eye. A black and white cat was coming up our walkway. Steadily he walked past the trees and toward us. I could not believe my eyes. A year had passed since we'd seen him but, sure enough, it was Rosie. My daughters were ecstatic and hugged and petted him. When they were done, Rosie sat by my feet, looked me in the eye and shook his head. Something jingled. I looked closer. He was wearing a collar with a license tag. He'd come back to let us know he had a family of his own. Those were my seventh and eighth lessons:

7) Let the special people in your past know you're okay.

8) Give thanks.

And, I did. I thanked him for the lessons he'd taught. Rosie stayed to visit for a couple of hours and then he left. We never saw him again.

~Deborah Lee Wilson

The Eight Lives of Stinky

*Are we really sure the purring is coming from the kitty
and not from our very own hearts?*
~Emme Woodhull-Bäche

I t was an autumn full moon. I awoke to the sound of my husband Joe making coffee. I reached for the clock—5:50. As I settled back onto my pillow I heard a muffled growling sound outside. I peered out the bedroom window and saw two coyotes on the front lawn. My initial reaction was one of amazement. They looked so small, so beautiful illuminated by the moonlight. As my eyes focused a little more I noticed a small lifeless black and white body laid out on the ground between them. My heart sank; we had three cats, each of them black and white.

I walked into the kitchen in a daze and asked Joe if he had let the cats out. "Yes, why?" he asked. My voice shaking, I told him there were two coyotes in the front yard and they had caught a cat. Immediately he ran towards the door. This wasn't easy for Joe, having had two back surgeries in recent years. "It's done, it's over," I cried. He threw open the door and began yelling. Would these animals attack humans? Should I call 911? Everything seemed so surreal, a surprise attack on our cat followed by another surprise attack on the coyotes as Joe charged at them. The coyotes ran away, one of them with the cat dangling from its jaws like a child's toy. Joe was right on their tail, yelling in a primal sort of rage which I'd never heard before.

He stopped suddenly and scooped something up and handed me our cat, Stinky.

I lay Stinky on the kitchen counter to get a better look at her. She was struggling to breathe and her body was limp and non-responsive. Her eyes were filled with fear. I quickly checked her body for any open wounds or signs of blood but I couldn't see anything.

I loaded Stinky into the car and told Joe we were off to the emergency clinic. He looked so forlorn, saying he just couldn't bring himself to go. He knew the vet would have to put her down. Stinky was Joe's cat, a gift from his mom who died two years earlier from cancer. Myonia was always rescuing animals. She just couldn't stand to see a stray or mistreated animal. She had brought this tiny ball of fluff over to our house in a cat carrier and asked us to "foster" the kitten for a couple of weeks until she could find her a good home. The minute my daughter Natalie and I peeked into the carrier and saw that adorable little kitten and simultaneously sighed, "Ohhhh... how cute" that was it. I looked up at my mother-in-law only to see the expression a drug dealer would have when he first introduces you to heroin. I'd been had and she knew it.

After a few days we decided it was time to name her. "How about Vivian, Mom's middle name?" my sister-in-law Kimberly asked. "How about Guilt?" suggested Joe. Nothing seemed to fit. The kitten fell in love with Joe. Anytime he stretched out across the bed to play with her she would climb all over his face. He'd say, "Yes that is a stinky butt you have there." Well, "Stinky" fit, and as she grew she developed a definite white skunk stripe along her back. She grew into a truly beautiful cat in spite of her name.

It was still dark outside as I drove east towards the clinic. I talked to Stinky, telling her how much I loved her, asking her to hang in there. She alternated between helpless crying and silence. I wasn't sure which frightened me more. Then I thought maybe it was selfish to want her to stay when she was in so much pain. With that realization I said to her that it was okay to let go and thanked her for the joy she had brought to our family.

Throughout the morning it felt as if I was outside my body;

someone else was guiding my actions. The light turned red outside the street entrance to the emergency clinic. At first I felt impatient. There were no other cars around except the one that happened to be in front of me. While sitting there I noticed its bumper sticker. I have never seen this one before or since. It read simply, "Life is Fragile." Just then the tears began to flow. "How true," I said out loud. The light turned green, the car ahead of me went straight and I turned left into the parking lot.

The veterinarian took Stinky back immediately to give her some medication for the pain and to take X-rays. Soon the veterinarian came out to brief me on Stinky's condition. He explained how coyotes violently shake their prey to immobilize them before actually killing them. The paralysis could wear off in a few hours or it could be permanent. We would have to wait and see. Otherwise he felt she was very lucky.

Next we visited our regular veterinarian, who concluded that due to the nature of the attack, our best option was to do exploratory surgery. My head started to override my heart. We had just spent several hundred dollars at the clinic and this was going to be a couple thousand more. But we had gone this far so we continued. The vet discovered three separate tears, one narrowly missing Stinky's gallbladder.

After surgery we were able to visit her in the operating room. Here was this poor sweet cat lying on a little operating table hooked up to IVs with warm air blowing under a baby blanket they had over her. She had a feeding tube in her neck for a couple of weeks. Dr. Attics said she needed to be pampered because she had just used up eight of her nine lives.

One day while I was lamenting the money we spent, Natalie put it into perspective by asking me, "Would you rather have the money in the bank or that fluffy cat purring happily beside you?" Enough said.

~Joanie Gibbs

The Life You Save May Be Your Own

People who love cats have some of the biggest hearts around.
~Susan Easterly

My cat Belinda loved to lie on an old rug right by the patio door. In that spot she could bask in the sun without actually going outside. She and I had no interest in danger. But when her life was threatened by illness, I faced her danger, and learned something about myself in the process. The life you save may be your own.

Belinda was eleven years old when she stopped eating, started losing weight, and developed a series of lumps on her stomach. A biopsy that cost $400 revealed mast cell tumor disease, a form of cancer. "She's going to die in two months without surgery," the vet told my husband and me. The operation would give her more time, but at more than $1,100, it sounded extremely expensive.

My husband teaches college classes and I'm a paralegal. We've never had children, but our budget felt pretty tight. After paying our mortgage, car payments, school loans and regular bills each month, there wasn't much left. At least that's what I believed.

I thought about the fact that Belinda was an animal. Where would we draw the line in taking care of her? She and her sister Magda had always been expensive, high maintenance girls. Each of their files at the vet ran to two volumes. We had just paid for Belinda's biopsy. The price of this surgery probably made it reasonable to say "no more." She'd had a good life, starting with her rescue from the tree where her wild mother had hidden her when she was a kitten. We wouldn't let her suffer; we would put her to sleep. It would be merciful and prudent. We would stay within our budget, keep our life manageable.

But something felt wrong. At first I couldn't put my finger on the problem. Then I knew. Grief was flooding through me. Knocked off balance, I sat down hard in an armchair and closed my eyes. Memories came. I saw Belinda and Magda as kittens exploring my apartment like eager little scientists.

Then I saw Belinda after her first flea bath, a small, bedraggled creature, her wet fur stuck together in clumps. I had expected her to run from me as soon as I lifted her out of the sudsy water. After all, she and her sister had only been with me a few days. When she didn't bolt, but instead mewed around my feet, I scooped her up into a towel, and rubbed her dry. In those moments, an unexpected tenderness broke open within me. When I bathed Magda, I felt the same.

Thinking of Belinda, with her light orange stripes, and black-and-white Magda sitting clean and dry after their baths took me back into an older memory: my dark-haired sister Rachel and blond-haired me eating bologna sandwiches in the kitchen after school. But this was a painful memory. I remembered my mother coming home from work late, opening the refrigerator, and yelling at us for eating too much. She was a widow who worked hard to support us, and it must have seemed to her that food vanished like snow in the sun, that there was never quite enough of anything. My overwhelmed mother did the best she could, but life with her was all about scarcity. I spent my whole childhood feeling too expensive and high maintenance. Rachel and I have always wondered if we were worth it.

Sitting in the armchair, I opened my eyes. "Mom," I said aloud although she had died years before, "I know just how you felt because I feel the same way." As an adult, it was easy to point to my check-book as the reason for pinching pennies, when the real reason was an emotional habit—a feeling of poverty that I carried with me always.

And I still felt a strong doubt about whether needy little creatures were worth the expense.

For so long I hadn't questioned my view that the glass of precious water was always half empty. Now, thinking about Belinda, I realized that my view was life-threatening—to her, and to me. I hadn't been in a bad car accident or been thrown from a boat, but my life—my faith that I was worthwhile, and that I had enough to risk giving—was in danger just the same.

"Mom, I know you loved me the best way you could, but I'm going to make a different choice here," I said.

I realized how much I loved Belinda, and what it meant to me to love her, to feel generous towards her. Somehow it was a way of believing that even expensive, high maintenance creatures—those who need surgery and cat food and those who needed bologna sandwiches—were worth it. Giving Belinda the surgery would be an act of faith, and a first step in trying to change my emotional habit.

My husband and I paid for the surgery. Our vet told us about a credit card for pet healthcare that charges no interest if the balance is paid off within a number of months. For me, trying to kick my scarcity habit in little steps, knowing we wouldn't have to pay interest helped me feel calmer about the expense. The new piece of plastic dubbed the "Cat Credit Card" took its place in my purse, and the line item "Vacation" disappeared from our budget for the year. I realized that even having money for "Vacation" in our budget meant I was luckier than I thought.

Belinda's surgery was long and difficult. The vet found another tumor. When I came to take her home she was shaven and weak like a concentration camp survivor, with so many stitches I didn't know how I was going to hold her.

Her recovery took every ounce of strength and patience Belinda and I had. There were many times I doubted my husband's and my decision. But even through the hours and days when all I could do was watch and wait for Belinda to heal, my leap of faith felt more and more right. Not only did she recover and share her sweet presence with us for eleven more months, but I felt I had found a pathway out of a dark and lonely place.

After those months, the cancer returned and it was clearly time to let her go. Now I often think of her, especially on mornings when I realize she's visited in my dreams. My memories of her help me find that pathway out of scarcity and doubt over and over again. Breaking habits is an act of faith. Belinda is my reminder that generosity benefits the giver most. And she lets me know that she was worth the gift and so am I.

~Rebecca Josefa

What I Learned from the Cat

Learning to Believe

Faith consists in believing when it is beyond the power of reason to believe.

~Voltaire

Homeward Bound

Miracles are not contrary to nature,
but only contrary to what we know about nature.
~Saint Augustine

My mom and her husband Danny had moved to a quiet neighborhood in Sheridan, Wyoming. Mom and Danny had two cats. Abbey, a twelve-year-old white Persian was actually my cat, but when I went to graduate school I left her with my mom. Dink was a six-year-old orange tabby cat, a gift from my brother. Over the years, my mom and Danny had become very attached to these cats—they were their kids.

One spring, while I was in Italy, I called my mom and I could tell something was wrong. She told me that Dink had disappeared and had been gone for a couple of weeks. Sheridan had just had a huge winter storm which kept people stuck at home with roads and businesses closed. My mom and Danny thought that Dink got lost in the snow, until they heard that the man across the street had been bragging about trapping and killing cats. In fact, this man had actually been bragging about "trapping an orange cat" (Dink, wearing an ID collar, often climbed the tree in this man's yard).

When my mom told me this story, I thought it was a little farfetched. The man swore he hadn't killed Dink, but rather he trapped Dink and drove him sixty miles to a mountain pass called Burgess Junction and let him out in the woods. All this happened just before the big winter storm. This story sounded really crazy to me. I was just so sad for my mom and Danny; they lost one of their "kids" and they had this crazy man who claimed to be responsible. Because of the winter storm and the conditions in the mountains, we all assumed that Dink died from the cold.

One month passed and my mom was still terribly sad, not only because of the loss of Dink, but because every time my mom or Danny would leave the house, they looked across the street at the crazy man's house and were reminded that he was responsible. A few more weeks passed and finally, my mom and Danny felt it necessary to move because it was too stressful for them. They moved just a couple of blocks away, but felt a sense of relief. Three months had passed since the loss of Dink and my mom decided to get another pet to love. Mom and Danny got the cutest little Pomeranian puppy — they named her Bear and she looked like a baby bear cub.

I arrived in Wyoming for a visit shortly thereafter. I could see my mom and Danny were settled in and happy in their new little home with Abbey and Bear (although Abbs and Bear are still learning to love one another!). We decided to drive the seven hours to Yellowstone and Grand Teton National Park. We spent the night in Jackson Hole, then went to Grand Teton National Park. We saw elk, buffalo, moose and Old Faithful; it was a great trip, but we decided to go home a day early because we were all just so exhausted from driving.

After hours and hours again in the truck, it was about midnight and it was super dark, without a single other car on those Wyoming country highways. Danny decided to take an alternate route on the way home. About fifty miles from home I dozed off.

I was immediately woken by shouts and realized we were stopped in the middle of the highway. The shouts came from my mom and Danny, who were calling for Dink.

As we drove down that alternate route, an orange cat had run across the highway. Mom and Danny saw him, screamed and stopped the car. They were calling the cat. In the dark, I could see the cat's eyes and I could hear him meowing. I thought "No way. We are fifty miles from home. Dink has been gone for three months. We are in the mountains. No way."

It was surreal. I dashed out of the truck with my camera, and filmed this amazing reunion.

Dink's homecoming was an adjustment for Abbey, Bear and Dink. Dink was still skittish, always watching his back, as I am sure he had to do in the wild. We found him about twenty miles from where he was supposedly dropped off by the crazy man. He had a tooth missing, a scratch on his jaw and a bump on his hind leg, but considering everything, he was in amazing shape.

This story makes me believe in miracles again. It's as if God was watching and guiding Dink and then was holding him on the side of the highway saying, "Hold on Dink, they are driving down the mountain now and will be here soon." Then it's as if God let go of Dink at the exact moment that we drove by.

As I type this, I am looking at Dink, stretched out and sleeping peacefully on the safe, kitchen floor. Amazing.

~Melissa Mellott

Take It Lying Down

If there were to be a universal sound depicting peace,
I would surely vote for the purr.
~Barbara L. Diamond

On a sweltering Florida summer afternoon I discovered two yellow eyes peering from beneath a cluttered shelf in our garage. They evaluated every move, daring me to approach a cool comfy spot on the cement floor.

"Hi there," I crooned. "I'm a cat-lover. Don't worry about getting chased out. I'm allergic to you and I'm just grabbing garden gloves." The yellow eyes disappeared under lazy furry lashes in response, then hovered half-open with the confident gaze of a princess posing at the door of her castle. I thought I detected a purr. So I ducked indoors for a quick drink and returned with a bowl of water for my guest.

By twilight, the long-haired black visitor greeted me like an old friend. She meowed softly and swished her feathery tail across my legs. The deed was done. "Sweet Pea" moved into the garage and into our hearts.

We had hosted other felines over the years. Sweet Pea ingratiated herself like her predecessors. She displayed a gentle, patient, affectionate good nature, while maintaining her independence and hunting skills at night. And we graciously received her gifts of mangled animal remains.

Before anyone realized it, Sweet Pea owned the garage and common areas of our house. We de-flea-ed. We de-furred couches and chairs. I religiously washed my hands and marveled that my asthma, sneezing, and watery eyes had not returned. The allergist remarked that Sweet Pea's gradual encroachment into my environment acted like allergy shots to de-sensitize me. I could enjoy petting a cat again! And I did, grooming her long fur to the soft rumble of her purrs. On one such occasion, neighbors who rarely walked past our driveway stopped in shock.

"Mimi! Our cat!" the woman shouted. "How long have you had her?"

"About a year," I replied, as Sweet Pea licked a paw and ignored us both. "She wandered into our garage and never left." I added defensively. Dollar signs for flea dipping and vet exams drifted into my head.

"We're so glad she's still alive!" Linda from three doors down the street continued. "She disappeared one day. Probably got tired of sharing with our other six cats. She was our first cat, which makes her seventeen years old now." Tinges of concern leaked from behind my smile, so Linda quickly added, "Oh, we're just so glad she's alive and has a nice home. You wouldn't like a couple more cats?"

At Sweet Pea's next yearly exam, I reported her advanced age. Doctor Conners and I had guessed short by five years, but Sweet Pea's elderly kidneys told the truth. The vet suggested giving Sweet Pea subcutaneous saline injections to keep her from dehydrating. Her kidneys required help so we instituted the "Kitty Kitchen Clinic." A saline bag hung above the sink with a long IV tube lassoed around the ceiling hook. My husband, son and I, even our cat-sitter, became proficient at "Juicing the Cat." At first Sweet Pea vehemently objected to being splayed on the kitchen counter top once a day to have her neck pierced with a needle. Once pricked into place, the needle let water run painlessly down the IV tube under Sweet Pea's skin for a few minutes to accumulate in a big water bubble above her left front paw. Sweet Pea quickly adjusted to IV juicing, settled into a compliant mode, and often purred right through the treatment.

Sweet Pea never wandered far from our yard... certainly not toward Linda's house and her six former roommates. But others stole into Sweet Pea's domain. Growling and howling pierced the night near our front door. Did neighborhood cats think they deserved Sweet Pea's goodies? We suspected as much, but my heart dove right to my toes one night when I saw a huge raccoon gobbling down her cat food! Wild animals were starving our poor little-old-lady kitty. Cat bed and food immediately moved into the garage at night.

"Now Sweet Pea is safe from rabid thieves," I thought. Ha! The growling and howling hit a crescendo inside the garage a week later. An escapee had torn out the window screen in two places and Sweet Pea's paw prints decorated the hood of my car. Was our geriatric feline that adventurous? Her food still disappeared too quickly. Could the raccoon climb through the garage window? The next morning, while Sweet Pea basked in the sunshine on the front step, I played detective. I scoured the entire garage for signs of an intruder. As I approached our outdoor refrigerator, I heard a hissing growl that practically sent me screaming down the block. Two beady eyes, a pointy snout, short thumbtack teeth and a foul musky odor surrounded a silvery fur ball hunkered down in a nest of leaves. A big opossum viciously defended his refrigerator corner. Apparently Sweet Pea escaped her nightly garage prison to avoid this unwelcome cellmate! I grabbed a broom and we fought for a good half hour. Finally the opossum surrendered, shuffling outside in a hasty retreat.

I marveled at the toughness of our now twenty-year-old cat. Sweet Pea had the heart of a lioness defending her territory. She survived intruders twice or three times her size. Yet she didn't let the battles color her cozy life in the sun of the front porch or the shade of our back patio. Sweet Pea oozed contentment whether she lay on the counter top for a juicing (now twice a day), or parked above my head on the back of the couch. She lived life one day at a time, in sun or shade, nibbled the same food, enjoyed a grooming, a nap, little things. Content! We both had entered our "later" years. She accepted her one-hundred-forty kitty years better than I was accepting my fifty-seven human ones. I knew I should appreciate my life like Sweet Pea enjoyed hers.

Then, an invisible invasion ambushed us. Sweet Pea and I got cancer. Sweet Pea's tumor grew under her tongue and mine attacked my right breast. I could have surgery, chemo and radiation, Sweet Pea couldn't. I could still eat and drink. Sweet Pea couldn't. So we called Dr. Conners for one last juicing at our home. In the Kitty Kitchen Clinic on her counter top, Sweet Pea slipped into Cat Heaven with a contented purr.

My cancer treatment progressed with more IV lines than I can count, more blood sample sticks than I choose to remember and unending hours in waiting rooms and treatment chairs. Even after chemo, radiation and two years in remission, I have returned to cancer treatment with metastases in my spine and a new attitude.

"How do you stay so positive?" folks sometimes ask. I smile. Memories of my geriatric Sweet Pea flood back. I remember the contented kitty who loved each day and purred through two years of sticks, pricks and IVs.

~Lynne Cooper Sitton

A Cry Goodbye

In the night of death, hope sees a star, and listening love can hear
the rustle of a wing.
~Robert Ingersoll

"Oh look at those adorable white kittens in the television commercial! How precious!"

But instead of running out to buy the product that was being advertised, I wanted to buy a cat.

A litter of white Persian kittens was advertised in the newspaper, and I couldn't wait to drive out to see them. The weekend finally arrived, and the first thing on my list was to return home with a new roommate, since I finally had the wisdom to send my former roommate on his way. After a disastrous relationship that left me in pieces, I had decided that my next roommate would be one who would love me unconditionally.

"Well, which one will you choose?" the owner asked. A difficult decision. Three fluffy kittens floated around in front of me like tiny clouds, two males and one female. The dainty little female with huge topaz eyes tiptoed over... and chose me.

Her name, Chantilly, and how appropriate since at the time my friends and I always wore Chantilly perfume! She was just like the TV kittens. I was given the papers, the important veterinary information, and as I was leaving, the woman announced: "Oh and she prefers homemade cat food. Here is the recipe. It's a long procedure, but she loves the taste!" I never took all that time to make my own dinner! I knew, however, that I would take the time to make hers.

My new friend adjusted quickly to her surroundings, deciding that the extra pillow on my bed was now hers. Every morning as I was getting ready for work, she would sit next to me watching me put on my make-up. It was almost as if she knew which item I would choose next. In the evening, if I was going out with my friends, I'd get a look from her as if to say: "Are you going out again? And when will you be home?" She was always on the stairs waiting for me to return. At night, when I'd take a bubble bath, Chantilly would sit on the edge of the tub trying to capture the soap suds. Such an affectionate little creature, she was always content to be right by my side.

But then I was scheduled for major surgery, which meant a ten-day stay at the hospital. My mother or my sister would go to my apartment to feed Chantilly in my absence. For six years, I had never been away from my cat, and I didn't want her to think that I had deserted her; I knew she would be well taken care of.

My last night in the hospital was a sleepless one; the woman in the next bed was snoring, another one was screaming, and I was given no medication to help blot out any noise. The sound I responded to was a very loud "meow," and I immediately recognized that it belonged to my Chantilly. I smiled because I thought my mother had sneaked her into the hospital for a most welcome visit. I waited and waited, but no one came into the room.

Arriving home the next day, I was disappointed that Chantilly wasn't on the stairs to greet me. "I guess she's mad at me," I remarked to my mother. Calling her name several times, I looked in all her favourite places, but no Chantilly. "I know you're hiding. Chantilly, where are you?" Tears streamed down my mother's face. Very gently, and with great sadness, she said: "Chantilly died last night. I think she missed you so much. It was as if she were trying to call to you, because just before she died she meowed so loudly." And that is the sound I heard at the hospital that very same night... Chantilly's cry goodbye.

~Lee Allen

Making the Connection

Are we not like two volumes of one book?
~Marceline Desbordes-Valmore

When I was six, my parents went away and left me with my grandmother. As the door closed behind them, I cried, "They don't want me anymore."

Gramma tried to soothe me. "Illness," she said. "Failed business. Taxes. Economy. Money."

Meaningless words to a child. What did I know? Gramma wanted me to stop crying and be brave. So I did and I tried.

After about a year, my parents came back and got me. But I still thought they didn't want me anymore.

Years went by and though I gained insight into the world of adults and adult issues, my heart still cried, "they didn't want me anymore."

Eventually, I married, though I never had children. Perhaps I never wanted any child of mine to face "they don't want me anymore."

But I did manage to establish a stable enough home environment that I dared to have cats, those furry child substitutes.

My first cat, Nina, lived to be fifteen and died in my arms.

My second cat, Nora, was a quite ordinary stray with long blackish fur. She showed up in our barn on the day that my first cat died. To this day, I believe that Nina sent out a message to the neighborhood: "There is a cat vacancy in this house."

Nora was so scrawny she looked like a kitten. So I took her to our farm vet. He also provides a clearinghouse for animal control in the area.

He examined her and said, "She's probably got worms. A good dose of wormer will take care of that. Then we'll feed her on a steady diet of good food and she'll plump right up. She's cute. We'll have no trouble finding her a home. But she doesn't act feral. You know our neighborhood is a dumping ground for unwanted animals from the city. Someone probably abandoned her."

They didn't want her anymore, my heart cried. "I'll just take her home with me," I said.

"She'll have issues all her life," he warned, "so you'll have to cater to her fears."

Right along with my own, I thought, and smiled. "No problem."

It wasn't so bad.

She was not as standoffish as many cats can be. I saw that as a plus despite the cat hairs on all my clothes and furniture. She spent a lot of time on my lap. Or in my La-Z-Boy when I was away at work.

Her most distinctive behavior involved her feeder dish. It was attached to one of those hoppers that replenish the food in the dish if the cat scrapes at the opening. Scraping the morsels of food out of the hopper allowed her to eat as much as she liked any time she liked.

Nora refused to scrape.

She needed the reassurance of a hand, preferably mine, reaching down on a regular basis and scraping the food down for her. That *deus ex machina* meant that she was on her own but not alone.

She had a very characteristic meow that meant "I need food." While meowing she would prance back and forth from my feet to her dish.

Typical cat behavior.

What wasn't typical was that she apparently didn't like the sight of the bare bottom of the dish. She would always start meowing when the dish was still about half full.

And then there was the fact that she was quite capable of scraping the food down herself. I actually caught her several times clawing out a morsel or two when she thought I wasn't looking. But as soon as I showed myself, she would sit back on her haunches and meow mournfully at the food dish until I reached down and scraped for her.

"You're a pain," I'd say.

I was sure she was smart enough, being a cat, to translate this into, "I know you just need me to show you I'm here."

"Meow," she'd reply.

I was smart enough, being a cat lover, to translate this into, "Sure, we both know that."

So if my husband and I went away for a vacation, we had to arrange for someone to come to the house every third day and scrape the dry chow out of the hopper for Nora.

This always occasioned such comments as, "What's the matter, is her paw broken?" Or, "My cat can manage that feeder by himself. Is she retarded?"

I invariably replied, "She has abandonment issues."

My friends would nod solemnly. This explanation always sufficed. They made the connection to me, their friend, who they knew also had abandonment issues. But I never made the connection myself. Or I never admitted consciously that I did.

Many years passed and I aged enough to retire. My husband and I began to travel a little bit more and stay away a little bit longer.

Getting someone out to our somewhat remote farm just to scrape food out of a hopper for a cat became increasingly more difficult.

And Nora became more difficult. She began to refuse the dry chow. Her aging digestive system needed fresh food every day.

Eventually, we had to make a trip to the West Coast to visit my oldest friend, who was suffering from Alzheimer's. I hated to leave Nora for three weeks at that point in her life. But I feared that my friend would soon not even recognize me.

We tried to make the best arrangement for her comfort and care that we could. We took her to a cat resort run by a vet who cared for her personally and watched over her health and wellbeing.

But Nora didn't understand the provisions we made for her. She saw our long disappearance as abandonment. Why wouldn't she? She had no idea where we had gone or why.

We came home to a cat as thin and weak as when we originally found her in our barn. Her heart was broken because she thought we had abandoned her.

I finally made the connection.

My parents hadn't abandoned me any more than I had abandoned Nora. They too had tried to make the best arrangements for my care that they could. They had loved me just as much as I loved my cat.

A lifelong weight lifted off my heart as it finally made emotional sense out of what my head knew.

~Karin L. Frank

Just Around the Corner

There is in every true woman's heart a spark of heavenly fire,
which lies dormant in the broad daylight of prosperity; but which kindles up,
and beams and blazes in the dark hour of adversity.
~Washington Irving

Named for Sir Edmund Hillary, the first man to climb Mount Everest, it seemed fitting that the big cat's favorite spot was atop the gate. From this regal position, Edmund watched over the patio and reminded everyone of his presence. The other cats recognized his dominance. Much larger than all the others, the gray king of the patio flexed his muscles and reminded them of his power. He had only to arch his back and any who thought of mutiny quickly dissipated.

But not one of our feline beauties appealed to Edmund. Perhaps none measured up to his kingly standards. He stretched himself across the gate and gazed at them as if they didn't even exist, that is, until "she" came.

She appeared at the food bowl from nowhere. With petite and delicate features, she seemed an unlikely choice for a queen; but Edmund was smitten from the beginning. Just the slightest "meow" from her had him down from the gate and by her side. Stealing away to places unknown to humans, Edmund made the new feline his true love. Weeks later, we found the kittens.

From that time on, we called Edmund's queen "Little Mama." The other cats realized that she was Edmund's favorite and they were obvious in their jealousy, blocking her from the food bowl and water dish. Because Little Mama was so small, she was no match for her rivals and stepped back, accepting their verdict.

And then from around the corner, the king appeared. He had left his throne to walk among the commoners. Cats scattered to make way for him. Edmund swaggered across the patio and lay down by the food and water, purring affectionately to Little Mama as if to say, "Come and eat, my sweet." He remained there until she had eaten her fill. And only then did he eat.

This scene was replayed day after day and grew so commonplace that Edmund no longer had to physically lie beside the bowls. The other cats knew that his queen had to be recognized, lest the king himself strut around the corner into their presence. A day came, however, that broke the cycle.

I peered out the window one morning to see Edmund dragging himself across the patio. His body was battered and bloody, so much so that I could only assume he had been hit by a car. His leg was broken and it appeared to be completely separated from his skeleton, attached only by skin and fur. Somehow, the king had made it home. He lay at the foot of the gate, too weak to jump to the top. We knew the inevitable—Edmund had to be relieved of his pain. We could not allow him to suffer.

For days after Edmund's death, Little Mama looked for him. At first, she continued to eat and drink as the reigning queen despite Edmund's absence. The cats allowed her near the food and water bowls, suspiciously looking toward Edmund's vacated perch atop the gate as if they expected to see him stealthily approach at any moment.

After a week, they were sure he would not return, and the queen's subjects turned on her, literally blocking the food and water dishes with their bodies. Little Mama tried to nudge her way between them, but the cats did not relent. A hungry Little Mama reluctantly retreated.

The hierarchical change was evident. Little Mama knew it too and hid. I looked everywhere that I thought she might be, calling her name over and over. After more than seventy-two hours, I was afraid she was gone forever.

At last, a hungry Little Mama appeared. On a porch located on the opposite side of the house from the patio, Little Mama approached me unobserved by the cats that wished her to starve. I brought food and water and watched her eat and drink, relieved that she had figured out a solution. As she nuzzled my leg in appreciation, I stroked her neck and thought how proud I was of her. She had learned to survive without Edmund's protection. "A good lesson," I whispered to her. "There are no guarantees as to what may lie around the corner."

Much like Edmund, I had always sought to protect those I loved. There were many times that I stationed myself just around the corner from my children so that I could rush in to protect them if necessary. I told myself that I would always be there to save them from harm, to shield them from pain. Perhaps, somewhere deep within my soul, I knew better, though I didn't want to admit it. A phone call forced me to face reality.

"Hello," I said nonchalantly.

After an odd silence, the highway patrolman spoke softly on the other end of the line. "Are you able to go immediately to your daughter's house?" he asked. "Her husband has been involved in a fatal accident."

The words sank in slowly. "Fatal?" I asked. "You mean he is dead?"

"Yes, ma'am," he continued. "Can you leave right now?"

"Of course."

I recall hanging up the phone and running to get my husband. After that, memories are less clear, the events from one moment blending into the next. I am sure that we called family. I am positive that we wept bitterly.

Despite the heartache of such immeasurable loss, my daughter had to make decisions for her husband's burial service. She wanted to say goodbye in private before the wake, which would be open to friends and other family. But it was several days before we received word that a visit had been arranged.

As we drove to the funeral home, I wished I could spare my daughter the pain of what she was about to experience. We parked and said a prayer for strength, then walked slowly down the sidewalk to the front entrance. A very kind attendant met us in the hall and offered to accompany us to the casket. "It's just around the corner," she said softly.

No amount of mothering could soften what lay ahead — that day, or in the weeks to come. I could not change what waited around the corner. I could not protect her. I could not hurt in her stead. Like Little Mama, my daughter would face life without her king.

And she would learn to survive.

~Elaine Ernst Schneider

77

Cat under a Hot Tin Roof

Grow flowers of gratitude in the soil of prayer.
~Verbena Woods

On June 27th, a truck from our local charity, St. Vincent de Paul, in Phoenix, arrived to pick up a mattress and box spring set I was donating after a move to a new home. I put my dogs in their crates and watched the front door to make sure none of my four cats got out as the men loaded the items onto the truck.

Life went on until Friday evening as I was clipping everyone's toenails. I counted five, not six, sets of paws. I went searching for Milli Vanilli, my shy Himalayan cat. I checked all her usual hiding spots as well as closets, cabinets, the garage, the backyard, behind appliances, but she was nowhere to be found. I started to get a little anxious because I couldn't pinpoint the last time I had actually seen her. It's not unusual to go a day or so without seeing her because she likes to hide. I thought back to each day that week. I knew I hadn't seen Milli since the mattress and box spring were picked up. I thought maybe she had hidden in the box spring because part of the backing had come loose.

I tried to reach someone at the charity that evening and I left messages regarding Milli on every phone number posted on the website related to thrift store donations. I then called one of the thrift stores and was told no one would be available until Monday. Since I wasn't one hundred percent sure Milli really was on the truck, I also I put ads in both local papers as well as some websites for lost pets, and went to the pound and Humane Society. I also posted fliers and knocked on all the doors in my neighborhood. I couldn't find Milli anywhere so I became even more convinced that Milli had stowed away on the truck.

On Monday, July 2nd, I called the charity in the morning and told the operator I thought my cat had accidentally been picked up on the truck on the 27th and asked if they would they please find the mattress and box spring I donated and check it for Milli. I know she probably thought I was one crazy cat lady but she took the report anyway and said someone would get back to me. I am very impatient and Milli had already been missing for four days in the heat of summer in Arizona so I called back three hours later to see if there was any news. Shirley told me that someone had seen Milli on the truck on Wednesday and she got spooked and ran into the warehouse. I drove to the warehouse with Milli's picture and her crate to begin the search.

The warehouse was massive, probably the size of a football field, with thousands of boxes, pieces of furniture, etc. I was not hopeful about finding Milli. I searched for two hours, but there was so much noise and commotion that the dock supervisor suggested I come back at around seven when it would be quieter. He also set up a humane trap with tuna fish in it. At around nine or ten, I went to the security desk, and explained the story to the guard, left my name, number and asked the guard to please watch for my cat on the cameras and call me if he saw her no matter what time it was. I went home extremely discouraged and concerned for Milli's safety.

At one in the morning, I got a call from the security guard. He had spotted a cat on the surveillance camera. I rushed to the warehouse where the guard showed me the footage and there was Milli making her movie debut, looking pretty good, I might add. We went into the warehouse and looked and called for Milli but she wouldn't come out. We went back and watched the cameras. I went home around four to get my dog, who was a pretty good tracker, but he couldn't find her either. I knew she wouldn't come out with all the people working during the day so I went to work.

After work, I took one of my other cats in her crate to the warehouse thinking Milli might respond to her. No luck. The next day was July 4th and the temperature was supposed to hit 115. The only people at the warehouse would be the security staff. I made sure they still had my name and number. I had done everything I could think of to find her. I had prayed for her safety but I felt like I wasn't being heard. I wanted to call my church and add her to our prayer list but I was afraid they would ask too many questions and realize Milli was a cat. I searched the Internet for special prayers to recite for missing pets. Instead, I found a place where people would pray for lost or sick pets, prayersforpets.org.

I posted Milli's story very late on July 3rd. I believed, even though she hadn't been seen in a while, that she would be found and for the first time in days, I was at peace. I knew I had done everything I could and it was now out of my hands. On July 4th I was flooded with the most touching prayers for Milli. There were no Milli sightings on the 4th but I was still hopeful and ready to go back the evening of July 5th to resume the search at the warehouse.

On the 5th, I received a call from the charity. Milli had been spotted again and they were trying to catch her. I hung up the phone and headed back to the warehouse. By the time I got there, they had caught her, and put her under a milk crate until I could get there. She was smelly, dirty and her eyes were matted with tears. She was downright boney because she hadn't eaten in eight days. I put her in her crate from home and took her around to all the people that helped get the word out to find her. It was a very happy ending and so many things could have happened resulting in a different, not so happy ending. I was so impressed with the determination and the compassion of all the people at St. Vincent de Paul who helped find my kitty and the people who offered up prayers for her. They are amazing people who really put faith and love into action. They acted as though finding Milli was as important to them as it was to me.

Milli did have to go to the vet for hydration but she came home, ate and drank well, and slept and purred by my side all night.

This whole experience taught me a lot of things. First, always check furniture for stowaways before you donate it, but more importantly, I was reminded of the amazing power of prayer and the goodness and compassion of total strangers which I had really begun to doubt. Her adventure proved to me that God still does perform miracles and answer prayers, and how much He cares about even the smallest of creatures.

~Brenda Denton

78

Victory Is Mine

One must love a cat on its own terms.
~Paul Gray

Pet people fall into two categories: dog lovers and cat lovers. As a youngster, I chose my side: dogs rule. Later in life, a mutual love of dogs was one of the many things that connected my husband Dan and me. In fact, the first bundle of joy we brought home as newlyweds was a ten-pound Golden Retriever puppy who never lost his youthful energy.

Sadly, our Golden died suddenly when he was eight, leaving our family pet-less for several years. In time, my husband and children, ages three and six, began pining for another dog. The idea tugged at my heartstrings—for a millisecond. Despite their pleas and fervent promises of care, I knew who'd ultimately be responsible for said puppy. Me. Dog lover or not, as a mother of two small children, a puppy threatened to capsize the boat of sanity I struggled to keep afloat.

However, I couldn't shake the feeling that pets and kids are like peanut butter and jelly. They're perfect together. Then one day an idea sparked—an idea that surprised even me.

We'd get a cat.

Yes, a cat would fit the bill perfectly: cute and furry (for the kids), and low maintenance (for me). I was happy. The kids were delighted. Dan? Well, if I'm a dog person at heart, he's a dog person—period.

Grudgingly, Dan gave in on one condition: that I sign a "contract" stating I would not become a "cat person" and promising one day we'd actually get a dog. A bit dramatic, but fair. I signed and started making plans.

The kids and I scoured pet shelters looking for the perfect cat. Finally, we came across a gentle, tiger-striped one who stole our heart. We knew we'd found our pet and named her Casey.

Naturally we were thrilled, but within a few days Casey began to sneeze and seemed congested. A trip to our long-time vet uncovered an upper respiratory infection. Dr. K treated her with IV fluids and advised, "Give it a few days. Things should get better." We did; they didn't. Casey stopped eating. Even attempts at hand-feeding failed. We returned for more medicine and hydration. As the days passed, her condition only worsened. Angry that I'd been given a sick cat, I called the shelter to complain. They agreed to take her back but admitted they'd probably euthanize her. Thanks, but no thanks.

By now Casey had stopped grooming. According to Dr. K, this signaled that a cat has given up. After almost two weeks of interventions, medically he'd done all he could. Time and options were running out, but Dr. K still had hope. He looked into her tired eyes and declared, "There's something special about this cat. I think all the attention may be stressing her out. Let's give her the weekend. Put her in a quiet room with her food and leave her alone. Let her sort it out and choose to fight... or not." He didn't say it, but I knew what "or not" meant.

So far, cat ownership hadn't provided the low-maintenance pet experience I'd agreed to. Yet that didn't matter anymore. During all the worrying and attempts to nurse Casey back to health, my canine preferences melted away and I'd fallen in love with this sweet, orange kitty. As I lay beside her on the floor of her quiet retreat, my aching heart pleaded, "You have to get better. Please choose to live."

By Saturday morning Casey perked up a bit. That evening she gave the answer I'd been hoping for: she licked her fur. The wise and compassionate wisdom of Dr. K proved just the right prescription. By Sunday, she started to eat kibble from her bowl. Yes! You're going to be okay!

It's been seven years since our "fight or flight" weekend. Physically, Casey made a full recovery and hasn't been to the vet for a sick visit since. Emotionally, she's still a timid cat, ever-wary of impending danger. The slightest noise sends her scurrying toward one of her well-worn escape routes. She presents herself in her own timing and some days is out of sight so much, I almost forget we have a cat. But often, when the house is quiet she'll appear. And in the safety of nighttime she'll leap onto my bed and curl up beside me, purring all the while. We have a bond, she and I.

During the years, in her quiet ways, Casey has taught me a lot about life. Through her I've learned:

- Worries melt away when you curl up in a patch of sun on the floor.
- Dogs aren't better than cats and vice-versa. They're just different. You can find love in your heart for both. The same can be said for different types of people.
- Those I might easily write off as standoffish or aloof can actually make wonderfully sweet companions.
- Sometimes I just need to let a friendship be what it is.

Recently, Casey taught me the most powerful lesson yet.

There's a small six-sided aquarium on our kitchen counter. I often find Casey sitting nearby, watching the goldfish—perhaps planning her next meal. One afternoon I heard an unusual noise in the kitchen and went to investigate. Imagine my surprise when I discovered our afraid-of-her-own-shadow kitty perched regally on top of the fish tank like a queen on her throne, her body barely able to fit on the cover.

Besides causing me to break into unbridled laughter, her image spoke volumes. In that moment I saw Casey shed her fur coat of fear, don a robe of glory, and triumphantly declare, "Victory is mine!"

We all have this choice, don't we? Usually we can't control our circumstances, but we can control our responses. Despite the brokenness, fears and burdens we carry, we can choose to give up in the darkness... or keep fighting through to the light. To run from trouble...

or curl up safely next to those we love. To stand by and longingly watch opportunities swim past us... or seize the high ground and brazenly stake our claim.

So thanks, Casey. The next time fear and uncertainty start to gain the upper hand, I'm following the example of the bravest scaredy-cat I've ever met.

~Kelli Regan

One Cat's Soul

No heaven will not ever Heaven be
Unless my cats are there to welcome me.
~Author Unknown

I was seventeen when a pastor told me, "Animals don't have souls and when they die, they turn back to the dust of which they were created." I didn't want to believe it. I tried not to believe it. I mean, what kind of a God would be that cruel? I was confused and torn. Until the day one cat showed me the truth.

Back then, my parents were officially divorced, I was in a new city of my mother's choosing, I was in a new school (a private school no less), and I didn't know anybody. I felt completely alone and my mom thought a cat would help.

"I went to the animal shelter today," she said. "And I found a cat just perfect for you."

We drove down to the shelter and when we arrived, she led me to a cage where a big, fat chocolate Siamese stared at me with bight, blue eyes.

"What do you think?" my mom asked.

"I don't know," I said. "How old is he?" I didn't think my mom actually meant a "cat." I was thinking more along the lines of a "kitten."

"He's an older cat, but Heather... He is so pretty. And look...." she pointed to his paws. "He has six toes on each paw. That means he's special."

Before I could say anything, she pulled open the cage, grabbed him, and plopped him in my arms. And that's how I first met Cappuccino.

For the next three years, Cappuccino saw me through high school, the start of college, a couple of apartments, several jobs, and even some boyfriends. I never really thought of his age. I just knew him as a grumpy old man. He was overweight. He was temperamental. He didn't like a whole lot of people. But, he was a permanent fixture in my unstable life.

And then one morning everything changed.

I woke up to something violently jerking on my bed. I jumped up and saw that it was Cappuccino having a seizure. I didn't know what to do. I held him until it passed, but he had another one and then another one. After the third time, it seemed to have stopped.

I took him to the vet. The doctor told me he found fluid in his ears. He explained that it might be applying pressure to his brain, causing the seizures. And the best part was there was medicine for it. I immediately relaxed. In my mind, the problem was fixable, life would go on as usual, and, after a couple of weeks, it seemed just that when the seizures completely stopped.

But I was wrong.

I went into the living room one morning and saw Cappuccino sprawled out. I called his name, waiting for him to flick his ear or flick his tail. But, he didn't move. I held my breath as I picked him up. His body went limp in my hands. His eyes were open in an unblinking stare. I thought he was dead. But that's when I noticed... he was still breathing.

I held Cappuccino and cried the whole day and night, praying and praying that he would snap out it. But by the next day, he hadn't changed.

I called the veterinarian. They told me that I could bring him in, but it didn't look good. I felt like I was swimming in a pool. I moved around the apartment in a daze, slowly gathering my purse and then my keys. Every second felt precious and priceless because I knew I was counting down the seconds of Cappuccino's final moments. And the pastor's words kept swirling in my mind like a vicious merry-go-round: "Animals don't have souls; they turn to dust...."

I tried to keep it together, but I couldn't. I cried uncontrollably as I sat in the waiting room with Cappuccino wrapped in a pink towel. About five minutes later, they moved me into a private room; apparently I was upsetting other people.

The veterinarian came in. She gave me a sympathetic smile and pulled some Kleenex from her jacket pocket.

"I don't want him to die!" I cried. "I just can't believe that nothing can be done to make him better!"

She opened his mouth and shined a light in both his eyes. She sighed and said, "I'm going to be honest with you. I don't think there is anything that can be done, but I'll ask the other doctors what they think." She took him and left.

I prayed for a miracle, but when she returned her eyes told me that there wouldn't be a miracle today.

"It's neurological," she said. "Cappuccino had what would be equivalent to a stroke."

"But he was getting better," I pleaded. "The seizures stopped."

"He may have had a very severe one. He's in a coma state."

"Nothing can be done?" I asked. "Nothing at all?"

She petted Cappuccino and said, "We could try and bring him out of it, but it would be very expensive. It could cost thousands of dollars and there's no guarantee that he'd ever be the same."

I barely had thirty bucks in my bank account, let alone thousands. I only had one option left.

I took a deep breath. "I have no choice but to put him to sleep."

"Is that what you want to do?" she asked.

I nodded my head, avoiding her gaze.

"It really is for the best," she said.

She left me alone for about ten minutes to say goodbye to him. The whole time I cried and petted him, telling him that I didn't want him to go.

The door opened. She came in with a syringe in her hand.

"He won't feel any pain," she said as the needle hovered above him.

The tears poured down my cheeks.

I didn't watch her give him the shot. I kept my face close to his and tried to etch his blue eyes in my memory before death glazed them over. And in seconds, death came like a flood. His eyes dulled. Cappuccino was gone.

But just then something passed through me.

It was like a breeze. It touched the top of my head and rippled down towards the tips of my toes. I felt warm, cuddly warm, and I had the greatest sense of peace, joy, and happiness. It was so pure and powerful... like nothing I have ever experienced before and not like anything I could ever adequately describe. I felt Cappuccino there. He felt free, completely boundless, and happy.

The feeling lasted only a moment. I looked at the doctor to see if she felt it too, but she said nothing, except that it was over and Cappuccino was no longer in pain.

I looked down at his lifeless body. I knew that he was gone. I felt him leave. But, I also knew that he hadn't disappeared and he wasn't going to turn to dust like he never mattered at all... like he never mattered to me. I was touched by the soul of a cat. That's all the proof I'll ever need.

~Heather J. Cuthbertson

Bug

If we treated everyone we meet with the same affection
we bestow upon our favorite cat, they, too, would purr.
~Martin Buxbaum

O
ur new kitten wouldn't eat. I thought she must just be scared. Ten weeks old, she had spent most of her life in a bush with her feral mother and littermates; it would take time for her to adjust to life with people. I offered her a variety of foods and tried not to worry. A Siamese Ragdoll mix, we called her Bug because that's what she looked like with the dark mask around her blue eyes and a smooth coat of ivory fur.

A day or so passed, and she purred whenever I held her; she meowed when I talked to her. But still she wouldn't eat. I took her to a vet who gave Bug antibiotics and said in twenty-four hours, she "should bounce right back." But the next day, not only had she not bounced back, she seemed so much worse I rushed her to another vet. When this one checked her temperature — 106 — the thermometer came out bloody. We both gasped.

"This kitten has panleukopenia," she said. "Feline distemper. It's fatal ninety percent of the time. Even if the kitten somehow survives the virus, there could be neurological damage. I recommend that you put her to sleep."

I flinched as I looked at Bug's tiny face and listened to this prognosis of doom, delivered by someone as emotionless as the cold white walls of the exam room. In less than a day, how had the outlook changed from "bounce right back" to "put her to sleep?" As the vet continued to explain about dehydration and secondary infections, I knew I couldn't make this decision alone. Bug had been a gift for my daughter on her fifteenth birthday. I needed to talk to her, though I could guess what she'd say.

I drove home with tears streaming down my face, Bug in her crate beside me. I tried not to look at her. Why of all the kittens in the county had we picked one that was so sick? I felt angry at the shelter for giving us an ill pet, angry at the first vet who said she only had an infection, angry at myself for not buying a Siamese kitten from a private home.

At a stoplight I forced myself to look at Bug. Even in the presence of my outrage, I had never seen such calm and trust as I did in her eyes. And I realized none of this was her fault, this tiny creature that weighed just two pounds now. She didn't want to be sick; neither did I. Suddenly there was no decision to make. I saw in her eyes not the ninety percent chance of dying but the ten percent chance of living. "I won't give up on you," I said out loud. Maybe I was just setting myself up for more disappointment. In the past few years I had seen plenty of that with my own illness. But I had to try and save her.

The next day, my daughter went with me to a third vet. This vet's office was big, beautiful, and expensive. My neighbor had made the sound of a cash register, "ka ching, ka ching," when she spoke of the place. After two years of not being able to work, cost was an issue. But I had remembered that the shelter gave me a free two-month policy from a pet insurance company to cover shelter-related illnesses, which this was. I would max out the $500 coverage, and then some, to help Bug.

The first thing the new vet did was order a blood test to confirm panleukopenia, which, because of vaccinations, had become as rare in cats as measles in humans. Stressing the phrase "no guarantees," he agreed to keep Bug in the hospital, on an IV, and give her fluids and antibiotics to help her ride out the virus, though he too said if she exhibited "a failure to thrive," she should be put down. At home I prayed every time I thought of her, but weakly. When the phone rang, I feared it was the vet calling to say she had died.

My daughter seemed naively hopeful—after all, she was a teenager, not a kindergartner. "When are we going to pick up Bug?" she kept asking, as if there was no doubt her kitten would come home. And Bug did return, after four days, three nights, and $489. "I told you so!" I'm sure my daughter said. But the kitten seemed so weak and frail, I wondered if we had made a mistake even keeping her alive. She definitely wasn't thriving.

The skin of her right ear had developed an infection and lay limply flopped over. The surface felt stiff, and when I tried to clean it, brown fur came off as well. Twice a day I had to clean blood off the naked ear. Three times a day my daughter and I used a syringe to squirt food and water into her mouth because she still wouldn't eat. All she wanted to do was sleep, a feeling I could identify with.

My sister said it was important that a sick animal feel the will to live. Wasn't that true for all of us? My daughter and I spent hours holding Bug. We told her we loved her. We combed her and sang to her. And slowly, my hope, which itself seemed like a sick animal, grew stronger as Bug did. Funny, but during this time a character on my soap opera read an Emily Dickinson poem where hope was referred to as "the thing with feathers that perches in the soul." That's exactly what my hope for her survival felt like, a little bird in my heart, faintly singing, until finally one day, the bird took wing.

Four days after her return, Bug walked over to her food bowl and ate on her own for the first time. I could have danced on the roof! The next day, she washed her little face and batted a felt toy that my son had made. Day by day, bite by bite, she got stronger. The ear that the vet said would never stand up again, perked back into place. Bug is six years old now and so plump and healthy that no one would ever guess she had once been so ill. She has a sweet and gentle nature and makes us laugh the way she sleeps on her back, paws folded against her chest, as if mocking death.

Shortly after her recovery, I felt a sudden panic as she slept one day in my arms. What if I had made the wrong decision and had her put down? But through her breathing, I heard a voice speak: "her life was never in YOUR hands," and I knew a higher power had brought us together. I had given Bug the care she needed to heal her ravaged body; she had given me the hope I needed to trust that my life was in His hands too. Most importantly, she had taught me never to accept a doctor's diagnosis of defeat.

~Linda Delmont

Saved by a Stray

Love makes your soul crawl out from its hiding place.
~Zora Neale Hurston

I grew up around cats. My mother had hers since she was nineteen and in her first marriage. That cat was with her through her second marriage, the birth of two children, and second divorce. When my mother's first feline died, she went through a string of cats as her mental facilities began to break down and her bipolar disorder gained control. In hindsight it seems that as each cat passed, a piece of my mother's sanity and will to live was buried with them. My mother never felt her children were as good as her pets and she reminded my brother and me about that often. We could never love her as much as her cats could, could never please her like they did. And, as much as we tried, my brother and I could never make our mother laugh as much as one cat, Sammy, did when he leapt about the house doing kittenish twirls before settling into her lap to purr and sleep.

My mother became so unstable and emotionally unavailable that I might as well have been an orphan in my own home. There were wild tantrums where she'd scream and break dishes or the television, or where she'd spout profanities and hit us. She also pulled us out of bed and from a sound sleep to throw my brother and me into cold showers while jabbing erratically at our hair with scissors.

One summer I went away to a Salvation Army camp with a number of other lost children, those from fragile households who needed respite from the constant insecurity of living with abusive parents or in a state of poverty. Everyone was guarded, too accustomed to being hurt by letting people in. These lessons of betrayal were learned before the age of ten. While I was at this camp my mother found Penny, a tuxedo kitten that appeared on the doorstep in the rain. My mother was ecstatic that she had a new soul mate. But Penny wasn't for her; that wasn't God's plan. When I returned home from camp, Penny and I locked eyes and from then on Penny never left my side.

I had never known what it was like to be so close to another living being. Penny loved me, and I her, and this did not sit well with my mother. When my mother would scream at me, this little bundle of fur would get between us and hiss and spit. My mother would then begin to scream at Penny instead. When my mother hurt me, as she often did, it was Penny who came to kiss the wounds or simply lie down next to me and purr as if she was telling me that eventually things would work out the way they were supposed to. Through every tear, cut, and bruise Penny was at my side. She also tried to prevent as much harm as possible. Besides hissing at my mother, she would kill every bee or ant that came near me. But some things she couldn't protect me from. My mother was a big imposing woman and one day she threw Penny off the balcony. Penny refused to die. I went down to retrieve her and she was bloody from the fall, but merely crawled into my lap and began purring.

I graduated from high school and went on to college with Penny still my constant companion. After college, I moved in briefly with a friend and found out that Penny spent her nights in my doorway keeping my friend's cat (known for scratching people as they slept) out of the room. She never wavered in her devotion.

Eventually I moved to Manhattan to start a new life. I had a job, friends, and a lot of flashbacks from my childhood. I entered therapy and still remember my therapist's first few words, "Wow, you're so well adjusted for what happened." He said that he'd seen people who had a lot less childhood trauma who couldn't function in society as well as I did. With each story I told of my childhood he said I lived a life consistent with being a prisoner of war. Yet, I survived, and the reason for my survival was Penny. When I thought there was nothing left in the world but pain, there was Penny at my side purring and comforting me. She protected me. She showed me that love existed.

When Penny died after a long battle with cancer I entered grief counseling. I told the counselor how wonderful Penny was.

"You realize she was your mother," the counselor said. It made sense. My mother was emotionally unavailable and downright dangerous to her children, and the only memory I have of my father resides in the scar under my lip. But Penny always took care of me.

"So I'm an orphan?" I asked. I had Penny for eleven years. I was in my twenties and not ready to be without my mother, my real mother.

I went back to therapy and my therapist agreed that Penny was indeed the mother figure in my life, a direct contrast to the normal role a pet plays as a surrogate child. I was Penny's child and she taught me well. Despite the abuse I suffered at the hands of my "human" mother, I grew up realizing that love exists and there is hope. I learned how to comfort and be comforted. I learned that sometimes you don't need words, just warm paws of support and the knowledge that there is something else out there. Because of this, I too can love.

This lesson is carved in marble for all to see. I buried Penny in Hartsdale Pet Cemetery and on her tombstone is written, "Penny taught me love." There is no better lesson I could have learned, and no better teacher.

~Victorya Chase

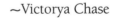

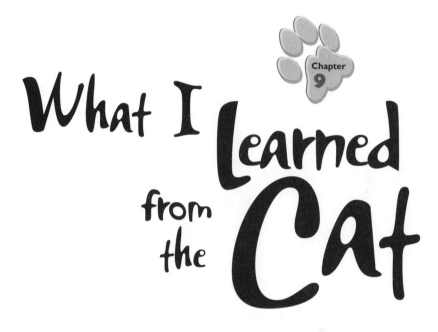

What I Learned from the Cat

Chapter 9

Learning about Love

*Nobody has ever measured, not even poets,
how much the human heart can hold.*

~Zelda Fitzgerald

82

Romeow and Julicat

True love stories never have endings.
~Richard Bach

Cats have no emotions. At least, that's what my husband
once claimed. I argued that my two cats experience emotions. They feel anger (a pair of amber daggers after an
application of flea treatment), fear (the neighbor's dog chased them
up a tree), and happiness (contented purring after a hearty meal). He
conceded my point, but maintained his opinion that cats don't feel
love. My tuxedo cat, Sebastian, would teach him otherwise.

The rumble of a diesel truck broke my concentration one spring
day. I glanced out the window and saw a young man carrying boxes
from a U-Haul truck into the duplex next door.

"Ah," I said aloud, "we're getting a new neighbor."

I turned back to my work, oblivious to the activity next door,
until an unfamiliar meow caught my attention. I looked across the
side yard at the duplex and smiled. A young gray cat with a white
face and pink nose sat inside on the windowsill, staring wide-eyed at
its new surroundings. So much to investigate in the backyard — frol-
icking squirrels, darting butterflies, and birds flitting from trees to
ground searching for building materials.

I stepped outside to introduce myself. Squeakette, my female
cat, followed me out the door.

The young man's name was Rob. His work brought him to
Tampa from Miami.

"I see you have a kitty," I said, pointing to the properly perched feline. "We have two, Sebastian and Squeakette. They're littermates."

Rob smiled and swept a hand toward the window. "Meet Juliet. She's an indoor lady. The window is her TV."

I laughed and said, "The wildlife in our eighty-year-old oak trees will keep her entertained."

I allowed Sebastian and Squeakette outside for daily supervised romps. Sebastian enjoyed climbing trees, chasing squirrels, and catching lizards. Squeakette seemed content to sit in the ferns, watching the hustle and bustle of the bio-network, pouncing on an occasional unsuspecting lizard. She rarely ate one, preferring, I suspect, to catch and release for another day. Sebastian hunted with a "don't-mind-if-I-do" attitude toward eating his prey. Lizards carry liver flukes, so I tried to prevent my cats from ingesting them.

When I caught Sebastian with a lizard in his mouth, I grabbed him. Applying just enough pressure to the sides of his jaws, I forced his mouth open to free the captive snack.

A few days after Rob moved in, I accompanied my cats to the backyard for their playtime. Sebastian snared his first catch of the day. I was about to grab him, when he stopped mid-snatch, letting his prey escape. He stood frozen, his amber eyes wide. I saw Juliet in her window gazing at him.

I watched, astounded. Juliet followed Sebastian with her eyes as he took one step, and then another, forward. He stopped and looked up at her again. If my cat could speak, he might have recited: "But soft! What light through yonder window breaks? It is the east and Juliet is the sun...." Like Romeo in Shakespeare's play, my Sebastian was thunderstruck. And Juliet had thrown the lightning bolt.

He seemed shy as he approached her, unusual behavior for my confident alpha cat. Standing on his hind legs, his white-mittened front paws on the wall beneath her window, he peered up at her. Her gaze never left him, and their eyes locked in communication.

Every day thereafter, Sebastian watched for her from the window in our home office. When she appeared on her windowsill, he threw a feline temper tantrum, knocking over the kitchen trashcan, pounding the door with his front paws, and meowing—nay, bellow-ing—until my husband or I let him out, supervised or not.

It took him several days to muster the courage to approach Juliet, until one day he leapt the four feet to the outside sill of her window and landed with masculine grace.

Every day, they sat gazing lovingly at each other through the screen, she inside, and he outside. I wondered what passed between them. Did they merely look into each other's eyes? Did he whisper sweet mewings to her? Did they love each other? With Sebastian neu-tered and Juliet spayed, I knew it couldn't be a call of the wild.

Even my husband watched in dismay. "What's going on with those two cats?" He scratched his head. "But cats can't feel love... can they?"

Juliet's owner had seen them, too. When he walked past the bedroom one day, he glanced into the room and stopped, surprised at the scene in the window. Rob said he watched the sweethearts for several minutes. "I've never seen anything like it before."

Five months later, their romance in full bloom, Rob told us his company asked him to move again, this time across the country. My heart sank. I wondered how Sebastian would react to Juliet's leaving.

On moving day, Rob knocked on our door to tell us goodbye. "You won't believe what happened," he said.

Having loaded everything into the U-Haul truck, he went back into the apartment for Juliet and saw Sebastian on the bedroom win-dow's ledge.

"It touched my heart to see your cat peering inside, searching for his paramour. I found Juliet in the living room on top of her cage. She seemed to know it was time to leave. I picked her up, carried her into the bedroom, and said, 'Would you like to say goodbye?' She leapt from my arms, clawing me with her hind feet." He showed us the lines of scratches on his forearm. "Juliet landed on the windowsill with a soft, cheerless meow. The cats nuzzled each other through the screen for several moments, and then Juliet turned to me as if to say, 'Okay, let's go before my heart breaks more than I can bear.' Sebastian watched me put Juliet into her cage and leave the room, his expression beyond sadness. I think he knew he'd never see his lady again."

For months after Juliet moved away and the new tenant moved in, I often caught Sebastian sitting on Juliet's window ledge, peering into the apartment in search of his lady. The new tenant didn't mind having the "Peeping Sebastian" after I explained his reason for being there.

Sebastian marked the small shrub outside that window as his territory. Other male cats were allowed on the property, but not near Juliet's window, which he guarded until his death.

Even now, when my husband and I walk through the backyard and see that window, he reminds me of the lesson Sebastian taught him... that cats do indeed fall in love.

~Janet L. Rockey

Where's that Elvis?

The smart cat doesn't let on that he is.
~H.G. Frommer

"Where is he? Where's that Elvis? I'm gonna get him." My son raced down the steps and grabbed Elvis off the couch where he was curled up in a tight ball dozing away. He started nuzzling Elvis, placing his face in close proximity as he talked. His voice rang out with affectionate tones sliding up and down the musical scale. Elvis replied, using his own vocalizing tones.

Elvis is my chubby, twenty-one-pound, seven-year-old tabby cat. He responds to my son's affection by placing both of his paws against my son's cheeks, staring straight into his eyes.

Elvis was hugged and rocked while my son talked to him for about five minutes before he placed him back down on the couch, where Elvis immediately curled right back into his tight ball and dozed off again. To many, this might've seemed like nothing out of the ordinary, but Elvis and my son have a certain bond which defies the odds.

Elvis has allowed my son to demonstrate physical signs of affection, and experience the emotion of love. And even more, he's encouraged my son to verbally communicate.

My son is diagnosed with Asperger's syndrome, a high function-ing form of autism. He resists receiving or giving any signs of affection with family members. Even as an infant he struggled against being cradled in someone's arms or being swaddled in blankets, preferring to be left alone on a blanket. Tactile stimulation was too intense for his body. He still abhors physical affection at age twenty-three, and will grunt and push you away if you attempt to offer him any.

No matter what time of day, Elvis doesn't resist my son's overly long hugs or tormenting play, and my son will eagerly search him out to play or cuddle.

My son prefers not to communicate using lengthy conversations; instead he uses three-word sentences or grunting tones, speaking in a monotone. Elvis encourages my son to release wonderful affectionate phrases. "What are you doing now, you fat cat? What do you want standing outside my door, you brat?"

Elvis waddles around the house because of his chubby shape, and would rather spend his days relaxing and sleeping than exercising. Still he eagerly takes the climb upstairs to go to my son's room, and will sit outside meowing until my son opens the door. They share a conversation, some wrestling, and then Elvis waddles back downstairs to me.

You see, Elvis declared himself to be my cat even though my husband was the one who wanted a cat. I wasn't keen over getting any pet, especially a fur ball cat. In fact, I couldn't stand cats, with their sneaky behavior, claw scratching and destructive habits, and all the cat hair they leave on furniture and clothes. I agreed, only because my husband swore he'd take on all the cat care.

Our first night home when Elvis was a six-week kitten, he managed to climb onto our bed and plant his body right on top of my head. Every night he assumed this same position while I lay there, utterly afraid to move, waking up with a stiff neck from my forced position. Somehow he managed to wiggle his furry body into my heart, becoming my self-proclaimed bodyguard, and of course my son's only friend. Elvis captured our hearts by revealing his unique form of cat love.

Over the years I experienced a few critical illnesses. While recovering in a hospital, my husband informed me, "Elvis is positioned by the front door, eying everyone who enters. He refuses to move from that spot, except to eat." Elvis stayed in the same spot until I returned home, and then he remained glued to my side in bed until I was ambulating. One time I had emergency stomach surgery, returning home with abdominal stitches. In less than a week Elvis developed a stomach obstruction which required emergency surgery, returning home with abdominal stitches. Both of us recovered in bed together, taking our pain medication and hobbling slowly through the house. I told Elvis, "You didn't have to go this far with your empathy. Surgery wasn't needed to feel what I'm going through."

While Elvis was ill, my son exhibited such tenderness and concern. He took extra care whenever he picked him up or placed him back down. Even though Elvis was in pain, he still allowed my son to handle him.

At times I believe he even looks at me as if he comprehends exactly what I'm saying. I tend to treat him more like a family member than a pet, talking to him as he follows me around the house. My husband is hysterical over my belief that Elvis understands everything, but I do believe it's remarkable how much he does seem to understand. He can read human emotions, and if he believes you need him, he will plant himself right by your side.

When my son was going to school, Elvis would waddle upstairs and stand right outside my son's door, meowing until he got up. On the days school was closed, I reminded him, "There's no school today, Elvis," and he quieted down and waddled back downstairs.

In the evening, Elvis follows me from room to room, looking up at me, asking, "When are you going to go to bed?" When I finally do, he climbs up on the bed and snuggles right against my side, being too heavy and big to sleep on top of my head now. He remains there as I mold my body around him, attempting to get comfortable. Why I don't push him aside, I can't quite figure out. You see, Elvis has reinforced in me what unconditional love is, by bonding to someone who dislikes cats, and especially to my son who detests physical signs of love. He's earned the warm spot by my side. That is, until my son creeps into my room asking, "Where's that Elvis?"

Elvis stretches his chubby body with his white and gold tabby coat, meows, and then makes the decision about who needs his unconditional love more.

~Claire H. Luna-Pinsker

Blessed Are the Merciful

Forgiveness does not change the past, but it does enlarge the future.
~Paul Boese

"I hate you!" I screamed in fury at my father. "You never let me do anything I want."

The slap across my face made my head hit the wall of his study. I fled in tears, and the hatred for my father cemented in my heart.

My dad and I had a rocky relationship. He was consumed with rage at what fate had thrown at him—a sick wife, kids to support, dreams thwarted. While sometimes he could be the most charming man in town, at other times he vented his rage with his fists. When my mom contracted Multiple Sclerosis, our peaceful family spun out of control. As the years passed and my siblings married or moved from home, I remained to help care for my physically sick mother and my emotionally sick father.

When my mother died, it was just me and my dad at home. I could barely tolerate him. All those years of mistreatment bubbled to the surface every time we were in the same room. While sometimes things were quiet, my pent-up rage hit him back as hard as he'd hit me that evening when I was sixteen.

Then came Baloo the Magnifi-Cat.

Baloo chose me at the town animal shelter one cold, gray Saturday. Just hours shy of execution, the scrawny black teen cat with emerald eyes loudly demanded my attention with an ear-piercing meow.

Despite my determination to adopt a kitten, I felt sorry for her and took her home.

When I got her home, Baloo took one look at the strange living room and dashed for the couch, where she hid for two days before finally creeping out to find her litter box, water and food.

"I hope you know what you're doing," my dad snapped at me as her tail disappeared under the skirt of the plaid couch.

As the snows of winter melted into spring breezes, Baloo became the catalyst for a growing relationship between my father and me. Baloo updates became the communications bridge between us. Stories of her many antics, from catching mice to her daily staring contest with the resident cardinal, gave us an excuse to talk without fighting. I'd come home and find my father cooing and talking baby-talk to the entranced kitty. He showed a gentle side of himself that I'd never seen before.

Gradually our relationship thawed. The past, however, with all of its pain and sorrow, kept us from fully healing.

One golden October day, Baloo taught me the most important lesson of my life: that mercy and forgiveness mean letting go of the past and removing what blocks us from love. As I sat at my desk at work, I had such a strong feeling that something was wrong at home that I couldn't sit still. I called home repeatedly, only to encounter a busy signal each time.

I called my dad's friend, who was also our closest neighbor. "Could you please check on my father? I can't get through, and it's odd to get a busy signal for more than half an hour."

My neighbor agreed, and I turned back to my work, feeling my anxiety rise with every breath. A few minutes later, my dad himself called me back.

"That darn cat," my father said. "She knocked the phone off the hook again."

"Like the time you cut your finger?"

The prior year, my dad has been working on one of his wood-working projects when his hand slipped on the table saw, and he'd severed his thumb. He'd managed to call 911, and while they whisked him to the hospital to stitch up his finger, Baloo had knocked the telephone off the hook. That time, I didn't know what her signal meant. Today I knew.

Something was still seriously wrong.

I couldn't ask Dad to put Baloo on the phone. I could only follow my heart.

"Dad, you know I love you, right? I just want to say I love you."

Words began tumbling from my mouth, burbling up like a hot spring from my heart. The barricade protecting my heart was lifted.

"I forgive you. I love you."

"What are you talking about, forgiveness?" he asked gruffly. "Why are you talking like this?" I could hear his confusion and discomfort. This wasn't how we spoke to each other. We joked when we felt pleasant. We snapped and snarled when we were annoyed.

We never said "I love you."

Baloo never knocked the phone off the hook... unless something bad was happening.

"I love you, Dad."

"What's gotten into you?" he asked. "You're acting all weird."

"Nothing. I'll see you tonight, okay?"

"Sure. Bye."

I didn't know what had gotten into me either, but when we hung up the phone, I burst into tears. As the minutes ticked on, I wrenched my mind away from the phone call and into my work. A few minutes later, the receptionist buzzed my line.

"Your neighbor is on the phone," she said, and she sounded upset. "He said it's an emergency."

"Jeannie, come home," my neighbor shouted into the phone without preamble. "Your father's been taken to the hospital. It's bad."

Somehow, Baloo knew. After hanging up the phone, my dad had turned to Mr. Matthews, said "I don't feel good," and collapsed from a massive heart attack. He died before the paramedics arrived.

Baloo taught me that my dad wasn't the ogre I'd made him out to be. As I saw my dad's behavior with her, I knew he was capable of love. Over the years, talking about the cat had let us build some sort of relationship from the ashes of my childhood. Now on his last day, Baloo had brokered a final link to healing and forgiveness.

They say animals are sensitive, and some people are sensitive to animals. I don't know if that's true for all animals or all people. I only know that Baloo used the only way she could to signal me that something was terribly wrong by knocking the phone off the hook. I never thought that a black stray cat who picked me out of the animal shelter would help me salvage my relationship with my father. Somehow, I was able in that last moment to say "I love you."

Baloo made my last words to my father words of love.

Mercy and forgiveness... mercy shown to a stray cat in the town shelter led to mercy and forgiveness in one of the most important relationships in my life.

~Jeanne Grunert

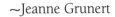

Bandit

It is impossible to keep a straight face in the presence of one or more kittens.
~Cynthia E. Varnado

"Aren't you going to kiss me goodnight?" I said with a lump in my throat. My husband twisted underneath the sheet and gave me a peck on the cheek. Then he turned his back to me.

"Goodnight," he said without any emotion.

I lay there quietly, trying to escape the tension between us. We'd had a big fight, over nothing really, right after dinner. And now we were in bed without any resolution to it at all. I would have stayed up for hours discussing what was wrong. He didn't want to talk about it.

This was a second marriage for both of us. Relationships are a lot of work, and this one surely didn't come easy. You'd think we'd have learned how to make things work after the errors we committed the first time around. But lately, a nervous strain entered our conversations when we did talk to each other. I longed for the days when laughter filled the air and our eyes lit up with joy at the sight of each other.

There was one thing in our lives that held us together like glue. Our cats. The newest addition, Bandit, got her name from the black and white outline of a mask on her furry little face. As a tiny, fluffy ball of a kitten, she fit in the palm of my hand. But she grew quickly, adjusting to life in the house with two other cats.

"Come here and look at this," my husband said one morning from the bathroom.

"What?" I replied with a tinge of annoyance. I was busy making the bed.

"Look at Bandit at the sink."

There was our slinky cat, perched on the edge of the porcelain with her neck craned all the way around.

"She's drinking right from the faucet while I shave," my husband said. "Have you ever seen a cat do that?"

"No, I haven't."

We both stood there, side by side in the small bathroom, watching our cat drink her fill. A smile perched on my lips and almost made it to my mouth. I noticed how tall my husband was standing there beside me, and how thrilling it felt to be close to him. I wanted to reach out and hug him, but the tension of the past few days still lingered. I turned away to finish making the bed.

Later that evening after work, my husband rested in his recliner watching television. Bandit jumped into his lap and then climbed to the top of the chair behind his head. The recliner was tilted way back, with the kitchen table about four feet away behind them. All of a sudden she sprang from the top of the chair.

"Did you see that?" I couldn't help but smile at the sight of this black and white flying acrobat cat, her four paws stretched out in all directions gliding through the air.

"No, but I felt her jump."

"She took a giant leap and landed gracefully on the table." I smiled at my husband, and he smiled back. The stress of the day didn't dissipate in an instant. Problems were still there: issues with work and money and other things. But it felt nice to share a moment.

A few days later, after getting into bed and a goodnight kiss that was slightly more tender, my husband moved his feet under the covers to warm his toes against my soft, flannel pajamas. I felt a thump and a pounce and then biting nibbles.

"Ouch, is that you?" I cried out in surprise.

"No, look."

Our little criminal found the movement of our feet enticing, like a game of cat and mouse. She nipped first one set of toes and then another, jumping back and forth between the two of us. I broke out in unbridled laughter.

"You little nut," I giggled as I pulled my feet up close to my chest.

"Come here," my husband said, "I'll protect you." He put his arms around me and held me close, but that didn't stop Bandit from pursuing our limbs. By that time we were both laughing at the absurdity of the situation.

"How are we going to keep her from biting us at night?" I asked with my face muffled into his T-shirt and the musky smell of lingering cologne filling my senses.

"I don't know. Let's lie real still and hope she finds something else to amuse her."

I curled up even closer and felt the protectiveness of his arms around me. They felt strong, warm, comforting. I thought about that furry nut robbing us of our sleep, but then silently thanked her for bringing my husband and me together again.

That little Bandit snuggled into our hearts like a burglar, but left more than she has ever taken. My husband and I had been working so hard on our marriage, dwelling on the serious side of so many issues, when Bandit woke us up to the fact that we could still laugh, we could still have fun, we could still smile and play. When I watch her sleeping peacefully, curled up in a tight ball, it's easy to see her angelic side, but that devilish imp is right there too, just under the surface. Kind of like my husband and me. We have our good days, and then we have days when we struggle, but underneath all of that, we love each other with all our hearts. And that's enough to keep us working on our marriage this second time around while taking moments for uninhibited laughter and joy.

~B.J. Taylor

86

Courageous Heart

When your kitty purrs to you,
doesn't it break your heart that you can't purr back?
~Candea Core-Starke

"I heard on the radio that the county humane society is housing ninety cats right now!" said my husband, Dick. "Want to go up and look? It's been way too quiet around here without a cat in the house."

Our Russian Blue mix, Daniel, had inextricably entwined himself in our family for sixteen years. After painfully losing him to liver disease, I had put off adopting another cat. My heart still ached with grief.

After two months, though, I had to admit I really missed the warm welcome and constant companionship that having a cat in residence assured. Although still not ready to adopt, I begrudgingly agreed to at least start looking.

The newscast was right! On the first day we visited, the attendant confirmed that the shelter was caring for ninety cats! All ages, colors, breeds, sizes, hair length, and background were represented. And they all looked at us with soulful, expectant eyes! Impossible to decide between them, I wanted to adopt each one—and at the same time I just wanted out of there with my heart intact.

Changing the litter box, vacuuming cat hair, grooming, paying veterinary fees, and arranging for pet care during our vacations didn't bother me. That part I could manage. More importantly and more honestly, was whether I had the courage to face loving and then losing another cat.

The idea of a spunky, playful kitty appealed to me though. Dear old Daniel couldn't have been called "playful" for several years. "Couch potato" more aptly described him. The movement of the sun chiefly motivated Dan to change positions. Perhaps a lively, curious feline companion would be a nice change!

So, over the next few weeks we kept going back to the shelter. Dick figured the right cat would "jump out" at us eventually. We even took home an application form, filled it out, and returned it. But in my heart I just wanted Daniel back.

On the first day we visited, I had noticed a cute, longhaired female. I automatically dismissed her from the running because I was convinced I wanted another shorthaired male. However, this seven-month-old sweetheart wouldn't take no for an answer. Each time we visited she gave us the look-at-me-I'm-very-very-cute routine when we got near the cage. Her long, bushy plume of a tail, feathered feet, tufted ears, and short, turned-up little nose differed drastically from Daniel's sleek, perfectly groomed looks. Dick finally gave in one afternoon and took her out of the cage.

The exuberant kitty immediately found a piece of dirt on the floor to bat around. Then she jumped on the back of my husband's chair and climbed onto his shoulder! "Playful" definitely described this cat!

We carried her around the room in our arms for quite a while. She loved it! Her outgoing, friendly personality delighted us! And stroking her extraordinarily soft fur comforted my cat-deprived soul! Playful, friendly, and comforting... an irresistible combination! How could we walk out of there without her?

"This is the one," I said. "Let's take her home." So we did!

Such an extraordinary feline deserved a not-so-ordinary name. We called her Isabelle. She immediately began an all-out campaign to win our hearts. The "cute" routine at the shelter only hinted at her charms.

Let's just say it had been a long time since we had lived with a spunky, young cat.

We soon found that Isabelle differed from Dan in more than just looks! She loved company of all ages, but especially children. At the sound of the doorbell, she ran to see who had come to visit her. No scurrying upstairs and secreting herself under the chair for Isabelle. Everyone received the royal welcome, not merely a glimpse of a disappearing tail. Isabelle rubbed along their pants legs, conned them into petting her, snooped into their bags and purses, and just generally made her presence known!

Isabelle also proved to be quite the entertainer. Throw her little bobble-head turtle and she fetched it! Run the model train and she stalked it till she derailed the engine!

And if no one had time to play with her, Isabelle didn't mind. She would simply rout a big rubber band out of the drawer, fling it in the air, catch it, and throw it up again. Or else she would drag out her much-loved and abused collection of furry mice. She amused herself for quite a while playing soccer with them until she lost them all. We would later find one in her water bowl, another under the TV stand, a few under the stove, and more under the refrigerator.

With her unique personality and winsome ways, she carved out her own place in our family and captured my heart. I learned that I could love again, despite the inevitability of losing my precious pet.

Isabelle provided us with the feline companionship we so desperately missed. She enjoyed "making" the bed, "helping" me dust, and pressing the computer keys. Working a jigsaw puzzle certainly piqued her interest! And she frequently accompanied my husband to the office for brief visits with the staff. Isabelle certainly didn't lack the courage to love wholeheartedly.

Tragically, unbeknownst to us, Isabelle had contracted feline leukemia and feline infectious peritonitis while at the overcrowded shelter. She suddenly went from lively and energetic to gravely ill. We lost her in two short days.

Isabelle passed away just before her second birthday—but, oh, what a lot of living she had packed into those twenty-three months!

She played intensely, loved unashamedly, hated vets fiercely, and fought bravely for her life to the very end. In the process, she taught me that, although it takes great courage, loving is worth any risk.

~Pam Williams

87

Reiki for Cats

The power of love to change bodies is legendary, built into folklore, common sense, and everyday experience…. Throughout history, "tender loving care" has uniformly been recognized as a valuable element in healing.
~Larry Dossey

I've always been interested in alternative healing. I know that it's not for everyone, but for me it affirms my view that there is some powerful force out there looking out for us, a force that we only have to ask for help and it will respond.

A few years ago, I decided to take the plunge and take a course in reiki—a non-contact form of energy healing. I loved the course and the way I felt the energy flowing through my hands as I placed them over people. The thought that in some small way I could possibly help someone was truly remarkable.

Our larger-than-life course tutor emphasised that we should practice all we had learned on family and friends.

"Not only that my dears, but if you have pets, give them some reiki. They will adore it," she said with a flourish.

I rushed home that evening filled with excitement, eager to practice on my partner and my two cats, Phoebe and Leo. My partner did admit that he could feel a sensation like cold water running down his back as I held my hands above his spine but did not seem overly keen to be my spiritual guinea pig on a regular basis! So I decided to turn my attention to the cats.

They do say that pets show the characteristics of their owner, and I have to confess that my two adorable moggies seem to display some of my personality traits to an exaggerated degree. Phoebe—or Feebs as she's known to those who love her—is a "chunky chick" who loves her food and adores a cuddle or two. She rules the roost and isn't scared to show everyone who's boss, whereas her brother Leo is scared of his own shadow and could do with a small brown paper bag to carry with him—just in case he has a panic attack. He falls over his feet and couldn't catch a mouse if his life depended on it! He's also the more intuitive of the two and we often spot him staring at the door or the phone moments before it rings.

The effect of reiki on my two mogs was interesting, to say the least. Phoebe, sensing an easy opportunity for a sneaky cuddle, was on my lap before you could say "relax." Normally, when on your lap, Feebs likes to return the cuddle and will continually nudge you and rub against you. As soon as I asked for reiki healing to pass through my hands however, she was like a rag doll (or rag cat in her case). Her entire little body seemed to become more fluid—in fact it was like holding a furry hot-water bottle as she chilled out (upside down, all paws in the air) in a seemingly altered cat-state! So unlike her was this state of Zen-like relaxation that even my other half commented that it must be working!

The following evening, I decided that Leo could do with some reiki too. He loves some guaranteed cuddle time—just him and "mom" and he settled down on my lap for a bit of a snooze. The reiki effect, however, was literally electric. As soon as I passed my hands over his back, he jerked his head up and all his fur began to stand on end. Then, flat-eared, he bulleted off my lap and out the door into the hall. No amount of coaxing would persuade him to come back onto my knee that evening. Perhaps he felt a surge of energy that spooked him. What was certain was that reiki was obviously not his cup of tea!

At that point in our lives, my partner and I had some difficult issues surrounding us. We had family worries as well as external pressures—it looked like my job would soon become redundant. In bed that night, I just could not sleep no matter how I tried. As I lay on my stomach I thought to myself, "I could really do with a bit of help here." In the darkness, I felt a pressure on my feet, working its wobbly way up my thighs and onto my back—where it settled. Just as I was about to freak out I heard loud purring. Craning my neck and trying not to disturb him, I realised that it was Leo. He lay snuggled on my back for about five minutes and then began the whole process again, walking up and down the length of my body before settling down. Ordinarily Leo never jumps onto the bed—preferring to snooze either in his little bed in the spare room... or in the laundry basket.

My sleepy partner who had been watching all this laughed softly and whispered, "I think you're getting cat reiki!"

"My God, I think you're right," I whispered back as Leo continued his unsteady progress up and down my back and legs. The cat reiki sessions continued every night for a week and then stopped as abruptly as they had started.

I don't know if it was the cat reiki but, over the coming weeks, the family worries and the job all resolved themselves in ways we could not have foreseen.

I never underestimate the power of love—be it from your partner, a friend, or your cat. These days, if I'm at all stressed, I climb into bed and before long have the sensation of four little cat paws marching resolutely up and down my body. While he still refuses any reiki from me (who knows, perhaps he is a cat master teacher and doesn't need my inferior ministrations), my little cat still gives me cat reiki when I'm feeling a bit under par. My next step is to undertake some training to be a t'ai chi teacher... who knows what the cats will make of that!

~Judith Keenan

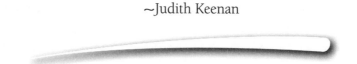

Lessons in Parenting

It is in the nature of cats to do a certain amount of unescorted roaming.
~Adlai Stevenson

When Kootenay bounded into our lives, my husband Richard and I joked that we could practice our parenting skills on him. We were newlyweds, and he was our first pet together. We reasoned that if we couldn't keep a cat alive it would be a sure sign that we should not have children. As it turned out, Kootenay was determined to burn through every life left to him.

Kootenay was an absolutely charming feline who showed his adventurous nature right from the start. As soon as we brought him home we knew he would not be happy as an indoor cat. Any time a door opened he dashed outside. He would often disappear for a few hours, and occasionally he would stay away overnight. This was not a good start to our lessons in parenting.

In an attempt to find out where he went, we got him a name tag with our telephone number. The calls started coming in right away. The conversations always went something like this:

The neighbourhood school crossing guard: "Your cat followed your kids to school this morning, and now he's hanging around in the playground. I'm worried that he'll wander onto the busy highway."

Me: "Umm, we don't have kids. He must have followed some of the neighbours. I'll be right there to pick him up."

Or like this one with a stranger from a few blocks away: "Your cat just came into our house and scared our dog."

Me: "I'm so sorry, I'll be right there to pick him up."

Stranger: "That's okay. He's such a sweet cat. He's napping right now and I wouldn't want to wake him. I'll call you when he wakes up."

On one occasion, he even acted as a reference for my husband. Richard had walked to the library, but when he got there, he realized that he had left his library card at home in his wallet. He couldn't sign out any books, and he couldn't get a replacement without ID. He and the librarian started chatting and it turned out that she lived near us, so Richard asked if she knew Kootenay. "Oh, yes," she replied enthusiastically, "he comes over for visits all the time. Lovely cat. If he's your cat, that's good enough for me. Here's your library card."

And on it went, Kootenay went everywhere, and everyone loved him.

Then one cold rainy autumn day he left the house, and there was no call from anywhere to come and pick him up. There was no call the next day either. It was still pouring when we scoured the neighbourhood, but there was no sign of Kootenay. Richard thought he might have heard a cat meowing in the nearby forest, but it was hard to hear much over the pelting rain. Richard was convinced that Kootenay was somewhere in the forest and he persisted in his search. Somehow he managed to locate him stuck up in a tree far from the trail. I could just barely see a dark shadow and hear his distant cries. We shuffled through the dark, wet undergrowth towards him, guided by the dim light of a single flashlight. At one point we tumbled down a steep bramble-covered slope that we hadn't seen in the dark. Fortunately we were dressed head to toe in rain gear, and the thorny branches cushioned our fall. We were scratched, but not seriously injured.

Kootenay was indeed stuck in a tree—a very tall limbless tree. There was no way to reach him. By that time he had spent two days up there. We didn't know what to do, but we had heard that the fire department sometimes rescues cats. We returned home and called them. They weren't particularly interested in venturing out into the forest on that cold rainy night, and they told us that he would come down when he got hungry enough. We were not prepared to wait and we devised a plan. We dragged the longest ladder we could find into the forest, but it was nowhere near long enough, so we went back home and sawed up lengths of sturdy lumber. We packed as many as we could into a backpack with a hammer and some long nails and returned to "Kootenay's tree." Richard climbed the ladder as high as it would go. Then, one by one, he started hammering the planks into the tree, and climbing them until he reached a soaking wet, cold and frightened kitty. He unceremoniously stuffed Kootenay into the backpack and they both climbed down.

Lesson 1 learned: We would go to heroic lengths to save a family member.

Things were quiet after that—for a while. Then there came another day when Kootenay didn't return home. Once again there was no call to come and get him. Our neighbourhood searches yielded no leads, and as the days went by, we started to give up hope. Then one evening, I came home and was greeted by a familiar odor: the tantalizing aroma of fresh cat food. I was puzzled. Did Richard get another cat? Had he taken in a stray? He greeted me and excitedly blurted out, "You'll never believe it. Kootenay came home. At least I think it's him. He's very skinny. He ate a ton and now he's sleeping on the bed." It was exactly two weeks from the day he disappeared.

"How did you find him?" I asked, incredulously.

"I didn't," he replied. "I heard a loud meow at the door and when I opened it, he dashed in and headed straight for the food bowl. He must have been starving."

Indeed he must have been. During the time he was gone, he lost almost half his body weight. We suspected that he might have sneaked into a house right before the owners left on a two-week trip. They would have come home to quite a surprise!

Lesson 2 learned: Never give up hope.

By this time we were seriously beginning to doubt our parenting abilities, but we rationalized that Kootenay was still alive, so we couldn't be doing everything wrong. We were becoming somewhat used to his exploits, so we were not overly concerned the next time he went missing. That time we did get a call. It was about a week after he left. Richard took the call, and I heard him say Kootenay's name. Before I got too excited, he gave me a thumbs-down signal, and I knew it was bad. Kootenay had been hit by a car many miles from home. A kind jogger had found his body and thoughtfully laid him down by the side of the road in a position that hid the collapsed side of his face. He almost looked as if he was taking a short nap before continuing his adventure. We took his body home and buried it in the forest under "Kootenay's tree."

We were so sad when Kootenay died. He had been with us for less than a year, but we missed him terribly. Worse yet, did this really mean that we wouldn't be good parents? We spent a long time reflecting on whether we should have done things differently. We could have kept Kootenay safely locked in the house, but he would have been miserable. He had the soul of an adventurer. He needed to explore and take risks. He had bravely ventured out into the world and lived the life he was meant to live. He was not destined to live a long life, but he lived a good one.

Lesson 3 learned: Sometimes you have to let your loved ones live life on their terms, even if that means dealing with difficult consequences.

In time we got another cat. Panda is also a lovely cat. He's now well into his teens and is not nearly as daring as Kootenay, and that's okay. He too is living the life he was meant to have. We also have two children who are also quickly approaching their teen years. They too are leading good lives.

Final Lesson learned: We can manage whatever life holds for us and our family.

~Dawn Livera

89

Duet for Fiddle and Viola

When a cat chooses to be friendly, it's a big deal, because a cat is picky.
~Mike Deupree

When you live on a farm, you choose your cats for mousing ability rather than for their cuddlesome qualities.

It's the reason I chose Fiddle, a skinny, green-eyed tortie with long paws and a fearsomely quick pounce.

Of course, I didn't know she was a good hunter when I got her. But her mother was a good mouser, according to my friend Nancy, whose grain storage was mouse-free, so it was worth the risk.

She was cuddly when she was a kitten, round, with soft fur. As she matured, her baby fat melted from her bones and she became a skinny, spooky, predatory cat. She reverted to her cuddly kitten self only when she was pregnant. When the kittens were weaned, she returned to her career as Lurker-in-the-Shadows. My grain storage was mouse-free.

When Fiddle was five years old, I had a run of spontaneous abortion in my ewes. The distressing part was that the ewes miscarried late in the pregnancy. In the middle of the thrill and hustle of lambing, all that new life, my favourite part of the year, came the shock of lamb after lamb emerging from the womb, tiny, perfect and dead. Over half my lambs never drew breath, or had any possibility of it.

Belladonna was one of the last to lamb and, like most of the others, she delivered early. She'd shown no signs of imminent delivery; no triangular hollow in front of the hip to indicate the lamb had dropped into position, no swollen udder, no nesting behaviour. She just pushed out a tiny black lamb, covered with the slime of birth, onto the manure of the barn floor and stood looking at it.

Without hope, I wiped the remains of the sac away from the muzzle and was astonished to hear a little gasp. The tiny thing shook its ears and produced a barely audible bleat. Belladonna strolled away. I tucked the baby, slime and all, into my jacket and headed for the house through the late-March snow.

I kept colostrum in the freezer for just this kind of emergency. While I was feeding the newly-dried lamb her first meal, Fiddle, who must have sneaked into the house on my heels, came creeping across the room and put a tentative paw onto my knee. Before she could pounce, I brushed her off.

"Not a mouse," I said to her, although I could hardly blame her for thinking of the lamb as prey. I could cup it in my hands with the legs dangling through my fingers. On my kitchen scale, it weighed a bare two pounds.

A newborn lamb has to be fed every two hours. A barn full of lambing ewes has to be checked every three or four hours. I was already strained from the lack of uninterrupted sleep. Keeping Fiddle out of the house was impossible; she was not Lurker-in-the-Shadows for nothing. Time and again I found her at my knee as I fed the lamb.

I kept the lamb in a box with a towel and hot-water bottle, in the spare room with the door closed. When I got up at night, I would check first to see if it was worth warming the bottle. I fully expected the lamb to die between one feeding and the next, but she hung on.

Finally the inevitable happened, and I failed to close the door properly when I went to get the bottle. Padding back upstairs in my nightgown, I was shocked to see a wide line of light falling across the hall floor from the guest room.

When I got into the room, I could see that my worst fears were confirmed. Fiddle was in the box with the lamb. From the sharp motion of her head, she was biting. It was probably already too late. I didn't want to look. But I would have to put her out with her prey — I didn't want blood and guts on my guest room floor.

As I looked down into the box, Fiddle looked up. Her green eyes were slitted and she was purring. Her paws were wrapped around the lamb, who shook her wet, cat-licked ears at me and bleated. At the bleat, Fiddle turned and took the lamb gently by the neck, as I had seen her do with her kittens when they wouldn't hold still for washing. Then she went back to work on the lamb's face and ears.

I waited until she was done, marveling, grateful and sleepily amused. When the lamb was washed to Fiddle's satisfaction, I gave her the bottle and tucked her back in. Fiddle curled around her, purring.

"Two points off your predator license, Fiddle," I whispered, stroking her head. I went back to bed for another snatch of sleep, leaving the guest room door open.

I named the lamb Viola.

~Elizabeth Creith

90

Blood Brothers

Just as the body cannot exist without blood,
so the soul needs the matchless and pure strength of faith.
~Mahatma Gandhi

The elderly man unceremoniously dumped the orange bundle of fur on the exam table. "All yours, Doc. You can take 'im, now."

I checked the record and the signed euthanasia papers I was holding in my hand.

Euthanasia was a sad, but unfortunately sometimes necessary, part of my job as a veterinarian.

"What seems to be the problem with Travis?" I asked gently.

"Problem is," he said gruffly, "he was my wife's cat, and my wife passed away last week."

"I'm so sorry."

"Yeah, well. I can't stand the sight of 'im. Just put him to sleep."

The cat was purring under my hands. "Would you like me to try and find a new home for him?" I kept my voice soft, not wanting to add to the man's pain, but detesting the notion of putting a healthy animal to sleep.

"I don't know who would want an old thing like him." The man shrugged. "I signed the papers. You do what you want." He turned and walked out.

I brought the cat to the back and did a full physical exam. He was in excellent overall condition. It was obvious he had been a beloved pet.

"You're never going to find a home for a ten-year-old cat," said one of my colleagues, stating the obvious and echoing the man who had brought him. "We can't even get rid of those kittens who were left on our doorstep last week. What are you going to do with him? This isn't a shelter, after all."

I shrugged. I had no idea what I was going to do with the cat. He rubbed up against me, still purring. "We'll figure something out."

A week later, Ruth Klein brought in her old seventeen-year-old cat, Morris. Morris had been suffering with feline leukemia for some time now, and more recently with intestinal lymphoma, an aggressive form of cancer.

Mrs. Klein's eyes were red-rimmed, evidence that she had been weeping. Wordlessly, she lifted her limp cat from the carrier and gently placed him on the table.

He was still alive, but barely. He had lost so much weight, he was now scarcely more than a skeleton, and his owner explained that it had been days since he had been able to hold down any food. His haircoat, once a rich luxurious ebony, was unkempt and dull. His eyes too were dull and sunken deep in their sockets, and I estimated his dehydration at ten to twelve percent—just barely compatible with life.

Mrs. Klein knew what I needed to tell her, but she wouldn't let me say it. She shook her head firmly. "I'm not ready to say goodbye."

I lifted the cat's lip. Once upon a time, he would not have so easily allowed me this close contact without a fight, but now he was too weak to protest. The gums were white.

"Mrs. Klein, Morris is in the end stages of a terminal disease. I'm so sorry. You don't want him to suffer."

She shook her head again. "No. Please. A few more days. Whatever you can give him. Please, make him more comfortable." Her tears streamed down her wrinkled cheeks and spilled onto his hair. "Please."

It was against my better judgment, but I of course respected her wishes. I hooked him up to an IV line and admitted him to the hospital.

"I've lost so much," Mrs. Klein told me, as we stood together a little later watching Morris. "I can't lose him, too. Not now. Not yet."

"We're rehydrating him, but he's terribly weak from blood loss. If we are going to attempt to keep him alive, he needs a blood transfusion."

"Then do it."

"He's losing blood into his intestinal tract, and his bone marrow can't produce any more because of the cancer. Mrs. Klein, his condition is terminal, no matter what we do...."

"Give him the blood transfusion."

After she had gone home, I consulted with the other doctors. We had no blood donors, and I was afraid we wouldn't have time to track down blood at another clinic.

"Does she have another cat we could use?"

"No," I shook my head. "Her cats got old together. Her other cat, Monty, died from kidney failure several months ago." Then an idea came to me. "Hey! There's Travis! We can use Travis."

The cast-off orange feline had become the hospital cat in the past week. He was strong and healthy, and surely wouldn't miss a little blood.

The transfusion went fine, and later that evening, I stood with Mrs. Klein as she visited Morris in the hospital's recovery ward.

"He's a bit stronger, now." She smiled, stroking his coat.

"Yes." But. But I felt I had to warn her. Not allow her to get her hopes up too high.

"Hopefully, we'll buy him a few more days...."

She cut me off. "I know. I know he's dying." Tears, a seemingly endless supply, ran down her lined cheeks, and her hand trembled. "He's all I've got, Doctor." Her voice was barely more than a whisper, and even though it was just the two of us, I had to lean forward to hear her. "I've lost everyone else. Morris is the only one I have left. My husband died last year from colon cancer."

I had heard about that, heard how bad it had been towards the end. "I'm so sorry."

She continued speaking, facing the cat instead of me, her voice a monotone, as if she was a really bad actress reciting her lines, carefully keeping all emotion out of it. "We only had one child. My son, David. We wanted more, but we couldn't have more. David was killed when he was twenty-one in a car accident. Then my husband died last year, and I was all alone, except for my cats. They kept me going. Someone to love me, someone for me to love. Someone to get up for in the morning. Maybe it sounds silly, but feeding them, caring for them, made me feel needed. It was all I had. Now Monty's gone, too, and soon..." Her voice caught, as her hand indicated the prone figure before us. "I can't lose him, too. I can't go through it again. Then no one will be left, and I'll be all alone. Maybe I should be dead, too."

"Mrs. Klein!" I was alarmed. "Please don't speak that way!" I looked around desperately for help. "You have a lot to live for...."

"No, I don't, dear." She smiled faintly, reading my fear accurately. "But don't worry. I'm not going to kill myself." She closed the cage door and turned away. "This is it, though. I'm through with cats. No more pets for me. It's just too painful."

I walked her back up to the front. On impulse, I took her the long way around so that we would pass Travis' cage.

"Oh, Mrs. Klein," I said. "I just thought you might like to meet Travis, our hospital cat. He's the one who donated his blood for Morris' transfusion."

"Oh!" She looked surprised. "It never occurred to me where you got it. So you just took blood from him?"

"Sure. We need to get it from another cat. Don't worry. Travis can handle it."

Sure enough, Travis was rubbing up against the bars of his cage, purring as always, looking fit as a fiddle.

"What do you mean, 'hospital cat'?"

"Well, his owners couldn't keep him, so he's been hanging out here."

Mrs. Klein nodded, already back on the subject of Morris' progress.

Morris did manage to hang on for a few more days, but he couldn't eat, and he became weaker and weaker in front of our eyes. Finally the day came when I had to tell Mrs. Klein that his blood count was falling dangerously low again. This time, there could be no transfusion.

"The new blood cells from the transfusion are dying or being lost into his intestines, and he can't make any more of his own."

She stroked his listless body, the tears falling. "It's time now, isn't it?"

I euthanized Morris, finally putting an end to his suffering, his owner cradling his thin body in her arms. He went peacefully, and I think it was a relief for all of us. I cried along with Mrs. Klein this time, and hoped she would be all right. She seemed so frail.

About a week later, Mrs. Klein marched into the waiting room, no sign of tears, and demanded to speak with me.

"Mrs. Klein?" I was surprised to see her. After all, she had no more pets. "What can I do...?"

She cut me off mid-sentence, which was her way, all business now, no time for small talk. "I'm here to adopt Travis. After all, he gave his blood to my Morris. The least I can do is give him a home."

~Debbie Kosinski

Ms. Whiskers

What greater gift than the love of a cat?
~Charles Dickens

I was raised in a very abusive home. I was afraid of my parents and I always felt very alone and confused. My mom and dad kept me empty inside with their constant emotional and verbal abuse. My parents taught me that I was worthless and that nothing I had to say held any value. I never felt loved and I never felt cared for—that is until Ms. Whiskers came into my life.

I will never forget the first time I saw Ms. Whiskers, a name I immediately gave to her. A beautiful high white tabby with four white paws, Ms. Whiskers had a presence about her which seemed almost human. Luckily for me, my parents liked cats so I was able to keep this precious little gift from God, and a special gift from God Ms. Whiskers truly turned out to be.

I bonded with her instantly and, amazingly to me, she bonded with me as well. Ms. Whiskers and I became instant friends and wherever I was, you could bet she would be right with me. She even followed me to the bathroom! Now have you ever seen a cat that devoted to any one in your entire life? I had never had such attention in my life and I loved it. Ms. Whiskers depended upon me to take care of her—to feed her, to make sure she had water, to keep her brushed and free of fleas and to keep her litter box nice and clean. But Ms. Whiskers gave so much more to me than I could give back to her.

Ms. Whiskers seemed to have a broken motor and she purred constantly when we were together. I noticed early on that she stayed away from my parents as much as she possibly could and that she was not free with her purring when they were close to her. I always felt that this fact was kind of a special bond between just the two of us; you know, like our own little personal joke. For the first time in my life, I felt unconditional love and I held onto that positive feeling deep within my heart.

Ms. Whiskers sure could "talk" too. She was always meowing to me like she was trying to tell me something. She would meow and meow and meow until I spoke to her or got down and petted her. I always imagined that she was saying how very much she loved me and how happy she was to be my cat. When I would come home from school I could sometimes hear her meowing to me as far as a couple of houses away. I did not know it at the time, but those meows slowly nurtured my broken heart and gave it the positive affirmation it so desperately needed and deserved.

I depended upon the attention and love Ms. Whiskers gave to me. She came along at a time when I needed her the most, and Ms. Whiskers was always looking deep into my eyes as if she were trying to get deep within my soul, as if she knew something far beyond human understanding. She communicated with me in those long, gentle looks and, as a result, I was finally able to connect with another living being. Of course, I did not understand these concepts for many years; all I knew at that time was that she loved me very much.

I can remember times after my father had beaten me when Ms. Whiskers would curl up close to my neck as I lay on my bed sobbing, and she would purr and lick my hand or face just as though she were trying to kiss those tears away. Ms. Whiskers comforted me so much during times like these and she really helped to keep me sane and stable in my very dysfunctional environment.

Ms. Whiskers was with me throughout my teenage years and gave me something to come home to every day; otherwise I think I would have run away. When I was old enough and about ready to leave and live on my own, Ms. Whiskers passed over to the other side. It was almost as if she were waiting for me to get out of my unsafe environment before she let herself pass on. Needless to say, I was devastated, and I mourn her death to this day. I will always be thankful to Ms. Whiskers for giving me all of her love and comfort and nourishment. She really taught me that I could trust others, and that I was a valuable human being, and I will keep her love in my heart and miss her forever.

~LaVerne Otis

What I Learned from the Cat

Learning to Let Go

No amount of time can erase the memory of a good cat, and no amount of masking tape can ever totally remove his fur from your couch.

~Leo Dworken

A Gift in Gray

A beating heart and an angel's soul, covered in fur.
~Lexie Saige

When my father was dying, I traveled a thousand miles from home to be with him in his last days. I soon discovered that even when you know what's going to happen there's still no way to really prepare for such an event. It was far more heartbreaking than I'd anticipated, one of the most difficult and painful times in my life.

After he passed away I stayed alone in his apartment. There were so many things to deal with: arrangements to be made, mounds of paperwork to sort through, bills to pay, belongings to pack, meetings with real estate agents and lawyers. Weeks passed; it all seemed absolutely endless. I was completely overwhelmed and unbearably lonely. I hated the utter silence of the apartment; how could rooms so full of furniture still feel so empty?

But one evening the silence was broken: I heard crying outside. I opened the door to find a little gray kitten on the steps. He was scrawny, beat up, and pretty pathetic looking. I remember thinking that he looked the way I felt. I brought him inside and gave him a can of tuna. He gobbled it ravenously and then almost immediately fell sound asleep right there on the kitchen floor.

The next morning I checked with neighbors and learned that the kitten had been abandoned by a previous tenant who'd moved out and left him behind. So the little kitten was there all alone, just like I was. As I walked back to the apartment I wracked my brain trying to figure out what to do with him. Having something else to take care of seemed like the very last thing I needed. But as soon as I opened the apartment door he came running and in a single bound leapt into my arms. It was clear from that moment that he had no intention of going anywhere. I decided to keep him—just until I went back home. I started calling him Willis, in honor of my father's best friend.

From then on, things grew easier. There were still long days of meetings and errands but no longer was I returning to a lonely, empty apartment. Instead I was now greeted with wild enthusiasm and an abundance of affection. There were still hours spent on the phone getting accounts in order, but with Willis purring contently in my lap the time seemed to pass much more quickly. At night, instead of restless tossing and turning, I slept more peacefully because he was curled up on my pillow or sometimes even on top of my head. And his crazy kitten antics made me laugh until my stomach ached—the first time I'd laughed since being there. His presence and companionship changed everything. I simply don't know how I would have made it through that bleak time without him.

When the time finally came for me to return home I had to decide what to do about Willis. Of course by that time it wasn't really a decision—there was absolutely no way I would leave without him. But if you've ever driven in a car with a cat you know what a challenge it can be. And when I thought of all the hours and the hundreds of miles ahead of us, I dreaded it. In spite of my trepidation, I packed us up and off we went. Much to my amazement, Willis never cried the whole way home. For the vast majority of the trip he just curled up in the back seat and slept. I think he was just happy to be with me. And I think he knew he was going home.

It's now been five years since my father died. And the scrawny little gray cat is scrawny no more. He's now a strapping twelve-pound boy and as handsome as can be. What a gift he was and continues to be. Over the years, several people have commented on how nice it was of me to rescue him. But he and I know what really happened—the truth is that we rescued each other. I may have given him a home but he gave me something greater—Willis taught me a powerful lesson for life. He taught me to trust. I now know that even in what seems like the darkest of times we should never lose heart and never despair. Because just when you need it the most, and just when you expect it the least, an angel can appear. And sometimes, instead of wings, they come on four legs and wearing a fur coat.

~Sherry Amen

Eddie's Philosophy

Who would believe such pleasure from a wee ball o' fur?
~Irish Saying

It got to be a daily routine question that I'd ask my husband, Bob, "Has the vet called with Eddie's biopsy results?"

"Not yet," he'd say.

On the day Bob answered, "Yes," I blocked his response from my brain. I had just come in the front door and hung up my coat. But then I saw that Bob was still standing at the door.

He came over and touched my shoulders. "It's not good," he said.

I felt something explosive hit me in my chest. "Just tell me straight," I said.

"Eddie has lymphoma. It's a very aggressive cancer. He has about two months at the most."

Now, I have worked in emergency rooms as a psychiatric consultant. I am used to trauma, that is other peoples' traumas.

But I had the oddest reaction. I thought, "If I put my coat on and go back out the front door, as if I hadn't come home yet, I could go back in time and what I'm hearing will not have happened." I really believed that.

Bob had me sit on the couch. But I was still unable to take it in. I could only see his mouth moving as he tried to explain what was going on with our cat—my little soul mate, Eddie. Every few seconds or so, the thought sank in, "Eddie is dying." But in an instant,

I went right back into never-never land. Completely dismissing any intrusive thoughts—of reality.

Each time it hit me again, I kept interrupting, "No! Not Eddie."

Bob continued calmly responding, "Yes."

Finally my tears turned to torrents. "He's supposed to be around for years. He is fine! He just saw the vet for a routine physical!"

In denial, I so needed to find a way to make it all untrue. I called the vet. "Are you sure?" was all I could think of to ask. He was sure.

I haven't told too many people about this. With the amount of trauma many of us have in our lives, I was afraid that friends wouldn't have compassion. And some that I did tell said, "It's just a cat."

We adopted Eddie from a shelter when he was eight weeks old. From day one, he has spent his life destroying our house. We spend half of our time cleaning up broken pieces of china he's shoved off a table and the other half keeping him safe. We have ugly plastic fencing on the top of our shower. This is because Eddie got a grand old kick out of flinging himself up to the top of the stall while I was taking a bath. Then he'd do a high jump into the bathtub.

He may hang in there for a while with treatment. He deserves that chance. I asked the vet, "Do you have any advice on grief?"

"Take it one day at a time. Eddie doesn't know he has cancer. He's not thinking like a human would. He's just happy—in the moment. He doesn't think about what might be or when or how. We could all learn a lot from him."

I must say that I look at Eddie differently at this point. I wish that it had not taken a dire diagnosis for me to do this. I believe, now, that we should look at all of those we love the way I do Eddie. When I hold him in my arms, I am acutely aware that he will die sooner than his time. Hence, I appreciate and savor each moment with him.

From now on, I vow it will not take cancer to teach me this appreciation for life. I just wish I had learned this before I was about to lose Eddie.

I don't want Eddie's purpose in life to be about teaching me to appreciate the moments. But, alas, he has been my greatest philosopher.

To Eddie, I say all the time: "Thank you for showing me that love matters more than stupid pieces of china or scratched furniture. Thank you for never being mad at me when you wanted me to pick you up and cuddle and I just walked right past you. Thank you for adoring me, even when I did wrong. For forgiving me when I did not put your needs first. For always teaching me that love is what is most important. And Eddie?" I whisper to him from my soul to his, "What will I ever do without you?"

~Saralee Perel

Peace in Leaving

Unable are the loved to die. For love is immortality.
~Emily Dickinson

The grief is sharp and bright in my chest as I stare at the word on the form: euthanasia. No matter how many times I reread it, it doesn't register. No matter how many times I tell myself I need to be here, I can't believe that I am.

The tech waits patiently until I pick up the pen and force myself to sign the paper, which will authorize the vet to put my cat, Chewie, to sleep. I answer her questions curtly as I try not to cry. Yes, I'd like to keep the ashes. Yes, I'll pay for it now. Yes, I'd like some water. Yes, thank you for your help. The tech finishes her work, brings me a glass of water, and leaves the room, shutting the door behind her.

Chewie sits stiffly in his carrying case on the table, and for a moment I cannot look at him. I unzip the top of the case and extract the red blanket that is wrapped around him. He's so ill he can't get warm on his own anymore, and he's snuggled under the fleece. When I open the side door to gently pull him out, he resists. "Please, Chewie," I beg him. "Please don't do this."

When he realizes there isn't anyone else in the room with us, he relaxes. It's completely silent until he coughs, hacking deep from his chest, and reminds me how ill he is. Incurably ill and in extreme discomfort. If that were not the case, we would not be here.

I embrace him, inhale deeply and pick him up. He is listless and sick but his legs still immediately wrap around me in a hug. I hug him back and we walk around the room together. I try to show him the cheerful painting hanging on the wall. "Do you see?" I ask him. He doesn't see. He coughs. I amble over to the bench in the corner of the room and sit down, Chewie still tucked safely in my arms.

I can't believe it has come to this, that our journey together is going to end in this pale, chilly room. Chewie has been a loyal companion to me since I was fifteen years old. I am now thirty-two. Over half my life has been tied to the ten-pound creature in my arms; he has been my constant through four cities, three degrees, and five schools. How can I possibly go through with this?

Chewie coughs again, faintly, and I remember why we're here: he is in the end stages of congestive heart failure and lymphoma. His lungs are full of fluid, and we're past all treatment options that would give him any quality of life.

This is the only mercy I can give him, the only peace, the only way to keep him from suffering more. It's not about me, and it's not about how much I am already grieving. It's about this dear cat who trusts me to help him.

When the door opens I clutch Chewie to my chest. The vet speaks softly as she approaches, and tells me she's brought along one of the techs who knows Chewie well.

"Will he know what's happening?" I ask.

"No," she promises, and I believe her. "Stay where you are. I can give him the sedative injection while you hold him."

I look at Chewie, and he picks his head up and stares me straight in the eye. I tell him I love him, that I'm not going anywhere, and that he shouldn't be afraid. He puts his head back down. I can't breathe or talk, and I shut my eyes as the vet approaches with the needle.

I start talking because if I don't, I'm going to be hysterical. I hold my cat and babble at the vet. She smiles and nods and after a few moments, I feel the tech take Chewie from my arms. He's fast asleep as they gently stretch him out on a gray towel on the table, but his eyes are open.

"Chewie?" I ask. He doesn't respond. According to the vet, he's alive but completely unconscious. I stay near his head and tell him how much he is loved, what wonderful dreams he's going to have, and how much I'm going to miss him.

I catch a glimpse of a syringe filled with pink liquid on the counter and look away again. That one isn't just a sedative. I try to pretend I don't know it is there, and the vet and the tech manage to complete all their preparations, shave Chewie's leg and set the IV outside my line of vision.

"I'm in the vein," the vet says somewhere over my shoulder. I nod and focus on the tabby markings on Chewie's head as I keep talking to him, as if nothing at all is wrong.

Nothing changes; nothing at all. Chewie's death is so peaceful I don't even see it happen. It is only when I notice the vet, at the edge of my peripheral vision, removing the IV from Chewie's leg that I think to ask.

"He's not with us, is he?" I ask, straightening up. The vet shakes her head. "No. His heart stopped almost right away."

He's still my cat for a few more minutes. I sit down on the bench with the towel, and the vet lifts him from the table, cradles him carefully in her arms, and hands him back to me. His head flops backwards and his eyes are wide, and he's a rag doll instead of a cat. I nestle him in my lap and as soon as the vet is out of the room, I start to sob.

I hold him on my lap and try to close his eyes, but they refuse to budge. I close my eyes instead, and I reflect that it seems that we did this fifteen minutes ago under much different circumstances. I pick him up, hug him and pace around the room just as we did before.

I don't want to leave him. One more hug. One more. I finally force myself to knock on the door, and the tech, who has been waiting outside, comes in. He takes Chewie from me, and we arrange him on his red blanket. It will accompany him to the pet cemetery so he will have something familiar from home with him; so the staff will know he is loved.

As I look at Chewie one last time, I can't help but notice how tranquil he is. He isn't coughing, he isn't choking, and he isn't gasping for air. He's splayed out on the red blanket, looking much more at ease than he did in the last days of his heart failure.

It's about him; it's not about me. The grief is sharp and bright in my chest, but he is finally free from pain. There is peace in that, for both of us.

~Denise Reich

The Emperor's Blessing

I pet her and she pays me back in purrs.
~Star Richés

Our cat Adventure was the epitome of feline nobility. He was a keen hunter and spent many days and nights guarding the perimeter of our acreage, but he was also a consummate lap cat with a resonant purr. The interior of our house was also part of his dominion, though according to Dad no cats were allowed in the house. That didn't stop us. Adventure ruled our chairs and our laps all summer long, and on school days he'd be waiting for us to arrive home. We just had to make sure he was out the door before Dad arrived home.

From the time he was a kitten, his pink nose was his symbol. Adventure was a black and white tabby, and his pink nose seemed to glow against the backdrop of white whiskers and chin. As children, my brother Scott and I joked that Adventure could substitute for Rudolph the Red-Nosed Reindeer and help Santa pull his sleigh on foggy nights. Therefore, when the cat was over a decade old and developed a chronic nosebleed, we teased him at first. The dignified Emperor of Cats had become a klutz, it seemed, and the slightest bump caused his nose to dribble.

As the months progressed, the nose bleeds got worse and it stopped being a joke. Mom took Adventure to the vet and returned with a grim diagnosis: cancer. Just as with pale-skinned people, cats with light-colored fur and pink noses are more likely to get skin cancer on their noses. There wasn't anything we could do other than make sure he was comfortable.

At the same time, my life began a dramatic shift. I met a wonderful man and became engaged. I lived in college dorms during the week, only coming home on weekends. My wonderful man joined the Navy, and it became apparent that after our marriage I would be living far, far from home. I buried myself in a heavy college class load and tried to pack and sort through my childhood belongings in my scant time at home, all while trying to plan for the wedding. To say I was stressed was an understatement.

Adventure was changing, too. Slowly, the cancer ate a black pit through his nose. He slowed down. He stopped being possessive at the dinner dish. He became more vocal, shifting from an almost-mute cat to one who would sit at the door and yowl for affection. Even as he deteriorated physically, he remained the same sweet, noble cat as always.

Some two months before the wedding, the realization hit me, and hit me hard. I was going to leave and move across the country. We were going to be very poor. I didn't know when I'd be able to return to California, and Adventure probably only had months to live.

I would never see him again.

This cat had been more like a younger sibling than a pet. The thought of leaving him forever was devastating, but at the same time I knew I was making the right choice. I loved my fiancé, and I had to move on with my life. But still, I felt guilty. As Adventure trotted over to welcome me home from another week at school, I knew I had to do something to help him and help my own grieving heart.

With most of his nose gone, Adventure was having great difficulty grooming himself. The short-haired cat who had always maintained an immaculate coat was now plagued with mats half the size of my fist, mostly located around his hindquarters and tail. I dug through a drawer and found my old school-picture-day plastic combs. I had a job to do.

From then on, I reserved a long space of time during my frantic weekends at home to spend with Adventure. It didn't matter if I had two papers due on Monday, needed to get the wedding dress fitted, and had to clear out another box of childhood belongings in my closet—Adventure needed me. I sought him out every weekend and set him on the big garbage can outside, and I began to comb his fur. He was ecstatic. He circled the canister lid, purring and pacing, and I combed him and worked out the snarls with every pass. He tried to eat the tufts of hair as they floated away and gave me gentle nips of gratitude. Adventure acted like his old self—happy, purring, and the center of my world. If it wasn't for the nature of my task and the condition of his face, I could almost forget he was dying.

But he was happy. That's what mattered. In that precious time, he taught me an important lesson: prioritize. Yes, the essays and the dress and the packing were important, but Adventure was foremost. I saw him as a kitten the day he was born. He licked tears from my cheek the day my grandpa died. We spent hours together as companions and explorers, wandering the back acres and climbing trees as a team. I was going to leave him behind. That was an undeniable fact. But I could leave with the knowledge that I loved him, and he loved me, and he would have the shiniest, cleanest fur coat possible.

My semester came to an end. The final weeks blurred by. On my wedding day, I had Adventure sniff my gown, and I applied a few of his spare hairs for good luck. The next day, my husband packed the moving van. Adventure, the vigilant guardian of the property, sniffed at the van's wheels and eyed the proceedings. There was no way he could understand I was leaving, and on some level, I couldn't fully comprehend it either. And then I left.

I talked to my mom on the phone almost every day, and I asked how Adventure was doing. The harsh heat of the summer was hard on him, but he endured. My brother and mom still let him indoors at every opportunity, and Adventure still ruled their chairs and laps.

In late October, my brother Scott gruffly disclosed, "Adventure was looking for you today. He went in your room and opened the closet and everything. He hasn't been in there since you left. He looked kind of puzzled, too."

After the call ended, I sobbed.

Two weeks later, Adventure was put to sleep. They let him in one day and he wouldn't eat his customary snack. The next day, it was the same. For a cat who was an unabashed glutton, this was the sign we had all been dreading. It was time.

Life continues, years pass, but memories remain. When everything seems fast-paced and frantic, I think back, and I can feel the plastic comb slide against Adventure's silky fur. I remember the peace in his eyes. All he asked for was love and a few minutes of time, and that lesson has stayed with me. Stop. Breathe. Dinner and deadlines can wait. I need to pet the cat.

~Beth Cato

Meow, Our Bonga Cat

The cat is domestic only as far as suits its own ends.
~Saki

My parents called me the morning our cat Meow died. I was in boarding school in my last year of high school in Zimbabwe. My mother didn't have the heart to call my brothers and sister who were in college in America. She wanted me to call them from home that weekend.

Meow had survived her first encounter with a poisonous snake without being injured but she was not so lucky the night she died. When my parents went to bed she had been out prowling the garden, so my mother left the bathroom window open for her. In the morning they found her cold, stiff body at the foot of their bed. She was so swollen, my dad said, she had probably been bitten by a snake and had made it home to die.

I phoned my sister, Ellah, in Philadelphia, first.

"Ellah, Meow died on Thursday. Mom and Dad found her at the end of their bed."

Ellah was quiet. I knew she was crying.

"Are you okay?"

"I'm fine," she sighed. "I am so sad. This really is the end of our childhood."

There are two types of housecats in Zimbabwe, fully domesticated cats that live and eat in people's homes and formerly domesticated cats that we say have gone "bonga" or feral. Our cat Meow belonged to a unique third category. She was a grayish generic-looking tabby cat with a white-tipped tail. Everything about her said "regular housecat" except her amber eyes, which held a hint of bonga in them. Meow enjoyed the security of a family but maintained her freedom, coming and going as she pleased.

We lived in Tynwald, a suburb about forty minutes outside Harare, the nation's capital. Tynwald properties were mini-farms. On our two acres—the average size for Tynwald—were my parents, my brother Richard, my sister Ellah, my brother Nhamu and me, the youngest. We had honeybees, pigs, chickens, turkeys, four dogs and Meow the semi-bonga cat. With plenty of undeveloped land around us, Meow had space to roam and would go hunting and exploring for days at a time. She always came back with a dead, or at least partially dead, offering of a mouse or lizard that she would leave for her best-beloved, my brother Nhamu. Although she belonged to Nhamu, Meow had a unique relationship with each of us.

From the time she was a kitten, Meow had been Nhamu's accomplice in terrorizing me. My earliest memories of the feline-boy reign of terror date back to when I was three. I couldn't tie my own shoelaces so Meow would "hunt" my trailing laces, crouching in doorways and pouncing on my feet when I least expected it. To add to my fear of walking from my room to the kitchen, Nhamu would hide in the laundry basket at the end of the long hallway, waiting to jump out and scare Meow. As soon as Meow appeared he would leap out and shout "Boo!" Meow would jump, I would scream, Nhamu would fall about laughing and then, completely unfazed, Meow would resume hunting my shoelaces. I never thought of telling anyone or asking for help. It didn't occur to me that anyone had more authority than Meow or more power than Nhamu, so I resigned myself to walking the gauntlet every evening.

Ellah had a better relationship with the cat. Meow allowed Ellah to pet and hold her, probably out of respect for their mutual bonga-ness. In turn, Ellah admired Meow's free spirit, recognizing a bit of her own independent self. At an age when girls can usually not see beyond prescribed trends, my sister dressed differently from everyone else. Her taste in clothing—homemade dresses, usually in black—was rivaled only by her choice of friends. She made friends with the strangest people and saw beauty in them all.

Unlike Meow, Ellah's bonga spirit lacked a sense of self-preservation. One day my great aunt and I were sitting outside the front door of the house shelling groundnuts. Ellah was leaning against one of the cars enjoying the sun and my mother was tending to her roses. Meow was behind Ellah on the hood of the car. Meow tensed up before we even saw a young black mamba, a very poisonous and aggressive snake, coming towards us. My great aunt recognized it at once. She yelled and ran, pulling me into the kitchen. My mom was running towards my sister who stood frozen, staring at the snake that was making a beeline for her ankles. Meow pounced and was between Ellah and the snake in an instant, giving my mom enough time to get Ellah into the house. We watched from the kitchen window as Meow expertly stalked and killed the snake without getting bitten.

Meow gained more respect from me and more affection from Ellah, but her preference was always for Nhamu. She adored him and would make sure she was close to him whenever she was home. She slept on his bed at night and napped on his lap while he watched TV.

Even when Nhamu went through his preteen everything-is-an-experiment stage and used Meow as his test subject, she remained loyal. I remember his attempts to disprove the theory that a cat will always land on its feet. Nhamu kept finding different heights to drop Meow from. First he stood on a chair and dropped her. Meow proved the theory correct. Next he stood on a table. Again the result was positive. He climbed on top of the refrigerator and dropped her. Once more she landed on her feet. Meow finally drew the line when he tried to get her up to the roof, jumping out of his hands and hiding for the rest of the afternoon. Afterwards Meow still followed Nhamu around the house and expressed her devotion by bringing him the limbs of unfortunate rodents after her excursions.

My oldest brother Richard was the least understood in our family. His teenage years were difficult and he had many clashes with my parents. I remember him closing himself in his room for long periods of time after arguments. I would sit outside his room wishing that he would come out so I could make sure he wasn't sad or lonely. Sometimes Meow would join me in my vigil, sitting in my lap. When she felt enough time had passed, she would scratch at the door and Richard would open it just enough for us to come in and sit with him. Meow and I would sit on Richard's bed and watch over him as he listened to music or flipped through magazines.

Since Meow's death, my country Zimbabwe has collapsed, Richard died in a car accident, Nhamu had a stroke at twenty-three and is now wheelchair-bound, and Ellah lives far away from me. Ellah was right. Meow's life represented our childhood. Meow saw and accepted each of us, bearing witness to the intense normalcy of family in what now seems to be an enchanted time. Our childhood is over but we still carry a little of Meow's bonga spirit with us.

~Mavhu F.W. Hargrove

Crystal's Compassion

If purring could be encapsulated, it'd be the most powerful anti-depressant on the pharmaceutical market.

~Alexis F. Hope

Crystal was a moody cat who hissed at almost everyone, except me. When she was little, I put her in her own room at night, because I always feared tripping over her. As she got older she slept where she wanted, but never with us.

Crystal was exclusively my buddy, confidant, and friend. On occasion, she would be friendly to my children, ages fifteen and eleven, but never towards my husband Jim—except on his birthday every year. For some reason she sensed the festivities and, wanting to be a part of the celebration, would sit with him.

Then the unthinkable happened. My husband became very ill and was diagnosed with terminal cancer. To everyone's surprise, Crystal began following him around the house. She seemed very concerned about him and sat by his side hour after hour guarding him—as if her presence could forestall the inevitable. After each round of chemotherapy, she checked on him when he felt sick and hovered at the table when he tried to eat. When he sat at our bay window praying in the morning, she was by his side, doing her best to comfort him.

After ten short weeks, Jim passed away, leaving me with two children, a bad back, and a shattered heart. The night he died I finally broke down. I went into our bedroom, where I sobbed long and hard into the pillows. Between sobs, I kept hearing a thump, thump,

thump, at the door. It was Crystal, trying to get in. Finally she gave one more push and succeeded in opening the door.

I felt her leap up on the bed with me. I rolled over to look at her and was amazed at what she did next. My loving cat climbed onto my chest and gently laid her paws over my eyes, trying hard to dry my uncontrollable tears. Her compassion was so evident and so direct, it soothed my pain more than I would have believed possible.

After that, she slept with me every single night for the next six years, until she died at age thirteen. Whenever I hear someone say cats have no feeling, I know better. I only have to think of Crystal, a cat who showed such compassion for my husband and for me in our times of sorrow.

~Carolyn Trezzo-Miserendino

Lost Friend

You cannot look at a sleeping cat and feel tense.
~Jane Pauley

The day we lost Colonel was a cold and miserable day in January. The year was only a few days old and somehow the magic left over from Christmas and all the promises of the new year ahead vanished as I gently lifted my small gray cat into the carrier.

His body was limp and his normally white beard was covered with yellow slime from the countless times he had vomited. The vet knew my husband, James, would be bringing him in, and as I closed the door to the carrier, I stroked the slate-gray fur of his forehead. He looked at me, pain filling his eyes, and I knew that we were saying our last goodbyes. I looked at my beautiful cat one last time, and tried to fight the tears sliding down my cheeks.

I busied myself with our two young boys of two and five. I spent the time trying to calm their worries about Colonel but as each minute slowly slid into the next, those worries only grew.

Despite all my reassurances, I knew that Colonel wasn't coming home. I prayed that I was wrong, prayed that Colonel wasn't as sick as I thought. I didn't want to believe that our young cat, not even two years old, was going to leave us. I had always thought that he would live to fill out his name and become the grouchy Old Colonel, much like our nine-year-old cat, Lobo, was the grouchy Old Prince. It wasn't fair that this cat, the same one who slept with my older son and allowed my younger son to use him for a pillow, was sick. It wasn't fair that I was going to have to tell them that he wasn't coming back.

Lobo was a wonderful cat, but he didn't have the same patience with kids. Colonel was Gabriel's cat more than he was anyone's, and I found myself worrying about what would happen to my five-year-old son's heart when his cat died.

When James walked through the door, tears shining in his eyes, the handle of an empty carrier clenched in his fist, I knew that my prayers had gone unanswered; Colonel was gone.

In a voice filled with grief, James told me that Colonel had had liver failure; there was nothing the vet could do but help him along. Tears stung my eyes and I felt a lump form in my throat as I thought about all the chin scratches he would never have. I thought of Gabriel and the nights he would spend alone without his living teddy bear, and the lump grew larger.

We told the kids and Gabriel was devastated. Tears choked his words as he asked us why, and tears choked our hearts as we explained that God had called the Colonel home.

The evening passed slowly and each moment found my thoughts returning to Colonel. Returning to the happy moments we had shared and all the moments we would miss. I thought about how empty our home would be without him and I worried about the nights ahead of us when no Colonel was there to snuggle against Gabriel.

When it was finally time for the boys to go to bed, sobs wracked Gabriel's thin body, and no matter how hard I hugged him, he couldn't stop. Instead, he shared with me all the grief that his small body held.

While James and I tried to calm Gabriel, Lobo entered the room and sat in the doorway staring at us. His yellow gaze scanned the room, and his tail flicked slowly as though in deliberation, before he slowly crossed the room towards us. Jumping onto the bed, Lobo did something that he had never done before; he lay down beside Gabriel and started purring. We stopped and the sobbing ceased. I said quietly, "Lobo is here to sleep with you."

Gabriel laughed, a tear-filled sound, then buried his face in the brown and gray tiger-striped fur. Lobo lay there, his purr deepening, the sound filling the room with assurance that all would be well. I scratched his ears and said a silent thank you to the grouchy cat who had sacrificed his space to bring a little comfort to the boy he shared a home with. Although Lobo had spent the last five years with Gabriel, he had never warmed up to this child who filled his life with noises and smells. He would avoid the kids, preferring to come to James or me for the occasional scratch. The fact that he was lying there, with a child grasping him tightly, proved that he was a remarkable creature.

I knew that Lobo wasn't Colonel for Gabriel, but on that cold night, Gabriel was able to sleep with Lobo by his side. The days continued and the heartache lessened. We didn't forget Colonel or how much we loved him, but we forgot the pain of losing him. Each night became a little easier and Gabriel cried a little less. Each night, Lobo would sit in the doorway, watching the little boy in his bed before finally climbing up with him. Each night, Gabriel would smile a tear-filled smile, curl up with one arm wrapped around Lobo and fall asleep.

Six months have passed and Gabriel can finally fall asleep more easily, but every night Lobo still curls up on his bed. Gabriel doesn't hold him like he used to, but Lobo's strong purr still fills the room as he fulfills the Colonel's legacy.

~Sirena Van Schaik

I Love Lucy

A cat is a puzzle for which there is no solution.

~Hazel Nicholson

Lucy came to us just like all our other babies had, from strangers who couldn't or wouldn't give them the loving homes they deserved. On a cold dark January night, there was a soft knock at the door and a woman with sad eyes quietly and gingerly handed me a tiny blanket with an even tinier bundle of fuzz. I took a quick peak, nodded my silent approval, and brought my new love into the warm kitchen to get acquainted.

As I held her in my arms I very carefully peeled back a corner of the blanket to see some of the biggest, roundest eyes I have ever seen gazing back at me. Her beautiful black face also had the longest, softest, whitest whiskers I could imagine. There was nary a peep as I explored her three-week-old emaciated body for any signs that she would need emergency attention and, silently thanking God, I found nothing to warrant further concern.

Without putting her down, I warmed up some kitten formula in the microwave as I retrieved one of the many kitty bottles I kept on hand just for these occasions. By the time the microwave had gone off, I saw that the rest of my furry family was quickly gathering round my feet to inspect the new arrival. They all knew this was their job, en masse. To inspect. To accept. To welcome with open arms, er, paws.

As little Lucy grabbed onto that bottle with a force I could never have imagined, belying her malnourished condition, my eighteen-year-old Sheila stealthily made his way to the front of the newly formed reception line. Yes. Sheila was a male whose badly bruised body had been found in a Dumpster. For months it was impossible to determine his sex. Once we did, "Sheila" had stuck. But being a mere male did not deter Sheila from providing motherly comfort to every newcomer in our home.

As Lucy virtually attacked her bottle, Sheila cuddled next to us on the oversized cushioned kitchen chair, placing his body on my lap directly under the hungry little bundle that I held. He furtively lifted a paw and patted Lucy's cheek, dutifully waiting for her to finish.

Three bottles later, Sheila followed me to the sofa as I placed Lucy on my lap, still wrapped in her original swaddling. I sat back and watched Sheila perform what had become a normal routine for each new addition. He licked, patted, cuddled, rubbed against, and finally just wrapped his long thoroughbred-like legs around the new baby until she was purring and snoring in his arms.

Lucy was the only newcomer who was eagerly accepted by my entire brood of eight cats. No hissing, no fighting, no jockeying for position on the household feline social scale. She was just a perfect little sister. As she grew, the girls all played with her and the boys protected her from the neighborhood bullies when we all had playtime in the front yard after dinner.

Then one beautiful November evening, my worst nightmare came true. We were playing with a new jingling ball that got lost in a bush. I returned quickly to my living room to get another one and within less than a minute, Lucy had disappeared. I didn't panic immediately; I calmly searched the bushes, then looked up into the sprawling old oak tree that shaded my front yard. Under the cars, my neighbors' flower beds, and even on nearby rooftops. Nothing. No Lucy.

I watched my other kitties for some sort of hint as to what they might have seen. The only hint was that they were sitting quietly, doing nothing. I knew this was odd behavior, but I didn't know how to decipher its meaning.

Hours turned into days, which turned into weeks, which turned into months. We visited every shelter within a hundred miles. Fliers with photos were posted everywhere. We even offered a very generous reward. All to no avail.

My heart was broken. I prayed that if she were still alive that she had been able to find another loving family where she could live out her days in feline bliss. Then I prayed that if God had indeed brought her home, that her end was merciful and painless.

I wasn't the only one grieving. Her surrogate mother, Sheila, was so distraught he began making loud crying noises and spraying the floor and walls near where Lucy's bed still remained. Nothing I could do would calm him.

It took until the following summer for my daily crying episodes to subside. Then on Labor Day I was making preparations for a neighborhood barbecue. It was very peaceful and quiet till about noon when I heard all my kitties begin to wail. It began as a low growl and it quickly spread through the group.

Till then they had been playing quietly in the backyard where they had been waiting for Dad to "accidentally" drop a burger from the grill. No longer quietly playing, they continued this odd growling until it reached a peak of wailing and pawing at the ground. My husband and I turned our focus from preparing the food to observing our very distraught cats. Then, en masse, they scurried around the garden, each grabbing one object, and one by one they filed in a single line from the garden, through the kitchen, to the living room where Lucy's bed still lay.

I stood in awe as they carefully and lovingly placed their "offerings" of flowers, geckos and grasshoppers next to Lucy's bed. They each then made an odd soul-wrenching mewing sound, and backed away. This overwhelming display of feline empathy and love was astounding to witness. Eight grieving family members were paying a final tribute to their dear friend.

They say all animals have a sixth sense. All I know is Lucy's sisters and brothers somehow knew the exact moment of her passing. She was gone for good and they found a way to say goodbye.

We never moved Lucy's bed. My cats had turned it into a monument of sorts for their lost friend. It still sits next to the big French doors where the sun shone through the brightest. And frequently, on a bright sunny day, I will see one of my babies walk over to the bed, as if beckoned, and talk and purr, as if in conversation with a good friend. I'm not surprised at all, really. Lucy loved lying in the sun in her bed, and a simple matter of death wasn't going to stop her from enjoying her favorite pastime.

~Marie Duffoo

My Father's Cat

The cat could very well be man's best friend
but would never stoop to admitting it.
~Doug Larson

My father was adamant. "No cats. No discussion."

"Fine," I replied, during one of my frequent visits back home. "We won't discuss it. I'll just get one. Besides, the cat isn't for you, it's for Mom."

That's how, despite my father's objections, a one-year-old female cat named Puss Puss was rescued from an animal shelter and entered my parents' life. But she did more than enter it, she took it over completely.

Like most cats, Puss Puss soon found the best seat in the house. That turned out to be my father's lap, surprising him as much as me. From his first few hesitant strokes of her fur, he soon became Puss Puss's most ardent admirer.

Not content to simply claim my father's lap, Puss Puss also got her own chair at the kitchen table. Since she was a cat of considerable girth, my parents had a special cushion made to accommodate her.

I learned that no conversation with either of my parents was complete without several references to Puss Puss. Everything the cat did, whether playing with her tail or eating all her food, proved how smart she was. Many a phone call began with "Did I tell you what Puss Puss did today?" and ended with "She's such a good cat."

I tried not to groan. Instead, I reminded myself the cat was good for my parents, emotionally and physically. With my father suffering from advanced polycystic kidney disease, the cat gave both of my parents something to focus on other than his thrice-weekly dialysis sessions, heart problems, and increasingly frail health.

As my father's world shrank, Puss Puss remained a constant. Too tired to use his computer or read, he had just enough energy to pet her.

A year and several visits later, I sat at the kitchen table with my parents and Puss Puss. I glanced at the fridge which my mother had festooned with family pictures. The glance soon turned into a closer scrutiny. Photos of the grandchildren had been shunted over to one side to make room for pictures of the cat.

There was Puss Puss in her cat bed. Puss Puss on her special cushion in the kitchen. Puss Puss on her chair on the porch, complete with a radio tuned to classical music—her favourite, according to my mother.

"Hey," I said, pointing to the fridge, "what about me? Where's my picture?"

My mother stared at the fridge for a moment. "There it is," she said, indicating one lone picture.

"That doesn't count," I said. "I'm only in that picture because I'm holding the cat."

My father smiled and continued to pet Puss Puss who, I swear, winked at me.

Over the next couple of years, Puss Puss reigned supreme. Like a jealous sibling, I poked her a few times when I visited, but only when my parents weren't around. Puss Puss would open one eye, glare at me in disgust, and go back to sleep, knowing her role as top cat was secure.

As my father's health deteriorated, the three of us spent much of my visits in his bedroom. He on his easy chair, the cat on his lap, and I sat on the bed. We talked about finances, about my mother, about what I'd need to do when... he never said the word "died" but we both knew.

While we talked, his hand rested on the cat's silky fur, occasionally petting her.

Towards the end, even talking sapped his energy. I just sat with him and the silence took on a softness, punctuated by the cat's purring.

When my father was in the hospital, dying, we waited until the ward quieted down for the evening and smuggled Puss Puss into his private room. Taking her out of her red carrier, I placed her on the bed. My father reached out to pet her and she settled by his side.

I think they both knew they were saying goodbye.

That's when I recognized Puss Puss's gift to him. Unlike my mother and me, she didn't tire him out by worrying. She didn't record his daily blood pressure. She didn't check every bite he ate or every sip he drank to make sure he was staying on his restricted kidney diet.

She simply loved him, unconditionally and wholeheartedly, and brought peace to his life and, at the last, to his death.

~Harriet Cooper

A Little Cat
Stole My Heart Today

When you're used to hearing purring and suddenly it's gone, it's hard to silence the blaring sound of sadness.
~Missy Altijd

A little cat stole my heart today. She was a one-and-a-half-pound tortoiseshell kitten and she had the kind of eyes that look deep into your soul. Maybe things happen for a reason. I am not sure, but maybe it was a lesson for me to walk in the shoes of my clients—to feel what they feel when they lose a cherished pet.

She came to me as a sick kitten from the Humane Society. Her owner was a friend who brought her to the clinic every day for treatment. She had panleukopenia and was vomiting, had diarrhea, and did not want to eat. We gave her fluids for dehydration, drugs to control the nausea and vomiting, and helped her to eat. I taught her owner how to give her subcutaneous fluids (fluids under the skin) so she could continue with her treatment when she went home in the evening. I thought this was an easy thing to do. Her owner had a hard time with it.

Her owner had to leave town to attend a funeral and left the little tortoiseshell kitten with me at the hospital. I could not leave her alone at the hospital all night since she was so little and would need treatments overnight. I took her home with me.

As a rule, I never take them home with me, but I was tired and did not relish the thought of driving back to the clinic several times that night. We bonded the instant I put her in a carrier and took her to my home. I had been able to distance myself until that point. I had a rough time giving her the subcutaneous fluids that night. I knew she needed them but I felt bad for doing it. The next day I placed an intravenous catheter in her neck so that I could give her intravenous fluids to keep her hydrated. This would keep me from having to give her multiple injections under the skin. She would not feel pain with the intravenous fluids.

The little kitten seemed to rally and get stronger. She even tried to play a bit. She loved attention and purred every time she was picked up. She traveled back and forth to the hospital with me every day. I thought we were headed in the right direction when she ate some dry food one day and then ate some tuna the next day. The staff at the hospital could not help but get attached. She craved attention and would meow and talk to you if she could see you. She even climbed the cage door when she got irritated enough that nobody was picking her up. I was pleased to see her making "happy feet" on the stuffed toy I had placed in her cage with her to keep her company.

After four or five days of seeming to improve, she declined again. She still purred but I could not get her to eat on her own. She slept a lot. She still looked at me with those soulful eyes. She had me wrapped around her little paws. Even in her decline, she purred. But she became anemic and grew weaker. Even a blood transfusion didn't help.

Her owner asked me to decide when it was time. She hated to throw the decision in my hands but she felt that I was the one who should decide since I was there. I was grateful for the trust but sad at having to make the decision. She was so young. She had barely lived life yet. I toiled with the decision. Was she just having a bad day? Were we holding on because in two weeks we had grown to love her?

Her eyes told us when it was time. Those soulful eyes had lost their spark. She purred once again for me that morning; it was like she was telling me it was alright. She had not purred the day before. I gave her an anesthetic injection into the intravenous catheter so that she would be under anesthesia. I did not want her to be scared. How many times had I done this before? I thought about how I always tell my clients that their beloved pet will slowly fall asleep in their arms. The last thing they remember is someone lovingly holding them in their arms.

I had cried after the first few euthanasias I did. After that you learn how to toughen yourself and hold back the tears for the most part. I had not cried in a long time. I always knew when I performed a euthanasia that it was for the right reasons, and that helped. It did not help me much with the decision I was making that moment even though I knew it was the right decision.

I spoke to her softly, in between the tears, as I gave her that final injection. I told her I was sorry. It was over in an instant. There was a hole left behind in my heart. An empty feeling. I had not felt such sadness in such a long time.

I was confronted with what my clients face when they make the same decision. Maybe the good that will come from this experience is knowing exactly what my clients are feeling. Maybe I will be even more empathetic. I doubt I will be able to hold back my tears the next time I humanely euthanize a pet. I will always remember those touching little eyes looking up at me. I will always wish there was something else I could have done.

~Bronya M. Redden Amos, DVM

What I Learned from the Cat

Meet Our Contributors
Meet Our Authors
Thank You
About Chicken Soup
Share With Us

Meet Our Contributors

Lee Allen is pleased and proud to have her first novel recently published; she will attempt to write the sequel. At present, Lee is working on several short stories, all true and from her heart, with the hope that they, too, will touch the hearts of those who read them.

Rachel Allord received her Bachelor of Arts in English from the University of Wisconsin, Stevens Point in 1996. She is a freelance writer and is hoping to publish her first novel. She enjoys traveling, eating sushi, tickling her kids and drinking the coffee her husband brews. You may contact her at allordfamily@sbcglobal.net.

Sherry Amen lives in the Pacific Northwest with her husband and three furry children: Nikki, an Oregon Humane Society adoption; Willis, her "Gift in Gray" and Nubby, adopted from the Cat Adoption Team, the Northwest's largest no-kill cat shelter, where Sherry enjoys volunteering.

Bronya M. Redden Amos received her Doctorate of Veterinary Medicine from Mississippi State University in 1992. She works in a nine-doctor animal hospital in North Carolina. She had desired to become a veterinarian at a young age and she is living her dream of helping animals.

Monica A. Andermann is a writer who lives on Long Island with her husband Bill and their cat Charley. When she is not writing, she most enjoys reading or spending time with friends and family. Her inspirational essays and poetry have been published in various anthologies and literary magazines.

Vy Armour, a former English teacher, is an adjunct communications instructor at the University of Phoenix. She lives in Arizona, where she owned Pages, an independent bookstore in Ahwatukee. She is currently a book reviewer for BookBrowse.com. Her passions include books, writing, food, golf, Mahjongg and most of all, family times. Contact her at vyarmour@cox.net.

Ronda Armstrong lives with her husband and two cats. A former school social worker she writes, reads, connects with family and friends, and dances. She has contributed to *Chicken Soup for the Soul: Tough Times, Tough People*, *The Des Moines Register* and *Tiny Lights* online. E-mail her at ronda.armstrong@gmail.com.

Joe Atwater is a horseman who breeds, raises, and races Standardbred horses on his ranch in North Carolina. Horses have been an important part of his life since adolescence and they take up most of his time. The rest of his time is taken up by his devoted wife, Elizabeth.

Valerie Benko is a former news writer turned freelancer. She has been published in the *New Castle News* (under maiden name Hoffmann) and on storiesthatlift.com. Valerie resides in Pennsylvania with her husband and her two cats.

Carolyn R. Bennett is a graduate of Regent University's School of Journalism and a Communications Director in Los Gatos, CA. She has published dozens of articles on church and missions movements around the world and enjoys photography, playing the piano and hiking. Contact her at missionseditor@calvarylg.com.

Nancy Bennett is an avid pet lover, whose pets include several rescue cats, Tim Tim, Nina, Maya and Scraps as well as Kali the dog. She lives on a two-acre farm on Vancouver Island, where she raises heirloom vegetables, and small rare bantam chickens.

Mitzi L. Boles lives in northern Arizona with her husband and daughter. She has a BA in Journalism and enjoys writing, teaching and family time (critters included). She shares her passion for writing with wildlife rescue, and recently had her first children's book about wildlife conservation published. Visit her at wondersofthewild.org.

Michelle Borinstein was born in South Africa, moved to the USA, and currently lives in Israel with her husband and their houseful of children. The author of a book, and numerous articles and poems, she would like to find a publisher for her children's books. She may be reached at mborinstein@013.net.

Arthur Bowler, a US/Swiss citizen and graduate of Harvard Divinity School, is a writer, speaker and minister in English and German. His writing has appeared in several bestselling anthologies and in best-selling books in Switzerland. Look for his book, *A Prayer and a Swear*, or visit www.arthurbowler.ch.

Aimée Cartier is an author, intuitive, and teacher. Her company, Spreading Blessings Media, is dedicated to providing tools for inspired living. She lives on an island in the Puget Sound and is currently at work on a book entitled *Getting Answers: How to get the answer to every question you've ever wanted to know*. More about her and her work can be found at www.spreadingblessings.com.

Megan Carty currently attends high school. Aside from theatre, she loves participating in track and field, figure skating, baking, and film production. One of her favourite pastimes involves cuddling with her three beautiful felines, Abby, Lucky, and Siara.

Beth Cato resides in Buckeye, Arizona with her husband and son. Her work has appeared in publications such as *Niteblade Fantasy and Horror Magazine*, *Crossed Genres*, *Six Sentences*, and the book, *The Ultimate Cat Lover*. Information regarding her current projects can be found at www.bethcato.com.

Cate Cavanagh is a syndicated columnist in the political and metaphysical genres. Her books, *Gifts of the Spirit* and *Her Godmother* continue to receive rave reviews. Cate graduated with honors from Pace University and is a member of The National Social Science Honor Society.

Victorya Chase is a writer recently transplanted to the old West. She has been a foster mom to many a feline, and is happy to pass on the love that her cat gave her.

Jane M. Choate, a mother and grandmother, has been entertaining family and friends with her stories for as long as she can remember. She graduated summa cum laude from Brigham Young University. She currently lives in Loveland, Colorado with her husband, Larry, of thirty-six years.

Harriet Cooper, a freelance writer/humorist, is owned by three delightful, though sometimes terrifying, cats. Her work has appeared in magazines, newspapers, anthologies, newsletters, radio and even a coffee can. When not writing, she is often hiding from her cats, all of whom think they write better than she does.

Susan Cooper has shared most of her life with cats. Due to family allergies, she has now gone over to "the bark side." She lives in Colorado with her husband and a Golden Retriever. Susan enjoys hiking and dancing with her dog, and visiting cats at her stable-hand job.

Elizabeth Creith raised sheep for ten years in Northern Ontario. She has written humour, how-to and short fiction as well as a children's book, *Erik the Viking Sheep*. She divides her time between writing and working in her pet store with her Australian Shepherd, Sky. Contact her at hedgehog.ceramics@sympatico.ca.

Tim Crooks's childhood was spent in the Middle-East, experiencing the Lebanese Civil War, Gulf War, and Palestinian uprising. He now lives in the marginally quieter location of Reading, England. He is a professional scriptwriter with credits for the BBC and International Bible Society. Find out more at www.wingandaprayerproductions.co.uk.

Heather J. Cuthbertson received two bachelor degrees from the University of Nevada, Reno in Criminal Justice and Psychology in 2003. She enjoys writing books for children and young adults. You can find more information about Heather at HeatherCuthbertson.com. Heather still has a hard time not crying when she tells Cappuccino's story.

Linda Delmont received a Bachelor of Arts from California State University, Long Beach in 1983 and is currently pursuing a Masters Degree. She has spent her career working in elementary education and has two children in college. Her suburban "zoo" includes one dog, two cats, two rabbits and six chickens.

Brenda Denton has a degree in Business Administration from the University of Arizona. She is a Database Administrator for a health insurance company in Arizona. She is an animal lover with five cats and two dogs, one of which visits hospice patients as a therapy dog. She enjoys writing about the entertaining antics of her pets.

Marie Duffoo is a full-time writer and career consultant. She is an animal activist along with being an avid cat lover and dedicates her life to the pursuit of happiness for her feline family members.

Terri Elders, LCSW, lives near Colville, WA, with her husband, Ken Wilson, two dogs and three cats. A public member of the Washington Medical Quality Assurance Commission, she received the 2006 UCLA Alumni Association Community Service Award for her work with Peace Corps. Contact her at telders@hotmail.com.

Debbie Farmer writes the syndicated column "Family Daze" and has been published in *Reader's Digest*, *The Washington Post*, many regional parenting magazines and several *Chicken Soup for the Soul* anthologies. Her book, *Don't Put Lipstick on the Cat!*, is available on Amazon.com or can be ordered from any bookstore. You can reach Debbie at debbie.farmer@yahoo.com.

L. S. Fisher lives in Sedalia, Missouri, with her ornery Manx cat, Katrina. She has published two books: *Alzheimer's Anthology of Unconditional Love* and *Essays from an Online Journal*. Widowed with two sons and four grandchildren, she writes for relaxation. Read more at www.lsfisher.com or earlyonset.blogspot.com.

Karin L. Frank attended UCLA and worked in the telecommunications industry for twenty-five years. After retiring she raised goats but has since retired from animal husbandry. Now Karin reads a great deal and writes poetry. There has always been a cat by her side.

Janet Freehling is a retired LPN. Pet therapy and animal rescue are her passions. Cosmo, a Maine Coon mix, and Oliver, a schnoodle, join her as Delta Society Pet Partners. Nine cats and two dogs—all rescues—share a home with Janet and her husband, Hal.

Mei Emerald Gaffey-Hernandez served in the US Peace Corps-Dominican Republic from 2006-2007 as a Community Economic Advisor. She continued to live in the campo of El Chispero until 2009, during which time she married (Papi), had a baby (John), and adopted several children (Chelo, Vitale, Rubia). Please e-mail her at meigaffey@yahoo.com.

Kimberly J. Garrow was a teacher in her previous life before children. Six kids (and many fur-babies) later she is the author of *A Mother's Journey: Through Laughter and Tears* and an inspirational, humorist writer. An excerpt of this story was published in the January/February 2008 issue of *MomSense Magazine*. Please e-mail her at kimberlygarrow@hotmail.com.

Joanie Gibbs writes from the heart about life experiences. She loves to read, quilt, paint and practice yoga. She lives in Oceanside, California with her husband, two kids and an assortment of cats, dogs, chickens and koi. Please e-mail her at jngibbs1@aol.com.

A graduate of UCLA, **Willma Willis Gore** is the author of seven children's books, and co-author of another twelve, including *Just Pencil Me In—Your Guide to Moving & Getting Settled After 60* and *Long-Distance Grandparenting.* She leads five writer workshops in her home in Sedona, Arizona.

Jeanne Grunert shares her seventeen-acre farm with her family, Shadow the German Shepherd, and her latest cat, a gray tabby named Pierre. She writes for many publications and provides marketing consulting for clients worldwide. She enjoys gardening, reading mysteries, and singing in the church choir. Please e-mail her at jeannegrunert@yahoo.com.

Mavhu F.W. Hargrove was born in Iowa City and grew up in Zimbabwe. She lives in Maryland with her husband and three children. She works on her first novel whenever her two-year-old gives her a chance. She looks forward to a time when she can move her family back to Zimbabwe.

Dena Harris is the author of several hilarious books on cats including *Lessons in Stalking* and the upcoming *Kiss My Kitty Butt: More Life With Cats.* She spends her days plotting how to sneak more cats in the house without her husband noticing. Visit www.denaharris.com or contact her at dena@kissmykittybutt.com.

Louis A. Hill, Jr. authored three books and many articles. He earned a Ph.D. in Structural Engineering, designed bridges and buildings and joined the engineering faculty at Arizona State University. He retired an Emeritus Dean of Engineering from The University of Akron. He is listed in Who's Who in America.

Rebecca Hill graduated from Georgia Southwestern College in 1991. She's written and self-published two books; a children's book called *Don't You Worry, Don't You Cry* and a novel entitled *Confessions of an Innkeeper*. Rebecca lives in Los Angeles with her husband, Tom Caufield, and their cat "Anais the Siamese." E-mail her at bohoembassy@verizon.net.

Teresa Hoy lives in the country with her husband and a large fur family of adopted cats and dogs. She exists to scoop out litter boxes and clean up hairballs, though she does enjoy writing, creating paper art, cooking, and traveling on the side. Visit her at www.teresahoy.com.

David Hull is a freelance writer who has been published in many magazines and writes a monthly newspaper column. He is a graduate of SUNY Brockport and has been a teacher for twenty-two years. His hobbies include reading, gardening and unsuccessfully attempting to avoid stray cats. You can contact him at Davidhull59@aol.com.

Rebecca Josefa lives in California and works as a paralegal. She and her husband go for walks and count cats they meet. On their best night so far they saw seventeen cats. Her current project is to read all the mysteries in her nearby public library in alphabetical order by author—after three years she is on B.

Judith Keenan is a freelance writer residing in the South of England. When not writing she enjoys craft and jewelry making and is currently working on ideas for her first novel. She shares her life with her wonderful husband, David, and would like to dedicate her story to Leo and Phoebe—two of the most fabulous feline friends.

Peg Kehret is the award-winning author of many popular books for children. She frequently includes animals in her books. Her cat, Pete, co-authored three of her books: *The Stranger Next Door*, *Spy Cat* and *Trapped*. Learn more at www.pegkehret.com.

Vicki Kitchner has a Master's Degree in Special Education and holds a National Board Certification in Exceptional Student Education. Vicki and her husband, Skip, divide their time between Florida and North Carolina where they enjoy backpacking, adventure vacations, fitness and reading. Please e-mail her at vicki@hikersrest.com.

Mary Knight is a professional writer, speaker and workshop facilitator. Her story is excerpted from her memoir, *Purr*, about her search for love and the cat that showed the way. Muggins is now eighteen years old and still purring. E-mail Mary at singleye@whidbey.com.

Debbie Kosinski received her Doctor of Veterinary Medicine from Cornell University in 1992. She currently divides her time between practicing as a veterinarian on Long Island, New York and being a mom to her two beautiful daughters, Bethany and Alexa.

Joyce Laird is a freelance writer living in Southern California. Her features have been published in many magazines including, *American Fitness*, *Cat Fancy*, *Grit*, *Mature Living*, *I Love Cats* and *Vibrant Life*. She is a regular contributor to *Woman's World* and to the *Chicken Soup for the Soul* book series.

Jane Lebak is a freelance writer and novelist. She has four children, three cats, one novel out of print, and one in print (*Seven Archangels: Annihilation*). Read about the mayhem on her blog, Seven Angels, Four Kids, One Family, at http://philangelus.wordpress.com.

Stacy Leslie is an English professor and writer. She generally writes fiction; "Chelsea" is her first published work of non-fiction. She holds an MFA degree in fiction writing from Antioch University Los Angeles and a BA in Journalism from the University of Georgia. She may be reached at slesliewrites@yahoo.com.

Dawn Livera is a parent, writer and artist who lives and plays with her family in Vancouver, Canada. One of her life's goals is to travel to every province and territory in Canada and to every continent in the world (except Antarctica—way too cold there!). Contact her at delivera@telus.net.

Former English teacher **Denise K. Loock** is a freelance writer. She is a graduate of both Cedarville University (BA) and Florida Atlantic University (MA). She enjoys gardening, reading, and playing Scrabble. She lives in New Jersey with her husband, their two teenagers, her eighty-six-year-old mother, and two cats.

Donna Lowich works as an information specialist, providing information to people affected by paralysis. She enjoys writing about her family and personal experiences. Other hobbies include reading and counted cross stitch. She lives with her husband in New Jersey. Her e-mail is DonnaLowich@aol.com.

Claire H. Luna-Pinsker is a retired nurse and author. She has multiple material published, enjoys photography and spending time with family. Having a son diagnosed with Autism makes awareness a topic of interest. Her sense of humor also adds to her video blogging commentaries. E-mail her at Lunarose22@hotmail.com or www.musicoflovewriter.com.

Michelle Mach is a freelance writer in Colorado. Her stories have appeared in several anthologies, including *Chicken Soup for the Shopper's Soul* and *Chicken Soup for the Coffee Lover's Soul*. Visit her website at www.michellemach.com.

Dana Martin graduated with honors from California State University Bakersfield in 2006 with a bachelor's degree in English. She is a freelance writer and the president of Writers of Kern. Dana enjoys baseball, her three teenagers, and the pleasure of a twenty-year marriage. Please e-mail her at DanaMartin14@gmail.com.

Katie Matthews is an avid cat lover, having owned five so far, and has learned more from them than they have learned from her. She will graduate in December with a teaching degree and hopes to inspire young minds to think for themselves. You can contact her at matthek@telus.net.

Melissa Mellott, M.Ed., earned her Masters degree in Higher Education Administration from Azusa Pacific University. She is the author of *The Little College Handbook: a First Generation's Guide to Getting In and Staying In*, and is a spa and travel writer based in Santa Barbara, California. Melissa can be reached at melissa@spadefined.com.

Lynn Maddalena Menna lives in Hawthorne, NJ with her husband, Prospero. She is a former educator with the Paterson Public Schools and is listed in Who's Who Among American Teachers. Lynn recently retired to be a full-time mother to Toonsie. Friends can contact her at prolynn@aol.com.

Amy Merrill-Wyatt received her Bachelor's degree from The Ohio State University in 1992. She currently teaches multimedia to middle school students in Holland, Ohio. In addition to acting as maid, chef, and masseuse to her two cats, she enjoys spending time with her husband and daughter.

Tory S. Morgan graduated from Vermont Technical College in 1997 with an Associates in Veterinary Technology. Today she runs an Arabian horse farm, specializing in rare color genetics. Tory continues to combine her love of animals with art and writing. Tory may be reached at shatormararabians@yahoo.com.

John Newlin is a graduate of North Carolina State University and Columbia University. After working throughout the world as an international businessman, he moved to writing and ministry. John's work has been published in about twenty different magazines. He also has a published nonfiction book. Please e-mail him at jwnewlin@msn.com.

LaVerne Otis lives in Southern California where she loves writing, photography, bird watching, gardening, reading and spending lots of time with her family. She has been published in many *Chicken Soup for the Soul* books and in various magazines. You may contact her at lotiswrites@msn.com.

Mark Parisi's "off the mark" comic, syndicated since 1987, is distributed by United Media. Mark's humor also graces greeting cards, T-shirts, calendars, magazines, newsletters and books. Lynn is his wife/business partner. Their daughter, Jen, contributes with inspiration, (as do three cats and one dog). Check out: www.offthemark.com.

Andrea Peebles lives with her husband of thirty-two years in Rockmart, GA. She works in the insurance industry and runs a garden wedding venue in the summer. She enjoys time with family, cooking, photography, reading and writing. She plans to write a photographic journal about the unexpected joys of living in a small town.

Saralee Perel is an award-winning nationally syndicated columnist and novelist. She is honored to be a multiple contributor to the *Chicken Soup for the Soul* series. Saralee welcomes e-mails at sperel@saraleeperel.com or via her website: www.saraleeperel.com.

Genevieve Read was born and raised in Cape Breton, Nova Scotia, and is currently living in Nerepis, New Brunswick. She is a mother, a wife, daughter and friend.

Kelli Regan is thankful for the victory Jesus offers and passionately shares that message with others through writing, Bible study and prison ministry. She's authored numerous articles and lives in Bucks County, PA with her husband, Dan, and their two children. She enjoys hiking, tennis, reading and gardening.

Denise Reich practices flying trapeze in her spare time, travels as often as possible, and loves The Cure so much she will trek cross-country to see them play. Her work has appeared in various publications in the USA and Bermuda, including *Pology*, *Mary Beth's Beanie World* and *The Indianapolis Star*.

A life-long animal lover, **Judy Reynolds** can't imagine her life without a pet in it. Judy enjoys gardening, reading, and walks with her dog. Under her penname Jana Richards she has published four e-books. Visit her at www.janarichards.net.

Janet L. Rockey is a member of the Florida Writers Association, ACFW, and Word Weavers. She has studied under authors Gayle Roper, Jeanette Windle, and Mark Mynheir at Florida Christian Writers' Conferences. Janet lives with her husband, Tom, and their two cats in Tampa, FL. Visit her blog at: rockeywrites.blogspot.com.

Linda Sabourin resides in the Oklahoma City metro area, where she returned after living in California for eighteen years. She makes her home with seven cats, who insist on having at least a bit part in anything she writes. She is a mother of two and grandmother of four.

Harriet May Savitz is a prolific contributor to *Chicken Soup for the Soul* books, and the award-winning author of twenty-six books including *Run Don't Walk*, produced by Henry Winkler, *The Story Blanket* co-authored with Ferida Wolff, and *The Gifts Animals Can Give*. Her books can be found at www.iUniverse.com, www.harrietmaysavitz.com or at www.authorhouse.com. Contact:greetingsfromasburypark@verizon.net.

Elaine Ernst Schneider is an artist and freelance writer. She is the managing editor of Lesson Tutor, a lesson plan site found at www.lessontutor.com. Her most recent books, *52 Children's Moments* (Synergy Publications) and *Taking Hearing Impairment to School* (JayJo Books and the Guidance Channel) can be found at Amazon.com.

Brianne Schwantes currently resides in Slinger, WI where she lives on a twelve-acre hobby farm, affectionately known as "The

Land." Brianne is pursuing her Master's degree in Communications at Marquette University. She is also a motivational public speaker and is working on her autobiography. Brianne can be reached at Brianneschwantes@gmail.com.

Mahnaz Shabbir engages audiences across the globe with personal accounts of diversity and inclusion. Mahnaz is president of Shabbir Advisors, a management consulting company, and is the mother to four sons. Barbara and Mahnaz have been friends for over twenty years. She can be contacted at mahnaz@shabbiradvisors.com.

Bobbie Shafer retired to a life of writing and caring for her two miniature horses, a miniature donkey, a miniature pigmy goat and several chickens, ducks, cats, dogs, and a little bunny. She writes children books, articles, and short stories and enjoys visits from her children and grandchildren.

Lynne Cooper Sitton's stories, verses and illustrations have been published in anthologies, greeting cards and Focus on the Family's children's website. Lynne was president of a South Florida American Christian Writers Association critique group for seven years and hopes her three granddaughters will cherish their family stories. Contact her at LynneCSitton1@aol.com.

Lynetta L. Smith lives with her husband, two daughters, and Rilian her cat in Nashville, TN. She loves writing, reading, music, and community theater.

Michael T. Smith works as a project manager in the telecommunications industry. In his spare time he writes inspirational stories and is currently working on a collection to be called, "From My Heart to Yours." To sign up for Michael's stories go to: visitor.constantcontact.com/d.jsp?m=1101828445578&p=oi. Read more stories at: ourecho.com/biography-353-Michael-Timothy-Smith.shtml#stories.

Diane Stark is a wife, a mother, a teacher, and a writer. Her essays have appeared in a variety of parenting and religious publications. Her first book, *Teachers' Devotions to Go*, will be released in the fall of 2009. She can be reached at DianeStark19@yahoo.com.

Nancy Sullivan enjoys multiple degrees and has written extensively over a long career in the disability arena. With one mystery novel near completion, she plans to write many more. Volunteering in animal rescue, Nancy delights in her own menagerie and is a Reiki Master Teacher. E-mail her at: nancy.writes@sbcglobal.net.

Jimmy Tang teaches social studies and English in the western suburbs of Chicago. He has also taught and lived in Sydney, Australia. Jim has degrees from Eastern Illinois University and National-Louis University. He enjoys travel, golf, reading and movies. He also coaches basketball. You can contact Jim at jtang@elmhurst.k12.il.us.

B.J. Taylor loves all of the animals in her home: one dog, three cats at the moment, and a beta fish. She is an award-winning author whose work has appeared in *Guideposts*, many *Chicken Soup for the Soul* books, and numerous magazines and newspapers. She has a wonderful husband, four children and two adorable grandsons. www.bjtayloronline.com.

Nina Taylor is the Editorial Director for Pneuma Books, the book producer for *Chicken Soup for the Soul*. In between raising her husband and three boys and editing books, she blogs her observations of mankind, writes poetry, and is working on a YA novel. E-mail her at nina@pneumabooks.com.

Carolyn Trezzo-Miserendino received her BS in Special and Elementary education from Northern Illinois University in 1973. She works for the Clothesline Project Chicagoland & Suburbs, a not-for-profit that educates viewers about domestic violence. She enjoys traveling with her daughter, visiting her son in Florida, yoga, cooking, and her kitties Angel and Chloe.

Carolyn M. Trombe published the only biography about a professional female baseball player, Dottie Wiltse Collins. Her work also appears in *The Cultural Encyclopedia of Baseball* and the *Encyclopedia of Women and Baseball*. She works in the Education Department for the State of New York. Her e-mail is ctrombe@juno.com.

Sirena Van Schaik is an honors graduate from Mohawk College in Early Childhood Education. She has been published in several anthologies and magazines and has found her passion in writing. She enjoys reading, spending time with her husband, two children and curling up with her cat Lobo. E-mail her at sirena.van@sympatico.ca.

Joanne Vukman received her Bachelor of Arts in Psychology from the State University of New York at Buffalo. She enjoys spending time with her two dogs, five cats, and three horses.

Samantha Ducloux Waltz (www.pathsofthought.com) is an award-winning freelance writer in Portland, Oregon. Her essays appear in the *Chicken Soup for the Soul* series, Ultimate Series, *Cup of Comfort* Series, and a number of other anthologies. She has also published adult nonfiction and juvenile fiction under the names Samantha Ducloux and Samellyn Wood.

Kimberley Ward works as an animal care professional. She enjoys both reading and writing and has a great interest in animal behavior and training techniques. She lives with her husband, three cats and two greyhounds in New Brunswick, Canada.

Pam Williams is a pastor's wife, freelance writer, Nana of three gifted grandchildren, and head of the housekeeping staff for "The Baxter," a black Maine Coon mix.

Deborah Lee Wilson resides in Everett, Washington with her husband and two cats. Her two grown daughters are recent college graduates. Deborah is a graduate of the University of Washington and enjoys hiking, bicycling, quilting and reading. She is currently working on a novel and plans to write more short stories.

Kristin L. Wilson lives in Nevada and is a happy stay-at-home mom to two young children, two dogs and of course, Baxter the cat. She writes as much as possible in as much free time as her busy family allows. She is working on a story for young adults. Please e-mail her at KristinLWilsonLV@aol.com.

Joanna G. Wright is a freelance writer from Indianapolis, Indiana, where she resides with her husband and two daughters. She enjoys reading, gardening, drawing and quilting.

Jeff Yeager is author of the book *The Ultimate Cheapskate's Road Map to True Riches* and is a frequent guest on television and radio, including NBC's *The Today Show*. He writes a blend of original humor and practical advice for enjoying life more by spending less. His website is www.UltimateCheapskate.com.

Jennifer Zambri-Dickerson grew up in Piscataway, New Jersey. She is a graduate of the University of Delaware with a Bachelors Degree in Animal Science. She currently lives in Delaware and works as a freelance writer and photographer.

Meet Our Authors

Jack Canfield is the co-creator of the *Chicken Soup for the Soul* series, which *Time* magazine has called "the publishing phenomenon of the decade." Jack is also the co-author of eight other bestselling books.

Jack is the CEO of the Canfield Training Group in Santa Barbara, California, and founder of the Foundation for Self-Esteem in Culver City, California. He has conducted intensive personal and professional development seminars on the principles of success for more than a million people in twenty-three countries. Jack is a dynamic keynote speaker and he has spoken to hundreds of thousands of people at more than 1,000 corporations, universities, professional conferences and conventions, and has been seen by millions more on national television shows such as *The Today Show*, *Fox and Friends*, *Inside Edition*, *Hard Copy*, CNN's *Talk Back Live*, *20/20*, *Eye to Eye*, the *NBC Nightly News* and the *CBS Evening News*.

Jack has received many awards and honors, including three honorary doctorates and a Guinness World Records Certificate for having seven books from the *Chicken Soup for the Soul* series appearing on the New York Times bestseller list on May 24, 1998.

You can reach Jack at:

Jack Canfield
P.O. Box 30880 • Santa Barbara, CA 93130
phone: 805-563-2935 • fax: 805-563-2945
www.jackcanfield.com

Mark Victor Hansen is the co-founder of Chicken Soup for the Soul, along with Jack Canfield. He is a sought-after keynote speaker, bestselling author, and marketing maven. Mark's powerful messages of possibility, opportunity, and action have created powerful change in thousands of organizations and millions of individuals worldwide.

Mark is a prolific writer with many bestselling books in addition to the *Chicken Soup for the Soul* series. Mark has had a profound influence in the field of human potential through his library of audios, videos, and articles in the areas of big thinking, sales achievement, wealth building, publishing success, and personal and professional development. He is also the founder of the MEGA Seminar Series.

He has appeared on *Oprah*, CNN, and *The Today Show*. He has been quoted in *Time*, *U. S. News & World Report*, *USA Today*, *The New York Times*, and *Entrepreneur* and has given countless radio interviews, assuring our planet's people that "You can easily create the life you deserve."

Mark has received numerous awards that honor his entrepreneurial spirit, philanthropic heart, and business acumen. He is a lifetime member of the Horatio Alger Association of Distinguished Americans.

You can reach Mark at:

Mark Victor Hansen & Associates, Inc.
P.O. Box 7665 • Newport Beach, CA 92658
phone: 949-764-2640 • fax: 949-722-6912
www.markvictorhansen.com

my Newmark is the publisher of *Chicken Soup for the Soul*, after a thirty-year career as a writer, speaker, financial analyst, and business executive in the worlds of finance and telecommunications. Amy is a *magna cum laude* graduate of Harvard College, where she majored in Portuguese, minored in French, and traveled extensively. She is also the mother of two children in college and two grown stepchildren who are recent college graduates.

After a long career writing books on telecommunications, voluminous financial reports, business plans, and corporate press releases, Chicken Soup for the Soul is a breath of fresh air for Amy. She has fallen in love with Chicken Soup for the Soul and its life-changing books, and really enjoys putting these books together for Chicken Soup's wonderful readers. She has co-authored more than two dozen *Chicken Soup for the Soul* books.

You can reach Amy and the rest of the Chicken Soup for the Soul team via e-mail through webmaster@chickensoupforthesoul.com.

Thank You!

We owe huge thanks to all of our contributors. We know that you poured your hearts and souls into the thousands of stories and poems that you shared with us, and ultimately with each other. We appreciate your willingness to open up your lives to other Chicken Soup for the Soul readers. And we loved hearing about your fabulous cats!

We could only publish a small percentage of the stories that were submitted, but we read every single one and even the ones that do not appear in the book had an influence on us and on the final manuscript.

We want to thank Chicken Soup for the Soul editor Kristiana Glavin for reading every story and poem that was submitted for this book and for her assistance with the final manuscript and proofreading. This book could not have been made without her expertise, her input, and her innate knowledge of what makes a great Chicken Soup for the Soul story. We also want to thank our assistant publisher, D'ette Corona, and our editor and webmaster Barbara LoMonaco for their expert editorial, proofreading, and organizational assistance, as well as Leigh Holmes, who keeps our office running smoothly.

We owe a very special thanks to our creative director and book producer, Brian Taylor at Pneuma Books, for his brilliant vision for our covers and interiors. Finally, none of this would be possible without the business and creative leadership of our CEO, Bill Rouhana, and our president, Bob Jacobs.

Chicken Soup for the Soul

Improving Your Life Every Day

R eal people sharing real stories—for fifteen years. Now, Chicken Soup for the Soul has gone beyond the bookstore to become a world leader in life improvement. Through books, movies, DVDs, online resources and other partnerships, we bring hope, courage, inspiration and love to hundreds of millions of people around the world. Chicken Soup for the Soul's writers and readers belong to a one-of-a-kind global community, sharing advice, support, guidance, comfort, and knowledge.

Chicken Soup for the Soul stories have been translated into more than forty languages and can be found in more than one hundred countries. Every day, millions of people experience a Chicken Soup for the Soul story in a book, magazine, newspaper or online. As we share our life experiences through these stories, we offer hope, comfort and inspiration to one another. The stories travel from person to person, and from country to country, helping to improve lives everywhere.